EDUCATION IN TIMES OF
ENVIRONMENTAL CRISES

The core assumption of this book is the interconnectedness of humans and nature, and that the future of the planet depends on humans' recognition and care for this interconnectedness. This comprehensive resource supports the work of pre-service and practicing elementary teachers as they teach their students to be *part* of the world as engaged citizens, advocates for social and ecological justice.

Challenging readers to more explicitly address current environmental issues with students in their classrooms, the book presents a diverse set of topics from a variety of perspectives. Its broad social/cultural perspective emphasizes that social and ecological justice are interrelated. Coverage includes descriptions of environmental education pedagogies such as nature-based experiences and place-based studies; peace-education practices; children doing environmental activism; and teachers supporting children emotionally in times of climate disruption and tumult. The pedagogies described invite student engagement and action in the public sphere. Children are represented as "agents of change" engaged in social and environmental issues and problems through their actions both local and global.

Ken Winograd is Associate Professor, College of Education, Oregon State University, USA.

EDUCATION IN TIMES OF ENVIRONMENTAL CRISES

Teaching Children to Be Agents of Change

Edited by Ken Winograd

Routledge
Taylor & Francis Group

NEW YORK AND LONDON

First published 2016
by Routledge
711 Third Avenue, New York, NY 10017

and by Routledge
2 Park Square, Milton Park, Abingdon, Oxon, OX14 4RN

Routledge is an imprint of the Taylor & Francis Group, an informa business

Library of Congress Cataloging in Publication Data
Winograd, Ken, 1951- editor.
Title: Education in times of environmental crises : teaching children to be agents of change / [edited by] Ken Winograd.
Description: First published 2016. | New York : Routledge, 2016. | Includes bibliographical references and index.
Identifiers: LCCN 2015042488 | ISBN 9781138944350 (hardback) | ISBN 9781138944367 (pbk.) | ISBN 9781315671970 (ebook)
Subjects: LCSH: Environmental education.
Classification: LCC GE70 .E415 2016 | DDC 372.35/7—dc23
LC record available at http://lccn.loc.gov/2015042488

ISBN: 978-1-138-94435-0 (hbk)
ISBN: 978-1-138-94436-7 (pbk)
ISBN: 978-1-315-67197-0 (ebk)

Typeset in Bembo
by diacriTech, Chennai

Printed and bound in Great Britain by
TJ International Ltd, Padstow, Cornwall

Dedicated to Dorothy and Arthur Traiger

CONTENTS

FOREWORD

In the course of the 25 years that I've been working on the climate crisis, I've also helped raise a wonderful daughter to maturity. (She did most of the raising herself, and her mother the rest, but I was around to watch). And so I've had time to think about what's appropriate when.

But, of course, I don't have the background to really know, and arguing from one case study is probably not the best possible technique. That said, it always occurred to me that the primary task for younger children was to get them to fall in love with the world around them. That's a task that's gotten harder as time has passed, of course, and we've become ever more mediated in our connection with the natural—a connection that for most of human history was primary, unavoidable, and overpowering. But it's still possible: possible to be out under the stars on a dark night and feel small, which must be one of the first sensations that made humans human. So I guess for me one of the tasks of educators would be to figure out how to entice their students into an engagement with the real. Where once, in the early days of our country, students arrived at the classroom rich in practical knowledge and needing some abstraction and mediation, now the opposite is the case. As teachers our job is perhaps now to add grit, not polish.

That's why I like the hard work reflected in this book so much. Teachers everywhere are tackling this most crucial of tasks: re-introducing young people to the idea that they are part of something large and wonderful. If that happens, I have no worries. We protect that which we love, and these young people will grow up to be the environmental defenders we badly need. It is a great labor, and I know I speak for many others when I say we are so grateful that you have chosen to undertake it.

Bill McKibben
Middlebury, Vermont
March 2015

PREFACE

I was born in 1951 during the Cold War, immersed in a culture of huge economic expansion and American exceptionalism. However, accompanying the collective optimism in the midst of US empire was an underlying dread of thermonuclear catastrophe. There was the constant quiescent anxiety for those of us who paid attention to the constant saber rattling and arms race of the two superpowers.

In my lifetime, there have been two crises that could be termed *existential*, in the sense that their outcome had immediate implications for the survival of all life. The first was the Cold War. In the midst of this long conflict, there was a 13-day period in late October 1962 when the US and the USSR faced off over Soviet nuclear missile installations in Cuba. During the Cuban missile crisis, it was transparent to a mindful 11-year-old that the world was on the brink of nuclear Armageddon. Living in central New Jersey and surrounded by its vital petrochemical industry, I knew that my family, friends, teachers, and everything I held near and dear had huge bull's-eyes on our rooftops for what US planners had termed 'mutually assured destruction.'

I was a worrier as a child, and it was easy for my emotional state to slide into despair, especially given the realities of the crisis. Unbeknownst to my parents, my anxiety went through the roof: I remember crying myself to sleep for some of the 13 days. Unlike now, when many parents peer and pry into the deepest recesses of their children's emotional lives, I don't remember my parents checking in with me about how I was feeling. I don't remember any words of reassurance or emotional support from them or my teachers. I imagine they were worried as well by the missile crisis, but it appears that the modus operandi for many caregivers was to avoid the subject with children and, instead, school and home activities went along, 'business as usual.' The crisis was resolved on October 28th, but for years afterward, I continued to have the same dystopian nightmare of people running to open-bed trains, escaping some vague threat to life and existence.

This leads me to the second *existential* global crisis: the specter of loss of an inhabitable planet as a result of humans' profligate exploitation and destruction of nature (and each other). Again, many of our children are aware of the crisis and increasingly so as weather disruptions increase in severity and frequency. Anxiety as a result of the environmental crisis appears to take two forms: the first is an underlying unease regarding the future shaped by the incessant news of environmental and economic uncertainty; the second is the more acute emotional experience when actually experiencing or even anticipating actual natural disasters, like cyclones, floods, earthquakes, droughts, and heat waves.

I was a student in public schools from 1956 to 1969. In spite of all the risks we faced from thermonuclear war, there was no curriculum or programmatic attention to the preparation of youth to live more effectively in this world gone mad. Peace education and youth civic engagement were virtually non-existent; teachers' preparation to support students emotionally was absent in teacher education programs; and community–school collaborations in disaster risk reduction programs were also absent. For children, instead of preparation to be activist citizens for peace and sustainable communities, the focus was on survivalist strategies that we now look back on with both nostalgia and incredulousness: e.g., family backyard bomb shelters and crawling underneath our school desks.

In part, the origin of this book was shaped by my experience of the Cold War as a child and the unpreparedness of schools to prepare my peers and me to live with care and responsibility *in the world*. This book is a response to the myriad of environmental challenges that our children face now or in the near future. The audience is elementary teachers, and the goal of the book is straightforward: *How do we prepare children to participate effectively as engaged citizens in a world that needs everyone ready and willing to defend a livable planet?*

I want to clarify some language that is used to describe the serious state of our planet's health. The environmental crisis is commonly referred to as 'climate change' in the media, everyday conversation, and in the education research literature. No doubt, carbon emissions and its 'blanket effect' on a warming planet is an incredibly serious problem and, perhaps, is a most immediate concern. Some of the chapters do use this nomenclature, climate change. However, some people maintain that the crisis is wider and deeper than just, say, carbon emissions and the imperative to reduce greenhouse gases and our carbon-based way of life. The book also imagines the *environmental crises* as reflecting a deeper global malaise: that of humans' disconnection from nature and from each other; and the pervasive violence done by humans to other humans as well as non-human life, violence often employed for profit and economic position. The book is an educational response to the commodification of life by our economic system, the treatment of both people and nature as resources to be used, profited from, and then discarded when fully extracted or no longer needed by the market. Sometimes explicit and sometimes implicit, the readings in this volume recognize that social and ecological (in)justice are mutually exclusive and cannot be separated. We cannot have social justice without also having ecological justice and visa versa.

Structure of the Book

The book is divided into six sections.

- Section I: Setting the Stage for Elementary Teachers, with Eyes Wide Open
- Section II: Place-Based Education: From Appreciation of Nature to Community Action
- Section III: Teaching Peace
- Section IV: Children's Activism: From the Local to the Global
- Section V: Explicit Teaching to Support Children's Emotions and Resilience
- Section VI: Opportunities for Professional Development: Teachers Moving Ahead, with Urgency

At the outset of each section, I provide an overview of the section and its chapters.

ACKNOWLEDGEMENTS

The goals of the book reflect the broad perspective that a reasonable educational response to humans' *disconnection* from the world is, conversely, a curricular experience that *reconnects* learners…with humans and the entire natural world. This germinal idea was compelling to the authors, and they readily volunteered their time and expertise. I appreciate the authors' faith in the project and their follow-through, sometimes enduring multiple revisions to craft chapters filled with much voice and strategies useful to elementary school teachers.

One of the themes of this volume is that teachers must be role models of what they envision their students becoming. So if we imagine our students learning to engage as activist-citizens in their communities, we teachers must do and be the same. My local environmental activist community, especially the folks in 350 Corvallis, reminds me almost daily of my responsibility to do this work. While individual behavior is important, it is only through collaborations and mass movements that real change can happen. The 350 group in Corvallis and many thousands of similar groups around the world are an inspiration to me to engage in the work because, simply, it is the right thing to do.

Credit List

Chapter 11 is adapted from Karen Malone (2012). The Future Lies in Our Hands: Children as Researchers and Environmental Change Agents in Designing a Child-Friendly Neighbourhood. *Local Environment: The International Journal of Justice and Sustainability, 18*(3), 372–395. Used by permission of the publisher.

Chapter 18 is adapted from Molly Brown (2014). The Work That Reconnects with Children and Teens. In J. Macy & M.Y. Brown (2014). *Coming Back to Life* (pp. 217–244). Gabriola Island, British Columbia: New Society Publishers. Used by permission of the publisher.

Figure 3.1: Environmental Identity Development Model © Carie Green. Used by permission of the author.

SECTION I

Setting the Stage for Elementary Teachers, with Eyes Wide Open

The chapters in this first section present overview ideas that encapsulate the goals of the book. In Chapter 1, Ken Winograd provides conceptual grounding of the core topics in the volume: the challenge to help children to reconnect with the natural world; place-based education; teaching peace; child and youth activism; and explicit support of children's emotions and resilience. In Chapter 2, Nel Noddings compels teachers to promote love of the earth, and she describes a wide range of strategies that may promote children's reconnection with the natural world. Noddings draws on references from philosophy and history to contextualize her eclectic ideas on what to do with children.

Carie Green and Michael Brody, in the third chapter, present a model for 'environmental identity development,' reflecting the idea that what teachers do to engage children in environmental education should, always, reflect their development readiness. They suggest that children must first learn to *trust* nature before they can defend it, and this relationship with nature is shaped by 'sustained meaningful encounters' with the natural world.

1

TEACHING IN TIMES OF ENVIRONMENTAL CRISES

What on Earth Are Elementary Teachers to Do?

Ken Winograd

In school curricula, "by what is included or excluded, students are taught that they are part of or apart from the natural world" (Orr, 1994, p. 13). A core assumption of this book is the interconnectedness of humans and nature, and that the future of the planet depends on humans' recognition and care for this interconnectedness. *Education in Times of Environmental Crises: Teaching Children to Be Agents of Change* aims to support the work of elementary teachers, teaching their students to be *part of* the world as engaged citizens, advocates for social and ecological justice.

While perhaps obvious in Buddhist and Indigenous traditions, most people living in the industrialized world, including me, would benefit from the reminder that all living and non-living things are interconnected: humans, plants, animals, insects, land, water and air, everything! And because of this interconnectedness, what happens to any one part of our world has consequences for everything. However, without both feelings and knowledge about the reciprocal relationship between human behavior and nature, humans are apt to lose sight of the effects they have on other sentient beings and, in turn, may behave in ways that harm the biosphere, perhaps irreversibly.

The stability of the world's climate, which for thousands of years has depended on a balance in this interconnectedness, is under siege. There are important educational implications of this breach in the web of life. This book provides teachers with perspectives and strategies for helping students learn to be more respectful to all of life and, hopefully, heal the breaches.

The Environmental Challenge

Our planet is becoming inhospitable for humans and most species of plants, insects, and animals. The motivation for this book reflects the assumption, however, that humans *will* survive this environmental crisis. The challenge, therefore, is to prepare our young children for a new world of great challenges and also great opportunities.

There are growing social movements around the world responding to the crisis with a sense of both realism and hope: realism that climate change is happening *now* and is going to get worse; and a hope that, out of the upheavals ahead, humankind *can* recreate a world shaped by democracy, sustainability, and peace, in harmony with itself and all nature (e.g., Cultural Survival; Williams, 2012). Humankind's metamorphosis to this new world, in part, entails education of young children to become citizens committed to social, environmental, and ecological justice.

The remainder of this chapter provides an overview of the key concepts and topics in the book, beginning with our notion of the 'effective' citizen.

The Effective Citizen

Our definition of the *effective citizen* is crucial in shaping how we teach and what we teach. Since the 1970s, students' identities have been constructed more explicitly in economic terms: as future consumers, future workers, future taxpayers (Molnar, 1996). In formal and informal education, student/citizens tend to become acculturated to an economic system that requires continual growth and development (i.e., capitalism) (Hill, 2003). Literate citizens in our market-based system work hard without questioning their subordinate positions vis-à-vis employers; hold the belief that "individuals are self-governing entrepreneurs who rationally assess the benefits and risks of their actions, make choices, and accept their consequences..."(McCarthy, Pitton, Kim & Monje, 2009, p. 39); and believe that competition is normal, and that it is an inevitable part of life to have winners and losers. In the dominant globalized economy, the characteristics of effective workers/ citizens include flexibility, adaptability, technical skill, and an absence of a critical/ activist orientation. As the marketplace has effectively infiltrated school culture, anything but these attributes is marginalized as fluff, of no value and, worse, dangerous (e.g., ethnic studies program in Arizona; art, music, and outdoor education).

Still, there have always been cracks and sometimes fissures in any dominant cultural framework. There *are* families, communities, schools, and teachers who teach young people to think for themselves, to question and challenge authority and texts, to work for social and environmental justice, to live in a way that challenges dominant ideologies such as consumption, materialism, and individualism. As I imagine the identity of a citizen that reflects the aspirations of this book, I draw on Elgin's (1981) notions of a 'life of simplicity,' reflecting personal and communal traits such as frugality, gratefulness, reverence for all life, caring, and local communities and connections. Reflecting Elgin, the readings in this book imagine the effective citizen who has the following behaviors and beliefs:

- Understands that people are part of nature, a small part of nature, actually;
- Understands that human survival depends on the survival of all life;
- Shows resilience and self-efficacy in the face of serious problems, both personal and public/societal;
- Can analyze texts and all experience;
- Is inclined to engage in actions with others to address social, environmental, and ecological problems; and
- Understands that we are one world, and that all peoples and nations must work together to share, help each other, and, indeed, be our sister and brother's 'keepers.'

Place-Based Education

This book and its readings (especially Section II) can be situated broadly in the realm of place-based education (PBE). While just two chapters are explicitly grounded in the language and concepts of PBE (Chapters 10 and 11), the other chapters describing children's activities, projects, and social actions comprise some (but not all) important elements of PBE. Basically, place-based education grounds curriculum and teaching in the geography, social issues, and problems of students' immediate communities.

Smith and Sobel (2010) identify five common elements of PBE curriculum:

- Curriculum is grounded in local issues and problems.
- With teachers, students are engaged as co-constructors of curricula.
- Student activity is characterized by inquiry and action.
- Adults from the community are involved as mentors.
- Activities stimulate "a sense of appreciation or positive regard about student's home communities and regions" (pp. 58).

PBE involves the direct experience and study of social and ecological problems in the local places that students inhabit. PBE promotes students' connection with 'place': the land, soil, animals, and social and cultural practices of where they live. Without a sense of connection with the "places where they live, there is little chance that the forms of care essential to environmental and social stewardship will emerge" (Smith, 2007, p. 192).

Traditional PBE reflects what Gruenewald (2003) calls *inhabitation*, which entails deep learning of one's place, learning how to live effectively, wisely, and sustainably in one's community. PBE traditionally has tended to avoid political controversy (e.g., learning about injustice and power relations, as is typically done in social justice education). However, Gruenewald has nudged the field of PBE to expand its focus to the *critical*, so students learn to critique bias and analyze problems as they reflect some injustice in their immediate community or slightly beyond. He names this critical aspect of PBE *decolonization*. Inhabitation and decolonization have a reciprocal relationship, with perhaps three key elements (bolded below).

> Students **study** an aspect of their local social and/or ecological setting...
> engage in **analysis** of problems which may reveal some injustice...
> and, then, take **actions** to address those problems.

Gruenewald and others (Smith, 2007) recognize the challenges of implementing critical PBE given the conservative culture of schools today and, as significant, the non-critical (traditional) orientation of teachers, teacher education, schools, and society. Still, even with the limitations of non-critical PBE, Smith (2007) recognizes that traditional PBE can still help students more deeply connect to their community, plant seeds of citizen activism, and engage students in active learning. "Encouraging children to take on the responsibilities associated with inhabitation opens the possibility for decolonization" (p. 203).

Critical Environmental Education

It is not enough for teachers to teach only the technical aspects of subject matter, or to restrict students' analysis of texts to the 'four corners' of the page, like is the emphasis of the Common Core Standards (US) (Au & Waxman, 2014). The goal of all education must be to teach students to raise real-world questions and problems and, then, to take action with others to build a more just and sustainable world. Reflecting students' age and conceptual readiness, this critical EE starts with the immediate classroom and then gradually extends out to the school, neighborhood, and larger communities. A criticalist environmental education has as its mission, social and ecological justice: so students learn to treat all life with care and respect, as engaged citizens in democratic and equitable communities (e.g., Gruenewald, 2003; Kahn, 2009).

Critical environmental education promotes forms of sustainability that entail "a 'balance' and 'integrity' in (the) use and renewal of social and natural resources and an understanding of the relational dimensions of society, culture and nature" (Dei, 2010, p. 94). Sustainability has to do with power relations and social relations, morality, our conceptions of the good life, "human conduct as 'good' and 'evil,' the tensions between 'domination of nature' and the 'intrinsic rights of nature'" (p. 95).

Orr (2002) argues that a truly sustainable world requires system change, leading to fundamental changes in how people and institutions relate to the human and non-human world. He imagines the lessons humans could learn from nature's self-sustaining system.

> Ecological design at the level of culture resembles the structure and behavior of resilient systems in other contexts in which feedback between action and subsequent correction is rapid, people are held accountable for their actions, functional redundancy is high, and control is decentralized. At the local scale, people's actions are known and so accountability tends to be high. Production is distributed throughout the community, which means that no one individual's misfortune disrupts the whole. Employment, food, fuel, and recreation are mostly derived locally, which means people are buffered somewhat from economic forces beyond their control. (Orr, 2002, pp. 9–10)

Orr's ideas here are reminiscent of Dewey's (1997) conception of democracy, in which "each (person) has to refer his own action to that of others, and to consider the action of others to give point and direction to his own" (p. 87). Orr calls for a renewal of *local* democracy in control of its resources and technologies; resisting the effects of globalized technological and economic control on communities; and the central importance of *place* in people's lived experiences.

Reconnecting with Nature

Kingsforth (2015) and others suggest that current environmental crises have long been shaped by three myths: the myths of *progress*, continuous economic *growth*, and human's *disconnection from nature*. The third myth addresses humans' relationship with nature, and how this relationship reflects one of two broad possibilities (Bai, 2001; Bonnett, 2007; Kingsforth, 2015; Macy, 2015). First, there is the dominant (Western) worldview that nature is something *outside* humans' identity. Much of humankind does not view itself as part of nature but, rather, outside and separate, standing apart and devoid of a sense of sacredness and reverence for the natural world. This disconnection makes it easy to relate to nature as a resource, as something to use, exploit, extract, and exhaust, in order to meet human needs and desires, no matter how gratuitous and greedy. The relationship of people to nature here is one of dominion and control.

The second conception represents humans as *part* of nature along with everything else; there is a sense here of connection with all life and the universe. While this is a challenging concept for modern humans, many contemporary people do experience this oneness, or unity, with the universe, like many Buddhists, Indigenous people, and deep ecology thinkers (e.g., Kingsforth, 2015). In fact, most religions preach the unity of all life, although many religious practitioners, at best, focus their justice lenses on humans and *not* non-human life. People whose relationship with the world is one of connection and care are more inclined to relate to the natural world with respect and even reverence. A 'humans as part of nature' identity is more inclined to use nature only to meet its needs and *not* for gratuitous consumption and profit.

Without ample and enjoyable experiences in nature, especially with parents or other mentors, children are less likely to grow up to be adult defenders of the natural world (Chawla, 2009). Without a personal relationship with the natural world, it is easy for people to become emotionally detached or acquiescent when industry proceeds in its inexorable quest to extract, degrade, and exhaust the earth's resources without any kind of balance or restraint. David Orr (2004) calls this disconnect between people and nature 'biophobia,' which ranges "from discomfort in 'natural' places to active scorn for whatever is not human-made, managed or air conditioned" (p. 131). Richard Louv (2008) argues that biophobia reflects the lack of experiences children and their parents have in natural spaces where they play, imagine, create, construct, or just be. By ignoring the teaching of nature and not explicitly enacting curricular experience that values nature, schools may inadvertently teach students and future citizens to have contempt for nature (Bigelow, 2014) which then leads people to participate without mindfulness, in the nature-as-resource, industrial–consumer culture.

Learning Peaceful Relations with All Life

Some people argue that the central environmental challenges facing humankind in the twenty-first century are shaped by inequality and violence (Andrzejewski, Baltodano & Symcox, 2009). This involves people and social institutions with more power doing violence to those with less power; wealthy nations violating the land and resources of poor nations; the violence done to people of color and women in most nations; the violence done to animals in factory farms; the violence to plants, animals, and insects due to deforestation and development; and the violence done by people to the ocean, the air, and land (Jensen, 2011). The damage is largely structural, since our public institutions, laws, and cultural practices have mostly capitulated to the needs of the market, which requires continuous growth, development, and excessive consumption.

Curriculum useful to teachers who are concerned about the myriad forms of violence done to the social and natural world is *peace education*. Peace education teaches learners non-violent strategies and ethics with which to engage with the world, with all life, both in their personal relations and also as participants in community and institutions (Brantmeire, 2005). Peace education can provide much insight regarding the social/cultural changes that are needed to address the roots of ecological degradation.

Frameworks for peace and sustainability education recognize the limitations of *social* justice as human-centered (i.e., anthropocentric) (Andrzejewski, Baltodano & Symcox, 2009; Brantmeire, 2013; Wenden, 2004), arguing instead that social and eco-justice are interrelated and parts of a larger system of oppression. These frameworks tend to find common ground in the idea that "ecological sustainability—the integrity of the natural world—[requires]...a biocentric orientation that makes the human species a member of the web of life, not its master or, even, its manager" (Verhagen, 2004, p. 54). *Healing the environmental crisis and healing social injustice are mutually reinforcing and interrelated goals.*

Children's Participation and Activism

Internationally and throughout history, children have long been involved in political work, actions that lie on a continuum from non-political community service to confrontational actions that actually put children in danger of physical harm.

There are many examples of youth and young children doing social activism that placed them in harm's way: e.g., the struggle to dismantle Jim Crow in the US South, the system of Apartheid in South Africa, and more recently Palestinian youth protesting Israeli occupation in the first and second Intifadas. Mother Jones led thousands of child coal miners in a march against child labor in 1903 (Bartoletti, 1999).

Robert Coles (2010) talked to Ruby Bridges about her experience as a first grader in New Orleans, walking to school each day, surrounded by federal marshals, subject to mobs of screaming white segregationists threatening her life. Her response to Coles, when asked what she thought about when she walked by the violent crowds: "I always think the same thing when I hear those people trying to scare me real bad. I always pray for those people" (p. 85). Ruby's support from her family and faith community appeared to make a difference in her remarkable resilience. During the Apartheid struggle, when teachers or parents were engaged with children (and youth) in social activism, it "increased the psychological resilience of young activists in the face of trauma and violence" (Wells, 2009, p. 135). Abebe (in Ensor & Reinke, 2014), referring to Ethiopian children's activism, argues for a conception of "children's agency as interdependent on the family and wider networks of long-term support" (p. 76). In the realm of social activism, dangerous or not, it appears that young children's participation *with their families, teachers, and peers* is important in helping to develop the skills, dispositions, and confidence to become engaged in their communities, as 'agents of change.'

In the international community, there is a near-consensus that children have the right to participate in community life, and the right to raise issues and concerns and then engage as participants in the resolution of these concerns. The United Nations Convention of the Rights of the Child (CRC, 1989), passed by 124 member nations (with the exceptions of Somalia, Sudan, and the United States), calls for children's right to participate in decisions that affect them (Hart, 2006).

Recently, there is an increasing effort to involve children as 'agents of change' in planning for disasters—before, during, and after they occur (e.g., Tanner & Seballos, 2012), especially in the current context of climate change and extreme weather. *Save the Children* is one NGO that has taken leadership to involve children in disaster planning in developing countries like Bangladesh, India, Vietnam, and Haiti.

> Child-centred DRR and CCA put children at the heart of risk reduction and resilience building. It is about focusing on the particular risks children face in particular contexts, and involving their voices and opinions in efforts to build resilience to the challenges of climate change and disasters. (Save the Children, 2013)

Bartlett (2008) also found that children's "active engagement and opportunities to be involved in active problem solving" is a "potent protective force...in situations of adversity, allowing (children) some sense of control in situations where they might otherwise feel helpless and preoccupied by anxiety" (pp. 511, 513). I point out these examples of political action by children in more dangerous settings for teacher-readers of this book who may work in more stable, less precarious settings. If children in high-risk environments in Africa and Asia can and do participate in various forms of social activism, I imagine that children in relatively low-risk political settings in the United States and the United Kingdom can also participate in social activism.

In the enactment of social justice action, especially in the relatively stable settings of developed nations, the educational literature is replete with descriptions of young children studying and then taking action on 'mature' topics like poverty, school violence, homelessness, and climate change *without* suffering debilitating emotions such as fear and anxiety. However, I am sensitive to concerns that young children not be subjected unnecessarily and prematurely to adults' problems and anxieties about the planet (Randall, 2011). Sobel (2008) warns of encumbering young children with the litany of ecological crises (melting ice caps, deforestation, oil spills, fracking, droughts, Lyme disease, etc.) that, perhaps, are more developmentally appropriate for students beginning in middle school. "No [environmental] tragedies before fourth grade," insists Sobel (1998). I agree.

Certainly, there is much ambiguity on when and how to engage young learners in the study of potentially 'sensitive' topics and then engaging learners in related social actions. The following guidelines may be helpful. First, teachers must know their students and families, including their background knowledge, emotional dispositions, and comfort level for particular civic actions. Second, teachers should ground children's activism in the local community and its particular issues, especially those issues that relate to children's interests. And third, teachers should never ask children to do the impossible, like 'save the planet.' If in doubt about young children and their readiness for civic action, a great resource is Ann Pelo's (2000) *That's Not Fair: A Teacher's Guide to Activism with Young Children.*

The Emotions of Environmental Uncertainty

The emotional implications of climate change for *all* people are huge, but children are especially affected. A National Wildlife Federation report (Coyle & Van Susteren, 2012) described children and the elderly as most at risk from immediate as well as long-term anxiety due to climate disruptions. The report estimates that close to 70 million children in the United States, alone, are susceptible to these emotional risks, and worldwide the numbers of children at risk are in the hundreds of millions.

There appears to be two basic ways of coping with the threat and the unfolding impacts of environmental disruption. First, *therapeutic approaches* can improve children's psychological adaptive strategies to regulate emotions. Second, engaging children in *social action* with others enhances self-efficacy, giving a sense of empowerment and positive emotions (Doherty & Clayton, 2011). Just two chapters (Brown in Chapter 18; and Ojala in Chapter 19) explicitly address therapeutic approaches. Most of the other chapters in the book address ways of enhancing children's emotional resiliency, but more indirectly through their engagement in local place-based civic actions.

Conclusion

Global environmental disruption is here and now, and it is going to get worse (Hanson, 2010). Given the apparent trajectory of what Macy and Brown call 'The Great Unraveling,' it behooves elementary teachers to support children's development of identities as caring, critical, and engaged citizens. As important, teachers should also consider the emotional risks to children of environmental upheaval and strategies with which to enhance their resiliency. The readings in this book provide a reasonable point of departure for elementary teachers who are ready to take on this challenge.

References

Andrzejewski, J., Baltodano, M. P., & Symcox, L. (Eds.). (2009). *Social justice, peace, and environmental education*. New York: Routledge.

Au, W., & Waxman, B. (2014). The four corners not enough: Critical literacy, education reform, and the shifting instructional sands of the Common Core. In K. Winograd (Ed.), *Critical literacies and young learners: Connecting classroom practice to the Common Core* (pp. 14–32). New York: Routledge.

Bai, H. (2001). Challenge for education: Learning to love the world intrinsically. *Encounter*, 14(1), 4–16.

Bartlett, S. (2008). Climate change and urban children: Impacts and implications for adaptation in low- and middle-income countries. *Environment and Education*, 20(2), 501–519.

Bigelow, B. (2014). How my schooling taught me contempt for the Earth. In B. Bigelow & T. Swinehart (Eds.), *A people's curriculum for the Earth* (pp. 36–41). Milwaukee, WI: Rethinking Schools.

Bonnett, M. (2007). Environmental education and the issue of nature. *Journal of Curriculum Studies*, 39(6), 707–721.

Chawla, L. (2009). Growing up green: Becoming an agent of care for the natural world. *The Journal of Developmental Processes*, 4(1), 6–23.

Coles, R. (2010). Learning from children. In K. Cahill (Ed.), *Even in chaos: Education in times of emergency* (pp. 83–88). New York: Fordham University Press.

Coyle, K. J., & Van Susteren, L. (2012). *The psychological effects of global warming on the United States. World Wildlife Federation.* Retrieved June 1, 2014, from www.nwf.org/pdf/Reports/Psych_Effects_Climate_Change_Full_3_23.pdf.

Cultural Survival: 40 Years. Retrieved September 8, 2014, from www.culturalsurvival.org/take-action.

Dei, G. J. S. (2010). The environment, climate, ecological sustainability and anti-racist education. In F. Kagawa & D. Selby (Eds.), *Education and climate change* (pp. 89–105). New York: Routledge.

Dewey, J. (1997). *Democracy and education.* New York: The Free Press.

Doherty, T., & Clayton, S. (2011). The psychological impacts of global climate change. *American Psychologist*, 66(4), 265–276.

Elgin, D. (1981). *Voluntary simplicity: Toward a way of life that is outwardly simple, inwardly rich.* New York: William Morrow.

Ensor, M. O., & Reinke, A. J. (2014). African children's right to participate in their own protection. *International Journal of Children's Rights*, 22(1), 68–92.

Gruenewald, D. (2003). The best of both worlds: A critical pedagogy of place. *Educational Researcher*, 32(4), 3–12.

Hanson, J. (2010). *Storms of my grandchildren: The truth about the coming climate catastrophe and our last chance to save humanity.* New York: Bloomsbury USA.

Hart, R. A. (2006). Rights of participation of children and youth. In L. R. Sherrod, C. A. Flanagan, & R. Kassimir (Eds.), *Youth activism: An international encyclopedia (Vol. 2)* (pp. 529–535). Westport, CT: Greenwood Publishing Group.

Hill, D. (2003). Global neo-liberalism, the deformation of education and resistance. *Journal of Critical Educational Policy Studies*, 1(1), 1–26.

Jensen, D. (2011). The tyranny of entitlement. *Orion Magazine.* Retrieved May 1, 2015, from https://orionmagazine.org/article/the-tyranny-of-entitlement/.

Kahn, R. (2009). Towards ecopedagogy: Weaving a broad-based pedagogy of liberation for animals, nature and the oppressed people of the Earth. In A. Darder, M. P. Baltodano, & R. D. Torres (Eds.), *The critical pedagogy reader* (pp. 522–540). New York: Routledge.

Kingsforth, P. (2015). Uncivilization—The Dark Mountain Project. Retrieved February 1, 2015, from http://dark-mountain.net/about/manifesto/.

Louv, R. (2008). *Last child in the woods: Saving our children from nature-deficit disorder.* Chapel Hill, NC: Algonquin Books.

Macy, J. (2015). Joanna Macy and her work. Retrieved April 22, 2015, from www.joannamacy.net.

McCarthy, C., Pitton, V., Kim, S., & Monje, D. (2009). Movement and stasis in the neo-liberal reorientation of schooling. In M. Apple, W. Au, & L. A. Gandin (Eds.), *The Routledge international handbook of critical education* (pp. 36–50). New York: Routledge.

Molnar, A. (1996). *Giving kids the business.* Boulder, CO: Westview Press.

Orr, D. (2004). *Earth in mind.* Washington, DC: Island Press.

Orr, D. (2002). *The nature of design: Ecology, culture and human intention.* Oxford, UK: Oxford University Press.

Randall, R. (2011). *Should we be working with children about climate change?* Retrieved July 2, 2014, from http://rorandall.org/2011/03/23/should-we-be-working-with-children-about-climate-change.

Save the Children (2013). Reducing risks, enhancing resilience: Save the Children's approach to disaster risk reduction and climate change adaptation. Retrieved June 23, 2014, from http://resourcecentre.savethechildren.se/library/reducing-risks-enhancing-resilience-save-childrens-approach-disaster-risk-reduction-and.

Smith, G. (2007). Place-based education: Breaking through the constraining regularities of public school. *Environmental Education Research*, 13(2), 189–207.

Smith, G., & Sobel, D. (2010). *Place- and community-based education in schools.* New York: Routledge.

Sobel, D. (2008). *Childhood and nature: Design principles for educators.* Portland, ME: Stenhouse.

Sobel, D. (1998). Beyond ecophobia. Retrieved August 23, 2014, from www.yesmagazine.org/issues/education-for-life/803.

Verhagen, F. C. (2004). Contextual sustainability education: Towards an integrated educational framework for social and ecological peace. In A. L. Wenden (Ed.), *Educating for a culture of social and ecological peace* (pp. 53–76). Albany, NY: SUNY Press.

Wells, K. (2009). *Childhood in a global perspective.* Cambridge, UK: Polity Press.

Wenden, A. L. (2004). *Educating for a culture of social and ecological peace.* Albany, NY: SUNY Press.

Williams, T. T. (2012). What love looks like. *Orion Magazine.* Retrieved September 25, 2014, from www.orionmagazine.org/index.php/articles/article/6598.

2

LOVING AND PROTECTING EARTH, OUR HOME

Nel Noddings

Children need to be informed and engaged in age-appropriate ways on issues of climate change. In this chapter, I will look at three broad areas of preparation for environmental citizenship that can be promoted and guided by elementary school teachers, and I'll conclude by recommending a renewal of richer, deeper aims in education.

Love of Nature

Children develop their relation to nature through both age and experience. E. O. Wilson (2002) describes *biophilia* as the love of life and lifelike forms, and he notes that it grows developmentally in children starting between the ages of six and nine as an interest in wild creatures and an awareness that they can suffer pain. It reveals itself between nine and twelve with a sharp growth in "knowledge and interest in the natural world" (Wilson, 2002, pp. 137–138). This development is encouraged by guided exploration and opportunities to engage with the natural world. Harmful experience or the avoidance of experience sometimes induced by fearful parents may lead to *biophobia*, a fear of the natural environment. It is important, then, to provide positive experiences to enhance the likelihood that children will feel confident in their interaction with the natural world.

Confidence is also supported by evidence of continued life and reproduction. Gaston Bachelard describes the human fascination with nests: "And so when we examine a nest, we place ourselves at the origin of confidence in the world, we receive a beginning of confidence, an urge toward cosmic confidence" (1964, p. 103). Bachelard also suggests "that the world is the nest of mankind." If we think that way, we will surely want to protect our world-nest.

Bachelard also reminds us that Van Gogh often painted nests and cottages, our human nests. Art and literature can play a large role in promoting biophilia. In addition to Van Gogh's paintings of nests and sunflowers, consider the wonderful bird portraits of Audubon and Monet's beautiful pond and garden paintings. Several writers in this volume will draw the attention of readers to the power of children's literature in developing a love of place. In children's literature, we all remember Winnie the Pooh, Piglet, Eeyore, and Tigger; Ratty and Toad; and Black Beauty, Lassie, Peter Rabbit, the Big Bad Wolf, the Little Red Hen, the Trumpet of the Swan, Old Yeller, and countless other childhood favorites.

Gary Nabhan and Stephen Trimble (1994) look directly at children and their fascination with both nests and shelters. In contrast to adults, children are usually not all that interested in scenery, in the grand vistas of mountains, distant rivers, and plains. While adults stand in awe gazing at such scenery, kids are scrambling about in the bushes looking for hiding places. Reading their stories of children shaping hideouts and creating peepholes, I was reminded of an episode in my own childhood. My cousin and I were playing ball, and the ball escaped us and landed in a huge blackberry bush. How would we retrieve it? My cousin (the boy-boss) held back some branches with his bat and encouraged me to crawl in. What a surprise! Inside, under the branches, was a completely clear, open space totally shut off from the outside world. Looking back on the experience, I think of the wisdom of Peter Rabbit, who induced his cruel captor to throw him into the bramble patch by begging him not to do that. Once inside, Peter was safe. No large creature could get at him there. It is this sort of experience, together with learning the names of the plants, rocks, and creatures among which they play that constitutes the beginning of a genuine environmental education for children (Nabhan & Trimble, 1994).

At least one study suggests that the tendency toward biophilia appears in poor urban children as well as in those more well-to-do. Indeed, their encounters with the ill effects of environmental degradation seem not to "squelch these children's diverse and rich appreciation for nature, and moral responsiveness to its preservation" (Kahn, 1999, p. 114). However, many urban children show biophobia as well. In particular they show fear of insects and rodents. When a class of urban sixth graders visited my home, I walked around the garden with them. Many were very afraid of bees and even ran from them. I explained how important bees are to the garden and told the students how I just hum along with the bees and do not get stung. "Just don't grab them and don't move too fast!" The kids calmed down but stayed well behind me.

Neither urban nor suburban students are generally aware that the pollution of urban streams is often at least partly due to the diligent preservation of suburban lawns. Few people have heard of the environmental pollution caused by the upkeep of lawns—the enormous quantities of water consumed, the choking out of other plants, the run-off of herbicides and other pollutants. Further, mowing our lawns pours incredible quantities of harmful emissions into the air that we breathe (Steinberg, 2002, p. 222). Michael Pollan comments, "Lately we have begun to recognize that we are poisoning ourselves with our lawns, which receive, on average, more pesticide and herbicide per acre than any crop grown in this country" (Pollan, 1991, p. 76). Sara Stein agrees with Pollan and would replace lawns with wildflowers and other meadow plants. She even recommends that we include puddles in our gardens so that butterflies have a place to drink (Stein, 1993, p. 176).

We should talk about these matters in our schools, but we do not want to cause discord in homes. Think how parents might react if their children refuse to mow the lawn or to fill in the small holes in the yard that could become puddles! Education is a multi-purpose activity, and we want our young citizens to learn how to communicate both critically and sensitively. If parents explain that they would be fined for neglect of maintenance if they were to abandon their lawns, children might sympathize by sharing the story of the Thoreau scholar who not long ago accumulated fines amounting to more than $20,000 for replacing his lawn with a more ecologically sensitive meadow-garden (Pollan, 1991, p. 67). Could we convert at least part of the lawn into an acceptable garden? What might that look like?

Place-Based Education

Nabhan and Trimble give an account of how Yaqui and Maya children learned about their environment through playful exploration, conversation with adults about the names of plants and animals, and a treasury of folk stories. "This was what *environmental education* was like before indigenous children were pulled out of their homes to go to boarding schools—before *environment* was partitioned off as a concern distinct from that of simply learning to live with the 'others'— the other-than-human creatures—around you" (1994, p. 83). Clearly, the sort of education they describe is not enough for life in today's technological global environment, but we can retain its essence and even use its basic ideas throughout the curriculum—exploration, conversation, storytelling, and empathy. A sound place-based education leads effectively into the wider world.

In the absence of wild areas and open spaces, many urban and suburban schools have established their own gardens where children and teachers (and sometimes parents) work together to learn about soil, water, and plants, and produce some of their own food. A school in Newark, for example, has a rooftop garden, and the children are proud to offer a variety of its products in their school lunchroom. Because the children select the foods they want from a nutritious array, there is not much waste, and what little is left over goes into a compost pile. The garden provides a center for both environmental and social education.

It is especially important to provide such opportunities in areas—and at times—when children are not allowed to roam freely in the outdoors—to climb trees, build their own shelters, and hide from imagined predators. In addition to whatever the school can provide by way of gardening opportunities, teachers should encourage students to use their own backyards or neighborhood parks as centers of observation. As I argued in *Education and Democracy in the 21st Century*, this should be *real* observation, not the fake sort in which students spend five minutes watching various caged insects and recording what they see. What could students learn about, say, cockroaches in five minutes of casual "observation"? Criticizing such a session, I wrote:

> What did the students learn about these hardy creatures? How long does an individual cockroach live? How many familiar types are there? How do they reproduce? Why are they so hard to eliminate? Do they bite? Are they dirty? People do associate cockroaches with dirt and, in fact, cockroaches are said to create an objectionable odor. But this may occur as a result of their cleaning themselves and leaving behind a smelly residue. Could students think of a way to test this conjecture? (Noddings, 2013, p. 90)

Kieran Egan (2010), too, has recommended the use of extended observation and study of the natural world:

> I just want to add the observation about our catastrophic ignorance of the natural world, and its cognitive consequences, as another reason to consider the educational value of LiD [learning in depth]. Especially if we choose our topics from the natural world, we can enable every student to build up both a quantity and a richly meaningful intensity of knowledge, which might go some way toward saving us from our current inability to think well about the natural world and our place within it. (pp. 17–18)

Place-based education invites interdisciplinary study; every subject in the curriculum can contribute to it and profit from it. It provides connection and meaning to studies that sometimes deteriorate to a mere memorization of facts. John Dewey argued strongly for the integrated study of geography "as an account of the earth as the home of man" (1916, p. 211)—not as a "veritable rag-bag of intellectual odds and ends" (p. 211). Nature study should be embedded in geography: "Nature and the earth should be equivalent terms, and so should earth study and nature study" (1916, p. 213). He pointed out that, while such study naturally begins in a local setting, it should move out to extend "the limits of experience, bringing within its scope peoples and things otherwise strange and unknown..." (1916, p. 212).

It is obvious that storytelling can be offered as a part of geography and nature study. So can art and music through the observation of artifacts and folk music. And there are fascinating bits of history that reveal dramatic changes in how human beings have perceived the natural world. Paul Theobald (1997) tells the story of how, in the Middle Ages, insects and rodents were sometimes charged and brought into court for damaging crops or destroying human surroundings. They were not to be exterminated without a hearing. Sometimes a defense attorney was appointed to defend the rats or beetles that were threatening a human enterprise. Theobald mentions several other writers who, while acknowledging that we would not want to revert to an age of superstition and physical hardship, suggest that we still might learn something from an age that recognized humanity's interdependence with other living forms. "Progress" should not be construed as a one-way path to a better life. We must continually ask of new ways: What is gained? What is lost? I recall, for example, the starry nights of my childhood in New Jersey. Today, even on a lovely evening on the Jersey seaside, we are lucky to see a few faint stars. Life is better in many ways, but there have been losses.

If we are serious about preserving the earth-our-home, we need to consider the inanimate world as well as the life world. Recent news stories have described the work of "clutter specialists"—people who help home-dwellers cut down on the deluge of unneeded belongings they have accumulated. In these accounts, we see vividly the two sides of progress. Surely, it is wonderful to have the variety of household machinery that relieves the hard work and tedium of daily living. We can hardly imagine life without refrigerators, vacuum cleaners, washing machines, dryers, mixers, mowers, and gas/electric ranges. But do we need the enormous collection of gadgets, toys, old clothing, broken tools, and other objects that clutter our living spaces?

Our society is plagued by over-consumption. But how will our businesses prosper if we do not buy their products? This is a serious problem for the environmental movement, and contemporary schooling may be making the problem worse. Instead of drawing attention to the many ways education might contribute to a richer, fuller life, we too often over-emphasize the monetary rewards of getting a higher education. And what is to be done with the monetary rewards? Too often the answer is to buy more, consume more, use more.

Another, related, problem for environmental education is what to do with the waste produced by a consumer society. Ted Steinberg (2002) underscores the ambiguities in past attempts to clean up our cities and residential areas. We no longer dump garbage in our city streets or employ "swill children" to gather and deliver it to farmers as we did in the 1800s. Disgusting and unhealthy as that practice was, it was not without a redeeming feature. Steinberg comments, "But this approach did have the virtue of giving social value to garbage, recycling it for human good, as well as providing a much needed source of income for working-class families struggling to survive in the city's Dickensian economy" (2002, p. 168). Today, recycling is a big and still-growing industry, and yet our oceans and wild places are loaded with trash, much of it virtually indestructible plastic. As Steinberg and other critics have noted, this is not a problem to be solved by individual consumers. It must be tackled at a powerful, global level. And it is not a problem merely for landfills: "Plastics may well represent a greater ecological threat at sea than on land...Tens of thousands of sea mammals, birds, and fish died as a result of the plastic tidal wave" (Steinberg, 2002, p. 232).

As we consider how to reduce consumption and waste, we should also think about how we might repair and preserve objects and tools instead of discarding them and buying new ones. Matthew Crawford, in his plea for a revival of interest in vocational education, notes that most well-educated people today have not learned how to fix things. "Fixing things," he writes "whether cars or human bodies, is very different from building things from scratch" (2009, p. 81). Such work requires attentiveness because the object is usually not of our own making, and we have to look at it and listen to it in order to understand what it needs to get back into working form. One can experience great satisfaction in restoring something (or someone) to working condition. Education today gives far too little attention to the skills of preservation and restoration.

An active commitment to the health of Earth arising from a mature bio-philia will lead us to preserve wild places, nurture home gardens, reduce harmful emissions, become more frugal in our consumption, and deepen our respect for both objects and other living things. It should also steer us away from war and its horrific acts of destruction.

Love of Place and Peace

Love of place should lead us to a love of peace. We do not want our deeply loved places to be destroyed. However, a love of place can lead in two very different directions. As children study their own place and learn to care for it lovingly, they must move beyond their own locale to the wider world in which other people care deeply for *their* places. Understanding the universal tendency to identify and protect one's own place should lead us to care for the Earth that is home to all of us. But, unfortunately, love of place is often converted to love of nation, a love of place defined by its political history and devotions. The two attitudes need not be in contention, but there is no question which gets the greater attention in schools. We pledge allegiance to a flag and nation, not to that part of nature in which we live.

The uneasy connection between love of natural place and nationalism is illustrated in a discussion that arises now and then over our national anthem. Officially, it is "The Star-Spangled Banner," but there are many who would prefer "America, The Beautiful" as our national song. (Some prefer the second simply because it is easier to sing!) Why do some of us prefer the words of "America, The Beautiful"? Children might be encouraged to look carefully at the words of both songs. Notice the emphasis on nation and war in "The Star-Spangled Banner": "ramparts, rockets' red glare, bombs bursting in air, foes' haughty host, war's desolation, pow'r that hath made and preserved us a nation, conquer we must, triumph"...all words indicative of pride in our *nation*. Then look at the words of "America, The Beautiful": "spacious skies, amber waves of grain, purple mountain majesties, fruited plain, brotherhood, God mend thine ev'ry flaw, till success be nobleness, undefined by human tears, from sea to shining sea." Can students see how we might cherish both songs but prefer the second because it is more consonant with a love of America as a natural place on an Earth we want to preserve?

Environmental educators should try to emphasize the love of place and life over the social/political love of nation. This emphasis need not involve dramatic criticism of national patriotism. To engage in such criticism would surely stir irate opposition, an even stronger reaction than one induced by a condemnation of lawns. Obviously, we can love our country as a natural place and as a political/social ideal but, historically, far greater emphasis has been placed on the political nation. Teachers should be aware, however, of the powerful critiques launched by critics such as Virginia Woolf (1966/1938) who pointed out how patriotic songs, parades, uniforms, medals, salutes, speeches, and celebrations support enthusiasm for war. Following Woolf, we might reduce our emphasis on national pride and increase attention to our nation's home:

> If we love a particular place, we know that its welfare is intimately con-
> nected to the health of the Earth on which it exists. This understanding
> may increase our commitment to a chastened patriotism. Because I love *this*
> place, I want a healthy Earth to sustain it...If the well-being of my loved
> place depends on the well-being of Earth, I have a good reason for support-
> ing the well-being of *your* loved place. I have selfish as well as cosmopolitan
> reasons for preserving the home-places of all human beings. (Noddings,
> 2012, p. 66)

The connection between environmental education and peace education becomes obvious.

The Larger Picture

Climate change and the many environmental crises should be of deep concern to people all over the world, and educators should invite children to become informed and engaged with its issues. The problem, serious as it is, is part of an even larger one in education. We have allowed the whole process of education to become complicit—even fundamental—in sustaining and promoting the con-sumer world. Everywhere today, Americans refer to education in economic terms. Why go to college? To get a well-paying job. Why study hard in high school? To get into a good college...?

Surely it is reasonable to hope that a good education will lead to a good job, but a good education should do more than that. We once believed that a good education would open the doors to a richer, fuller life. We would become better people through that good education. Somehow, we have lost that faith or, at best, given it low priority. We educators should wage a campaign to renew it (Noddings, 2015).

Helping children to know and love the natural world should, of course, be part of that campaign. The activities of gardening, exploring, observing wildlife, and sharing stories are themselves part of a richer, fuller life. As Dewey counseled us, education is not mere preparation for life; it *is* life.

Children should also be involved in keeping their school and neighborhood clean and free of clutter. They should be encouraged to learn how to use tools and repair things. If we are serious about protecting our life-spaces, we should provide shops, kitchens, and gardens in our schools as well as studios for the arts. Many people today are unaware that a shop for "manual training" was once a standard facility in many elementary schools. We need to remind ourselves of what Dewey described as the four-fold interests of children: communicating (talking as well as listening), making things, inquiring, and expressing themselves (1990/1902). Active involvement with the natural environment provides wonderful opportunities to engage all four interests.

Supporting the active engagement of children with the natural environment should be part of a larger program of education that respects the full range of human talents and interest. Instead of forcing everyone into a standard curriculum in the name of "equality," such an approach suggests that education should help children to find out what they are good at and help them to develop their special talents.

Finally, a fuller, richer education would encourage devotion to our lived-places, both local and global. Without denigrating our national allegiance, schools should be committed to a passionate shift in emphasis away from pride in a nation and toward a loving dedication to our country as natural living-place and to the Earth on which it depends for life.

References

Bachelard, G. (1964). *The poetics of space.* (Maria Jolas, Trans.). New York: Orion Press.

Crawford, M. B. (2009). *Shop class as soulcraft.* New York: Penguin Press.

Dewey, J. (1916). *Democracy and education.* New York: Macmillan.

Dewey, J. (1990). *The school and society* and *The child and the curriculum.* Chicago: University of Chicago Press. (Original work published in 1900 and 1902)

Kahn, P. (1999). *The human relationship with nature.* Cambridge: MIT Press.

Nabhan, G. P., & Trimble, S. (1994). *The geography of childhood: Why children need wild places.* Boston: Beacon Press.

Noddings, N. (2012). *Peace education: How we come to love and hate war.* Cambridge: Cambridge University Press.

Noddings, N. (2013). *Education and democracy in the 21st century.* New York: Teachers College Press.

Noddings, N. (2015). *A richer, brighter vision for American high schools.* Cambridge: Cambridge University Press.

Pollan, M. (1991). *Second nature.* New York: Delta.

Stein, S. (1993). *Noah's garden: Restoring the ecology of our own back yards.* Boston: Houghton Mifflin.

Steinberg, T. (2002). *Down to earth.* Oxford: Oxford University Press.

Theobald, P. (1997). *Teaching the commons.* Boulder, CO: Westview Press.

Wilson, E. O. (2002). *The future of life.* New York: Alfred A. Knopf.

Woolf, V. (1966). *Three guineas.* New York: Harcourt Brace. (Original work published 1938)

3

A TWILIGHT DANCE IN THE SNOW

Thinking About Environmental Identity Development

Carie Green and Michael Brody

Dusk in the far north comes early in the wintertime; by three in the afternoon it is dark. If one does not act quickly during the short daylight hours, the window for outdoor play has withered away. Or has it?

"What would you like to do during the winter break?" I asked my three young daughters during a dinner conversation. My seven year old, Heidi, suggested a museum, my five year old, Juniper, a hike, and my three year old, Jade, just giggled.

My own bias showed through their suggestions. A hike? How about a late night stroll in the woods? Enthusiasm was apparent and so after stowing away the food and dishes, we proceeded with putting on the layers of winter gear appropriate for outdoor adventure in the Arctic. Missing gloves, struggle with boots, and limited time caused some apprehension in our decision to go outdoors. However, we overcame the struggles and emerged outside. The dark was calm and chill; giant snowflakes softly meandered to the ground, caressing our rosy cheeks and brows. It was a perfect night for exploration!

Placing Jade in the sled, we proceeded on toward the dark cluster of trees, the leafless birch glowing white in the night and the towering spruce covered with clumps of thick glistening snow. "Which way do we go?" Heidi asked as we entered into the trees. "That way," I answered, pointing towards the wider trail, the perfect width for a family parade. "You lead the way," I suggested to Heidi. "I am scared," she replied. "It's not scary—it will be fun," I reassured her.

Drawing strength from her countless experiences in nature, she proceeded ahead slowly and cautiously with her small flashlight. Gaining comfort, her speed quickened until she was eventually running through the deep shimmering snow. Juniper cowered behind, a little more apprehensive than her sister; she clung to her father for comfort. My husband, Aaron, reassured her, and she eventually ventured out independently on her own, following in the boot prints of her older sister. Jade remained quiet and content, bundled warm and safe in the sleigh.

Along the path, the oldest paused, pointing her light into the shadows of the black trees; everything appeared a bit differently in the dark. We briefly stopped and silently turned out the flashlights to fully take in the setting. How amazing were the reflections from the moon, beaming bright on the iridescent snow. The small and great trees alike stood as silent silhouettes, like guardians of strength in the night. All was crisp and quiet and fresh and peaceful. We continued onward. The two older ones became braver, gaining a new awareness and sense of self in the forest at night.

Eventually we came upon a wide clearing where the snow was nearly two feet thick. A winter wonderland, the children's energy soared to new heights as they ran in circles, carving snow angels and furrows through the soft powder. Jade awakened too, curious of the new setting. I reached down my hand to her; she was still a bit apprehensive about stepping out of the sled, so I modeled how fun it was to carve a path where none existed. She smiled excitedly, stood up, and danced her own pattern through the flakes, forming her own connection and experience in the snow. We then intertwined our paths together in a shared pattern of a twilight dance in the snow.

Their father took the sled to the top of the nearby hill, racing to the bottom. The older two took turns climbing up and sliding down, carving a slippery white trench. The littlest indicated she would like a turn; looking up she said, "Mama hold me." I took her hand and helped her find her way through the thick powder to the top of the hill. At the top we rode down together. I held her close, providing reassurance and comfort during our novel nightfall adventure.

This vignette shows the diverse ways in which children develop their environmental identities alongside parents, caregivers, educators, siblings, and peers during the early years of life. Starting with *Trust in Nature* as a foundation, children are propelled to find their own sense of *Spatial Autonomy* and develop *Environmental Competencies* through sustained meaningful encounters with the natural world. In the vignette above, each of my children appeared to progress in different ways through various stages of the Environmental Identity Development Model (Green, Kalvaitis, & Worster, 2015) (as depicted in Figure 3.1 below).

For instance, as we ventured into the forest at night, all of my children began at the *Trust in Nature* stage. This was evident when Heidi stated, "I am scared." Juniper also revealed her initial discomfort or mistrust in nature by clinging apprehensively to her father. Jade, the youngest, was perhaps the most anxious, choosing to stay within the comforts of the sled. However, it did not take long for Heidi to run ahead independently and find *Spatial Autonomy*, or her own sense of place, in the dark night. She experimented by turning out the flashlight and taking in the "new" setting. Likewise, after finding reassurance from her father, Juniper also ventured along the trail, following the lead of her older sister. Then in coming into the wide-open snowfield, the two displayed *Environmental*

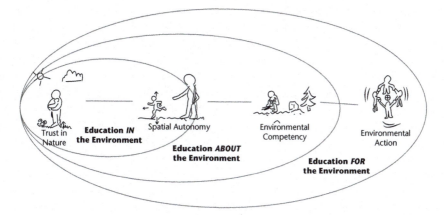

FIGURE 3.1 Model of Environmental Identity Development © Carie Green, 2015.

Competency, skills and confidence to use the environment to carry out their own goals and enrich their experience. Heidi lay down to make a snow angel and Juniper ran fervently carving new furrows in the snow. They both took a turn sliding down a nearby hill.

Jade also progressed through the various stages of the EID model much differently than her sisters. She possessed a less developed sense of *Trust in Nature*, which prohibited her from independently achieving *Spatial Autonomy* or *Environmental Competency*. However, with the comfort and security provided by her family, she took small steps in carving out her own space in the snow and gaining a shared sense of environmental competency through a joint sleigh ride.

In this vignette, I argue that *Trust in Nature* plays an essential role in children developing a positive and healthy environmental identity. Unfortunately, not all children have opportunities to build a trusting relationship with nature through shared and supported encounters. Therefore, I urge caregivers and educators to consider the individual needs of children and take the necessary time and care to help children build and refine their sense of security and comfort with the natural world.

Reference

Green, C., Kalvaitis, D., & Worster, A. (2015). Recontextualizing psychosocial development in young children: A model of environmental identity development. *Environmental Education Research*. DOI: 10.1080/13504622.2015.1072136.

SECTION II

Place-Based Education
From Appreciation of Nature to Community Action

Place-based education (PBE) is a broad curricular field. It encompasses both social and ecological units of study. Sometimes, place-based work simply (and not so simply) consists of children's experience of and reconnection with local places, like experiences in nature. PBE can also entail more explicit study of local issues and problems, including children planning and implementing actions in response to these issues and problems. The focus of Chapters 4 through 7 in Section II emphasizes students' reconnection with *nature as place*, a type of place-based education with a focus on the ecological. In Chapter 4, Simon Boxley, Gopal Krishnamurthy, and Mary-Ann Ridgway describe schools that are based on the philosophy of Jiddu Krishnamurti of India. Krishnamurti schools promote a vision of the 'integrated' person by allowing opportunities for solitude, quietness, and reflectiveness in nature. From this perspective, the role of the educator is that of embodied questioner, moving the learner to greater self-knowledge without ever exercising 'authority over.'

Jolie Mayer-Smith and Linda Peterat in Chapter 5 describe a multi-year project in British Columbia, Canada, in which elementary school children have year-long experiences working on a local farm, learning agriculture from (retired) mentor farmers, thus helping these young learners sow 'seeds of stewardship.' In Chapter 6, environmental educator Ted Watt, who has for many years partnered with elementary schools as a 'naturalist in residence,' describes the excitement of students who are engaged in outdoor education. Watt suggests that schools ought to consider employing environmental educators, just as they do physical education and music teachers. Still, Watt recognizes the potential of teachers to develop the interest and capacity to themselves lead the kinds of teaching he illustrates in the chapter.

Art educator Geraldine Burke's work (Chapter 7) reflects PBE that focuses on nature appreciation and how art can help learners develop their aesthetic relationship with the natural world. Burke describes her work with pre-service elementary teachers and, then, the work of these young teachers with their elementary students, doing art as a means of learning about local school habitats, thus becoming more aware of local wildlife needs. She also shows how students can learn the ways that Indigenous and non-Indigenous communities connect to animals and land through their art. Linda Wason-Ellam (Chapter 8) shares Burke's respect for Indigenous cultures but, now, in the teaching of a unit on water to a fourth grade class in Saskatchewan. Students learned about water from both Indigenous and traditional Western scientific perspectives. There is much that non-Indigenous peoples can learn from Indigenous peoples and philosophies, especially their reverential relationship with the land, and Wason-Ellam's work reminds us of these important land-centered worldviews.

In Chapter 9, Candice Satchwell examines the relative merits of three approaches to climate change education: broad school-wide programs that aim to forge an ethos of sustainability; one-off activities or visits from local activist groups; and engaging children as 'researchers' on more long-term projects. Not discounting any of these approaches, Satchwell argues that they all have a place in the larger agenda of climate change education. Satchwell's work is both straightforward and potentially powerful, by providing children with opportunities and spaces to simply *notice* and *reflect* on the environment around them. The chapter also examines the quintessential challenge of school learning and 'transfer': to what extent do students transfer school experience and learning to their subsequent behavior at home with their families.

Christy Radbourne (Chapter 10) and Karen Malone's (Chapter 11) chapters are explicitly grounded in the language of PBE and, importantly, in its child-as-activist orientation. Radbourne, an elementary school principal in Thunder Bay, Ontario (Canada), examines a series of place-based activities done by her students, teachers, and community. In one project, students collaborated with a local pizzeria in a buy-local campaign. Karen Malone describes the participation of kindergarten and fifth grade students in the planning of a new residential development. The aim of the project was to provide an opportunity for children to have authentic input into the design of the new development so that it will incorporate the visions and dreams of children growing up in the area. The project was implemented through a series of research workshops with residents and children from the local community.

The power of PBE, as described by the chapters in this section, comes in the collaboration among students, teachers, and community participants, involving intergenerational mentoring relationships and explicitly aimed at teaching young children how to do civic engagement...as 'agents of change.'

4

LEARNING CARE FOR THE EARTH WITH KRISHNAMURTI

*Simon Boxley, Gopal Krishnamurthy, and
Mary-Ann Ridgway*

Almost all of us feel responsible for our family, children and so on, but do not
have the feeling of being wholly concerned and committed to the environment around us, to nature, or totally responsible for our actions. This absolute
care is love. Without this love there can be no change in society.

(Krishnamurti, 1981, p. 33)

Do you know that even when you look at a tree and say: "This is an oak
tree," or "that is a banyan tree," the naming of the tree, which is botanical
knowledge, has conditioned your mind that the word comes between you
and actually seeing the tree? To come to contact with the tree you have to put
your hand on it and the word will not help you to touch it.

(Krishnamurti, 2010, p. 20)

Seventy teenagers and 18 adults from over 20 different countries pour out of a ram-
bling old Georgian manor house at Brockwood Park School. A seven-minute walk
leads to Inwoods Small School with four adults and 30 primary-age children from the
local neighborhood. Both of these sister schools sit in the countryside of Hampshire,
England, and are two of the handful of schools worldwide founded on the principles
of the Indian-born educator, philosopher, and iconoclast Jiddu Krishnamurti. Half
of this motley group of young people and adults adorn blindfolds and the other half
guide them by touch as they begin their exploratory walk around the school campus.

It is indeed the autumnal season of mists and mellow fruitfulness; the earth
is wet with the morning dew and yet many of the walkers are barefoot. The
more they walk, the less the guidance and greater the independence. Soon the

guides allow the walkers to explore pace and direction and to navigate by themselves, merely looking out for their safety. Halfway through the walk, after about 30 minutes, they switch roles. The blindfolded walkers are guided to touch, smell, hear, and occasionally even taste different life and organic forms from their natural environment. The touch of branches and bark, the smell of compost and wet grass, the sound of birdcalls and twigs crackling underfoot, the taste of crushed pine needles and even untrodden soil, are invitations for a heightened sensory and sensuous engagement with the world around (while temporarily keeping the sense of sight in abeyance).

Next, activities that engage the sight are included. This is another opportunity for learning firsthand from the world context rather than secondhand from textbook and text. There is now occasion to navigate our inner and outer landscapes as one whole movement, with questions to be asked together by teacher and student, such as, "Is there an observation, not partial, but with all the senses? Is there an observation without the past [memory, experience and knowledge]?" (Krishnamurti, 1979); "Let us find out if it is possible to look at that flower without naming it" (Krishnamurti, 1961, p. 5). Sense-based maps can be drawn, studied, redrawn, and navigated, indicating the play of our senses, feelings, and thoughts in exploring the worlds within and without, and in understanding the place of our senses in learning a sense of place.

This chapter offers a glimpse of the learning experienced by children whose schooling has been more or less shaped by the educational vision of Krishnamurti. However, the authors—two of whom work in such schools and one of whom has worked only in UK state schools—believe that features of this pedagogy might be employed in many types of educational settings to support children in developing a love and respect for their world and community.

What Makes Krishnamurti's Pedagogy Distinctive?

The approaches to learning in and about nature associated with Krishnamurti emphasize *awareness, presence,* and *being with* nature. The responses they illicit from children to environmental degradation, both global and local, are not predetermined or expected. In a sense, it would be fair to say that the relationships that children may go on to build with nature are symptoms of the wider processes of self-awareness, self-learning, and self-knowledge that are so central to Krishnamurti's teaching.

In what follows, you will find a challenge to the idea that simply acquiring or 'owning' knowledge of global environmental issues will assist in advancing ecological health and well-being. We will enquire into whether particular types of experience of nature—those which are open and undirected, and draw attention to one's awareness and presence—might yield a consciousness of one's environment which is characterized by love, and which may lead to a sustained effort on all our parts to care for the Earth. We believe that it is unlikely that we will care for that which we do not love. So, should elementary teachers give up on teaching about the big environmental issues altogether in favour of learning about oneself? Individual teachers will make their own judgements about that, but counter-intuitively the pedagogical experiments conducted in Krishnamurti schools suggest that such an approach might nurture and sustain an integrated attitude towards environments!

We all arrive in this world eager to learn and to understand with significant capacities to observe, to listen, to be alert with all our senses. In the formative years, there is very little judgment in our endeavors to understand our surroundings, and our interests are hardly selective; we are curious and open to whatever is in our pathway. We start out in life awake, aware, and alert to our full potential. In the highly intellectually stimulating environment of schools, where rational thought is considered a powerful tool, there is a shift from this (natural) sensorial, unambitious approach to learning, to something that demands great verbal capacity, quick thinking, and the ability to measure one's 'progress' so that we can join the competitive paths to 'success.' Can schools that serve young children make a conscious shift away from the metrics and fast pace of this type of education, to a learning environment that allows children's immersion in unmeasured and uninstructed periods in nature? To allow periods when the child can marvel at the jewels of dewdrops under their feet, touch the fresh sticky buds of a blossoming tree, feel the earth on their hands, or watch the intricate movements of a caterpillar, not just once and consider it 'done,' but with a never-ending sense of wonder and discovery for the living world, and a growing and strengthening communion with it?

There is an emerging awareness in education that schools need to be more than just institutions that impart knowledge and skills to young people—even, perhaps *especially*, knowledge about the environment and its destruction—that learning how to learn and how to relate with one another is also significant to our future planetary well-being, job satisfaction, and sustained family interactions. Greater emphasis is being given to 'problem solving,' empathizing, and developing one's talents. This is a necessary widening of the responsibility of schools; however, mainstream schools still come packaged with methods, instructions, measurement of achievement, and an overall intellectual striving. How can schools address the here and now of relating with each other and with the planet, without the motive of a personal future gain? Those of us who work in Krishnamurti schools have found that if we give children uninterrupted time in nature—time to play, question, experiment, observe, sit quietly, reflect—guided but not heavily instructed, then so much of that learning that we painstakingly plan to take place in the classroom naturally occurs outside, in both serious and playful ways.

At Inwoods, for example, we hold that for there to be a significant change in how we relate to each other in society, we need a substantial shift in emphasis from the teacher-directed, knowledge-based, and time-managed grading system of the authoritarian approach in the classroom, to a more open, explorative, and uninterrupted enquiring approach in the outdoors that our environment naturally lends itself to, and which seems to put everyone on an equal footing when we get out there together. Understanding others goes hand in hand with learning about oneself. To learn about both oneself and one's world, teachers need to offer a relaxed and non-judgmental atmosphere, where there is neither fear of failure or humiliation, nor the pretence of flattery. Children need to see who and what they are, based on a thorough observation of facts. Nature is probably the best *hostess* of this great inner work as it doesn't compare, undermine, or label. Given the opportunity, children can sit for great lengths transfixed by the business of ants; they may observe their movements, perhaps mirror in some way their own behaviour, marvel at their qualities, and be conscious of their vulnerability too in relation to their own powerful potential to cause devastation to a whole colony with one small gesture. Through just observing and being, the connection with the living world grows and alongside this an expanding sensitivity for oneself, our companions, and this marvelous planet.

What We Do

The following regular happenings in a school setting form the foundation for an ever-deepening connection in nature and don't require specific knowledge or skills as an educator. What they do require is adults' trust in the child's natural inclinations to learn, the ability to hold that sense of wonder, to listen, wait, and also learn with the child.

Daily Walk In Nature

The daily walk in nature need not be for very long or very far but, somehow, it takes on a regular aspect of the school day (see Figure 4.1). It could be that the children are dropped off at the beginning of the day at the furthest point from their classroom on the school grounds, or they are collected there. Or a nature trail is created that winds its way through natural formations, no matter how small or few, in the local area. This daily walk will inevitably grab the attention of the children at different points in the seasons and not necessarily in predictable ways. The regularity of this happening, like a healthy reliable breakfast, will become wholesome nourishment for the senses and allow for frequent unplanned moments of rejoicing in the changes and movements of plant and animal life. It is important not to force the observations and sharing or to believe that every child has to be equally included or engaged at each discovery. This is not a classroom or group setup with 'learning outcomes' to aim for. A leisurely atmosphere with a spontaneous sharing of observations will have a contagious effect of inspiring each individual to notice and wonder, without adult prompts. Just trust and wait.

FIGURE 4.1 Daily walk (photograph courtesy of Mary-Ann Ridgway).

Hikes

Regular hikes in the year along country paths or in city parks, once introduced to the curriculum, become a favourite of the educational trips. While the daily walks help focus the awareness on details in nature within a particular and familiar environment, hikes put those details in the context of a landscape. The children will inevitably move faster as they eagerly explore the space and find out what lies beyond the bends and hills of their paths. Landscapes vary and change with the season and climate so there is a lot to discover throughout the year. Appropriate gear for protection from sun, rain, and cold are the only essentials so that there is enough comfort to sustain an adequate length of exposure outdoors. Children's natural inclinations to move and spend energy means that the connection with nature is quite clearly physical; along the way, children will spot trees to climb, rocks to scramble over, hills to roll down, and streams to paddle in. For the novice young hikers, the landscape may be more of an exciting playground than anything else, but with enough exposure and gentle guidance, they will discover that it is alive with life and also requires sensitivity and care to navigate. Once they discover birds nesting in the trees that they climb, they will explore the branches with additional attention and care. Rocks where insects have been found to hide will no longer be kicked and abandoned but carefully upturned and replaced. Plants that are observed flowering and attracting bees, rather than grabbed or picked in abundance and discarded, will be sporadically gathered for a more thoughtful purpose. Thus, the playful physical explorations of nature's elements grow to also become respectful investigations of landscapes with an understanding of one's relationship and responsibility there.

River Walks

A narrow, shallow, and meandering river or stream littered with rocks and boulders is an adventurous and highly sensorial environment to take any age group of children. The basic intention is to navigate one's way up or down the river, preferably barefooted, wearing shorts or rolled up trousers. One can decide on the challenge ahead of the journey: e.g., not to get one's feet wet so to hop between rocks, trees, and fallen branches; or to only follow the water's flow while taking advantage of those sturdy fixtures to hold onto for balance. The enduring flow of the water as it curves, falls, tumbles, and bubbles along its varied and rocky pathway creates a whole range of therapeutic natural sounds that soften or increase with every bend and drop. The alert attention needed to carefully steer one's way, coupled with the stereo sound effects of the water, transports one into another world that drowns out most other human fabricated noises and, indeed, many of those thoughts that accompany them. The aim is not to travel very far but to pick one's way cautiously and slowly and to lose oneself to the bounty of sensations that the river can offer. Children are generally easily fascinated by water pathways and patterns, and their actual experiences and appreciation will inspire a wealth of water-related questions and observations.

Solo Observation

Any activity outdoors lends itself to an occasional pause to sit alone and observe in quietness (see Figure 4.2).

The buzz and business of children hanging out together will inevitably keep wildlife at bay; quiet children can bring stillness to the proceedings and a safer atmosphere will be created for birds to venture closer, insects to emerge, and larger animals to amble or scurry by. Children grow to appreciate the collective agreement to respect each other's chosen personal spaces, so that observing can happen uninterrupted by social interactions. As children become acquainted with these solo moments, they become quite adept at finding comfortable spots to settle in: snuggled in nooks of trees, straddled on a low hanging branch, tucked inside a bush, leaning against a warm rock, etc. The shift from movement and

FIGURE 4.2   Solo observation by a student (photograph courtesy of Mary-Ann Ridgway).

noise to stillness and quiet, once experienced, feels like an essential addition to the outdoor programme. As well as an undisturbed opportunity to observe, it can inspire a change in attitude and perspective of the natural world; the self, normally eager to dominate and possess, quietens down a little in the presence of such natural beauty, intelligence, and majesty.

Natural Play Elements for the Playground

Rather than asphalt and prefabricated industrial play structures in our playgrounds, children will benefit far more from grass and earth under their feet and a whole range of inexpensive natural elements such as sand, water, mud, chalk, wood, and stones at hand. Provided with these natural 'play features,' there is scope for much learning as children build dens and structures out of wood, mold mud, carve and grind chalk, dig trenches, and build dams to harvest water. They will use their imaginations and develop practical knowledge of these elements to engage and collaborate with each other, resulting in playgrounds becoming rich places of uninstructed investigations and social learning. Obviously, this sort of playground activity risks clothes becoming wet, muddy, or dusty and so we need to bear this in mind and not let our concern for the children's daily garments get in the way of their freedom to explore and experiment. Protective gear, such as waterproof trousers and jackets, or spare clothes to change into, will help towards addressing this issue, as will an often necessary conversation with parents regarding having a different mindset on what's more important in the child's life.

Nature Drawing and Writing

In conjunction with all the nature-related activities, equip children with nature journals for drawing or writing what they observe or reflect on when they choose to (see Figure 4.3).

These journals can help to focus children's attention on observing factually what is around them, and over time their depictions in pencil and words will become more accurate. These journals are personal records, better left unmarked by others, not judged, corrected, or commented on. Simply offering a moment to share for anyone who wishes will enlist growing confident contributors that inspire one another with reflections.

A Favourite Place

Our attention is easily captured by the evident seasonal changes such as the sudden explosion of blossom in spring, the ripe strawberries in summer, the bed of colourful leaves in autumn, and the emptiness of the trees in winter. However, how many of us are aware of the more subtle indications of nature's response to the changing climate and evolving ecosystems? Offer children frequent intervals in the year to observe from a chosen place and they will begin to see interactions between species, notice the variation in the arrival of plants, and begin to develop a personal connection with creatures, thus enriching their experience of the seasons and deepening their appreciation of the workings of nature. To sit in one place with no prescribed goal and relatively little that stimulates is a challenge to both adults and children who have been accustomed to an ambitious,

FIGURE 4.3 Drawing/journaling by the river (photograph courtesy of Mary–Ann Ridgway).

competitive, and hectic upbringing. Gaming devices and media entertainment contribute to this overstimulation, resulting in short attention spans and boredom if there isn't an immediate reward. So being able to stay with the seemingly unobtrusive elements of nature will develop alongside a lessening of self-fulfilling activities.

Excursions into Natural Places

Occasions in the year to embark on a several-day immersion in a natural setting raises a range of learning opportunities less likely to occur in the limited and somewhat artificial school context. This could be camping in wilderness, or staying at a small sustainable farm where some basic facilities offer a gentler introduction to living simply and close to the land. Compost loos, washing in a river, wood fires for warmth and cooking, harvesting one's food, and simple shelters shared with creepy crawlies and allowing us to hear the wind, rain, and nocturnal animals are all elements that offer a more direct contact with and awareness of the natural world. There is a danger that the comfortable environment of the modern home and school promotes self-absorbed behavior and increasing expectations and demands on others for an easy and consumer-dependent life. The intention of these excursions is to engage the children in meaningful life situations and with tasks that reawaken the senses, challenge the body, and open the mind to a learning that is passionate and integrated. Children are creatures of nature who are unfortunately made to live in artificial surroundings. But expose them to the raw elements while having to manage their basic needs, and a very natural, almost primordial response takes place, inspiring them to find their place harmoniously among the extended wild community. Learning that takes place in relationship with life is not conceptual or abstract but very real and meaningful and intimately woven with a sense of beauty and wonder of the mystery of the living world.

Having to function together in an unpredictable environment also deepens the relationships between individuals. The cultural roles become secondary to the natural ones that move us to cooperate and take care of each other; adults will find themselves giggling and wondering with the children, and children will find themselves spontaneously taking on unrequested responsibilities to support the group.

It is important that when organizing such a trip children are included in aspects of the planning and discussions regarding its intentions. Rather than striving to make a trip comfortable and entertaining, consider the children as responsible participants in the creation of a meaningful adventure together. They are then more likely to have the openness and willingness to face any discomforts and challenges that arise.

Growing

Having some element of growing food as part of their education helps children to contribute to their own survival, live with the seasons, understand the cycles and challenges different organisms face, and feel a connection to the world. Watching something grow from seed to harvest can feel miraculous and inspiring; by being part of it, children are also seeing the outcome of their care (see Figure 4.4).

'Picky eaters' will often try vegetables they grow that they would never otherwise taste, let alone eat. Children can take ownership even if they don't have their own section of the vegetable garden. They can consider the whole garden part of their responsibility, allowing for more cooperation and teamwork. Children can choose many of the plants that are grown, as well as receive expert help in areas such as timing, rotation, companion planting, nourishment/watering techniques, and pest control. Having various types of garden spaces expands what can be grown as well as the concept of what a garden is, such as vegetable patches, forest gardens, tea borders, herb gardens, and mixing wild, ornamental, and food crops in the borders/pots of a school's grounds. Combining gardening with topics such as evolution, genetics, reproduction, chemistry, physics, species identification, health, medicine, and care enhances learning, enriches the gardening experience, and links it to the rest of education and life.

Gardening "teaches a student patience ... it teaches humility, as it is a collaboration with nature and therefore a check on our hubris; it insists on the student

FIGURE 4.4 Shoveling dirt in a school garden (photograph courtesy of Mary-Ann Ridgway).

being *present* (emphasis added) ... it encourages care and openheartedness, making space for other species to thrive" (Primrose, 2014, p. 32). When Gary Primrose talks of presence, of course he doesn't mean that children will simply occupy the space, but that they will be *aware* of their presence, and meet nature with that awareness both of themselves and their responses, and of the reality of the environment—its cold and discomfort, its rot and decay, as well as its beauty and expansiveness. Krishnamurti pedagogy emphasizes this presence in nature; it would be easy to say "self-presence" but that awareness of individuated self may give way to a sense of a self (or rather an absence of self) that is more thoroughly integrated into and a part of nature, present to itself.

Reflections on Nature as Teacher

Gary Primrose, who for many years both taught and tended the grounds at Brockwood Park, developed the idea that in the immediacy of contact between learners and their subject matter, the subject becomes the authority, rather than the teacher. Put aside for a moment any Vygotskian concerns you may have about the necessity of mediation and, instead, reflect on the meaning of the possibility of the subject as authority. For Primrose (2014), if that subject is nature, in children's very direct relationship with that subject matter, *nature becomes teacher*. This may be humbling for those in the school more used to being recognized as an authority. As they relinquish this role to nature in the kinds of activities we have discussed, teachers become co-enquirers with children *into* the lessons that nature can teach.

Like other Brockwood and Inwoods teachers, in his work with nature-as-teacher, Gary Primrose focuses on the unique experience each child develops in immediate contact with a place over a sustained period. Writing individual journals, collecting materials for installations: none of these things are particularly distinctive to Krishnamurti pedagogy—one of the authors of this chapter has done these things many times in state schools with young children in the UK. What is distinctive to the Krishnamurti pedagogy is *the patience to allow time for awareness and sensitivity to places to grow, and for senses to become alert and attuned to quietude, intricacies, the tiny and delicate as well as the vast and awesome.* We are very aware that through no fault of teachers, such patience is in short supply in the condensed, fast-paced world of many schools.

Identification and Learning That Is Inclusive of the Local Ecology

Ecosophical writers such as Arne Naess (1988) examine the idea of *identification.* They are interested in the ways in which we see ourselves in and through features of the world beyond our physical body, how we identify with others—animals, plants, objects, landscapes—to such an extent that we can "lose ourselves" in them. For Krishnamurti, though, identification is the means by which an illusory sense of a permanent self is generated. Krishnamurti is critical of these processes of identification because they would appear to perpetuate a harmful imagined self. So, here's a challenge. If we educators take children into natural settings and invite them to identify with the many non-human species which surround them, are we thereby reinforcing the belief in this imagined self upon which the various experiences of nature centre?

Krishnamurti's approach suggests that such a challenge may be met if the way we approach nature resists appropriation and ownership. Paradoxically, his approach of observation and identification may indeed appear somewhat detached: "[n]ow can you observe the tree without naming it? Just look at the tree, sir. Just look at it and see if you can look at it without the operation of a single word or memory, just look. Can you?" (Krishnamurti, 1979). In making such an enquiry, Krishnamurti seeks not for a sentimental attachment to nature, nor an identification associated with ownership of knowledge about individual plants and flowers—valuable and interesting though such knowledge may be—but a letting go of selfishness and egoism, of possession and authority over nature. A shift towards the humility of teachers in the experience of nature suggests a wider movement towards the humility of all humanity, an awareness both of nature and its riches and a willingness to *let them be.* Insofar as his pedagogy calls for 'attention' rather than 'critique' in a conventional sense, 'looking' rather than analyzing, it is amenable to a non-interventionist pedagogy of nature.

In a sense Krishnamurti's schools embody a set of Arcadian ideals: they are places of beauty, connectedness and earth-awareness, calming human desires and balancing them against the needs of the environment. In the beauty of the pedagogical revelation of nature, Krishnamurti envisions the loss or, alternatively, the explosion of self into the cosmos, or nature, which is reflected in this passage from one of his last talks in India in late 1985:

> With the grandeur, the majesty of a mountain or a lake, or that river early in the morning making a golden path, for a second you've forgotten everything. That is, when the self is not, there is beauty... Like a child with a toy, as long as the toy is complex and he plays with it, the toy absorbs him, takes him over... We are also like that... We are absorbed by the mountain... for a few minutes; then we go back to our own world.
>
> (Krishnamurti, 1988, p. 73)

There is a great educational significance to this observation. It is a paradoxical process of self-learning without self: identification without ego. Perhaps many of us will remember this experience from childhood, that of 'losing oneself' in a place, or a game, of identifying with the wider processes that surround us, before 'coming to yourself' again. Krishnamurti suggests that if one doesn't understand the nature of this experience—perhaps the same experience described by ecological educators from Leopold's (1949) "thinking like a mountain" to Naess' (1995) "self-realisation"—it's because one has too much knowledge; rather, one should be simple, for "[i]f you are very simple, deeply simple in yourself, you will discover something extraordinary" (Krishnamurti, 1988, p. 73).

Krishnamurti (1987, p. 60) speaks of a war on nature and on humanity, of mankind's self-destruction alongside the destruction of the earth. For Krishnamurti, integration of the human into humanity and her integration into nature are inseparable. Integration into nature is integration into humanity: "If you are in harmony with nature, with all the things around you then you are in harmony with all human beings. If you have lost your relationship with nature you will inevitably lose your relationship with human beings" (p. 107). So what does this 'harmony with nature' consist of? And how can education help to bring it about? Krishnamurti's holistic pedagogy reflects Michael Bonnett's (2004, 2007, 2013) criticism of science as contributory to environmental and social crises, and David Orr's (1994) concern about the misuses of scientific 'cleverness.' Unlike Bonnett and Orr, Krishnamurti places particular emphasis upon what one might call individual spiritual education as an ecologically healing force. "[E]ducation is the cultivation of the whole brain, not one part of it...Science is what has brought about the present state of tension in the world for it has put together through knowledge the most destructive instrument[s] that man has ever known" (Krishnamurti, 1987, p. 125). So, his schools value science no more than any other branch of knowledge but value science less than awareness of the self. This approach necessarily applies to the science of climate disruption or mass extinction, or indeed any of the critical planetary problems, the impact of which has become so much better understood in the years since Krishnamurti's death. So, ultimately, the most important work of ecological learning is self-learning.

School in the Wider Context

Only a tiny proportion of teachers have access to environs like the Krishnamurti schools; but many can find urban parks, or even some fields or woods within walking distance. The authors recognize the challenges this presents, and there are clearly even greater practical difficulties in making time to allow awareness to develop in an overcrowded curriculum. It is inevitable and unavoidable that public education systems, formed and fed by the political contexts within which they sit, will themselves redound with political meanings and convulse with political contradictions. So, how do educators meet the challenge of opening the schoolroom door to *nature-as-teacher* in such a climate? Primrose asks, "[A]re we teachers politically literate and balanced enough to bring awareness to the student about these different paths [to sustainability], and in so doing, to avoid indoctrination?" (Primrose, 2014, p. 31). In doing some of the types of activity discussed in this chapter, and first and foremost by allowing teachers and children the time and space to make enquiry their own, we believe that children will indeed find their own as-yet unmapped paths to a sustainability of heart, mind, and conduct.

References

Bonnett, M. (2004). *Retrieving nature: Education for a post-humanist age.* Oxford: Blackwell.

Bonnett, M. (2007). Environmental education and the issue of nature. *Journal of Curriculum Studies, 39*(6), 707–721.

Bonnett, M. (2013). Sustainable development, environmental education, and the significance of being in place. *The Curriculum Journal, 24*(2), 250–271.

Krishnamurti, J. (1961). *The collected works of J. Krishnamurti.* Dubuque, Iowa: Kendall/Hunt Publishing Company.

Krishnamurti, J. (1979). *Is thought the instrument of right action? Conversation 1344, Brockwood Park, England, 26 August 1979.* Retrieved May 15, 2015, from www.jkrishnamurti.org/krishnamurti-teachings/view-text.php?tid=1344&chid=1043.

Krishnamurti, J. (1981). *Letters to the schools. Volume One.* Den Haag: Mirananda.

Krishnamurti, J. (1987). *Krishnamurti to himself: His last journal.* London: Victor Gollancz.

Krishnamurti, J. (1988). *The future is now: Last talks in India.* London: Victor Gollancz.

Krishnamurti, J. (2010). *Freedom from the known.* London: Rider.

Leopold, A. (1949). *A Sand County Almanac and sketches here and there.* New York: Oxford University Press.

Naess, A. (1988). Identification as a source of deep ecological attitudes. In M. Tobias (Ed.), *Deep ecology* (pp. 256–270). San Marcos, CA: Avant Books.

Naess, A. (1995). Self-realization: An ecological approach to being in the world. In G. Sessions (Ed.), *Deep ecology for the 21st century: Readings on the philosophy and practice of the new environmentalism* (pp. 225–239). Boston, MA: Shambhala.

Primrose, G. (2014). Nature as teacher: Extending the learning community. *Journal of the Krishnamurti Schools, 18,* 29–33.

5

SOWING SEEDS OF STEWARDSHIP THROUGH INTERGENERATIONAL GARDENING

Jolie Mayer-Smith and Linda Peterat

> *Through planting you learn lots of lessons...It teaches you about the environment and how it interacts with things around it. Like how the insect interacts with the plant and how the plant interacts with us and how we really depend on each other.*
>
> (Rita, grade 7 student)

Rita is a 12-year-old girl who is sharing her understanding of a fundamental principle of ecology, namely that life on our planet is sustained through the delicate balance of interaction and interdependence. Rita didn't study ecology in her grade seven classroom. She learned about the environment and plants, insects, and interdependency while working to grow vegetables beside Edward, a lively 78-year-old who had spent most of his life cultivating the fertile soil of the Fraser Valley in British Columbia, Canada.[1] Rita and her "farm friend," Edward, are part of the Intergenerational Landed Learning on the Farm Project, an initiative that since 2002 has partnered children from inner-city elementary schools with retired farmers and community gardeners on an urban farm, to learn about growing food and, through this experience, develop deep concern and care for the land and all its inhabitants. This intergenerational gardening project began as a small 'experiment' in environmental education to explore the roots of stewardship.

In this chapter, we describe the origin and evolution of the Intergenerational Landed Learning on the Farm for the Environment Project. We share the lessons we have learned and provide practical illustrations of how to sow seeds of stewardship through gardening from more than a decade of working with a dozen teachers, over 1,000 elementary children, and 700 volunteer gardeners.

Sowing Seeds of Stewardship

Intergenerational Landed Learning on the Farm for the Environment was a germ of an idea 13 years ago, but since then it has grown, blossomed, and borne fruit, providing many lessons on the ways and means of stewardship education. The seeds of this initiative were sown in 2001, following a visit we made to the University of British Columbia Farm, a 24-hectare parcel of land belonging to our university and the last urban farm in our Regional District. While historically a place of extensive research, this land had been neglected and was under threat of development. As science and home economics educators, we had been invited to visit the farm and offer advice on how it might reinvent itself as an education site. The pastoral space we saw was fresh, green, and alive, and our walk around the grounds inspired visions about breathing life into dreary discipline-heavy curricula and textbook-based classes. This site seemed an ideal place for urban school children and teachers to participate in authentic and meaningful lessons about growing food, healthy lifestyles, and environmental care.

To plan our project, we drew on our overlapping interests in science, environment, food education, home economics, and global issues. Our shared concern was that despite a pending worldwide environmental crisis, young people seemed unaware and uncaring about their interactions with the planet. This blindness towards the environment was alarming and caused us to ask, why was it that we (chapter co-authors) felt emotionally close to the earth? We thought about experiences that influenced our values, beliefs, and behaviours. Our conclusion was that time spent outdoors when we were young, playing, working, and experiencing nature in the garden, often in the company of older family members, was significant and left us with enduring memories.

Based on our memories of learning about nature in spaces beyond classrooms, we decided to adopt a "place-based approach." Place-based learning can infuse environmental education with elements of empathy for the earth and community-mindedness (Gruenewald, 2003; Woodhouse & Knapp, 2000). We reasoned that a farm could offer rich opportunities for tangible hands-on participation with the land and a space for nurturing the living and non-living world, activities we believed were essential for developing environmental consciousness (Morris, 2002). Berry (1987) described the lives of farmers as being guided by the unspoken law, "Land that is in human use must be lovingly used" (p. 164). Thus, we imagined retired farmers being part of our project. We knew rural spaces were shrinking in the face of suburban sprawl, and that in our aging population the numbers of people with deeply felt experiences were dwindling. We believed there were retired farmers and avid gardeners in urban spaces who retained their passion for land-based traditions. We wondered whether these city-based farmers and community gardeners could help teachers cultivate in children an understanding of what it means to care for the land and our planet. Our thinking was further informed by McNamee's (1997) argument that human–earth connections develop gradually over time, and that the emotional connections fostered by caring interpersonal relationships in families are important preparation for ecological caring. We decided to try and replicate these relationships through an intergenerational partnering of adults with farming or gardening backgrounds and children.

The premise and theme of our environmental initiative is that *eating is an environmental act*. This theme builds on Wendel Berry's (1990) notion that eating is an agricultural act, and this idea has been further developed by Michael Pollan (2006). All aspects of food, including our consumptive, social, and cultural practices and habits, influence the health of the planet and all that inhabit it. We envisioned that discussions about what we eat, why we eat what we do, where food comes from, the costs of food production, and the implications of particular food choices were topics that young people could understand and engage with if they planted food gardens and sampled food they had grown themselves. We also believed that conversations about land, food, and the earth could be easily integrated across the curricula.

Cultivating a Plan

We began in 2002, naming our project Intergenerational Landed Learning on the Farm for the Environment to reflect the elements we believed would support children in becoming caring stewards of the planet: firsthand experience with the land in the presence of seasoned mentors in an agrarian setting. Our plan was to start small and work with one class of students from a nearby school. At the farm, we had a dozen raised beds, empty and waiting to be cultivated in the Land Food Community Garden. We received a small grant to support our activities. These funds were frugally designated to purchase tools, seeds, and soil amendments, bussing costs to bring a class of children to the farm, and part-time salaries of three project assistants. Envisioning that learning about nature and care for the land through gardening would take time (at least a full growing cycle), we recruited a teacher who was comfortable bringing her students to UBC Farm to participate in multiple *farm days*.

Finding experienced farmers for the project was more challenging, however, as we discovered that "retired" farmers continued to farm. Through word of mouth and advertising at community centres, we located four men and three women who were experienced farmers and master gardeners, and excited about sharing their knowledge of growing food and caring for the land with a group of young students. Thus, in year one, the participants in Intergenerational Landed Learning on the Farm consisted of one science teacher and 18 grade seven girls from a local private school, seven farmers, and a small group of personnel who helped manage the site. The volunteer farmers and gardeners, designated as "farm friends," met the students for the first time at UBC Farm on a cool, sunny morning in January 2003. Farm friends were partnered with groups of three girls, and these teams worked together for the duration of the project. From January through June our intergenerational teams met and worked in their gardens. It was a learning experience for us all.

Growing Together

Starting Small: The First Two Years

From January to June 2003, farm friend teams met 11 times at the farm and on three occasions at the school. Time together was spent in conversations about growing practices, building cold-frames, planning inside an on-site greenhouse, sowing seeds and transplanting seedlings, and planting and caring for the culti-vated plots. Regardless of the weather, teams spent time every farm day tending their crops. During one visit, the students interviewed their farm friends about their lives on the land. Each group made their own decisions about their garden plots: what to plant, how to plant, when to thin, when to add soil amendments. Groups discussed the merits of various cultivation practices and how to deal with garden "pests" and insect friends. Lively debates about organic and traditional growing practices were part of everyday conversation among farm friends and between groups. As the garden plots grew and flourished so did the relationships between the children and their farm friends.

The teacher took part in the digging and planting, and she watched with inter-est the discoveries taking place every farm day. As the year unfolded, she planned and implemented classroom activities that linked the farm events with the provin-cial curriculum. Each group of students maintained a team journal documenting their gardening activities, and near the end of the project in June 2003, farm friends joined the students at school to watch multimedia presentations the chil-dren had designed about their experiences and learning on the farm. On the final day, a small early harvest celebration was held at the farm. Parents accompanied the students, met the farm friends, and enjoyed sampling foods the children had grown in their raised beds.

By the close of our first year, the project had yielded a rich early harvest of healthy vegetables and an equally rich set of lessons about education for stew-ardship. Not everything had worked as planned, but important takeaways were evident in the words and actions of the participants. The children and their senior companions had become close, trusting friends who were committed to their growing projects and deeply connected to the farm. The teacher was ready to return with another class of 18 grade seven girls the following year. Having expe-rienced a full cycle of farm days and more knowledgeable about the complexities of the non-formal learning environment, she felt prepared to develop explicit environmental and science lessons that could be integrated with the gardening activities.

In the second year, we started farm visits earlier in the school year to give the groups a chance to experience the fall harvest, prepare their garden beds for winter, and plan earlier for spring planting. To encourage more integration of school and field learning and more environmental conversations, we met with the teacher and farm friends to share ideas on what they might do with their teams. The teacher proposed that a more "scientific" approach be adopted in the gardens. Students were asked to generate a 'research question' and conduct small experiments with their farm friends. To bring more attention to the environmental theme of the project, farm friend groups were encouraged to have explicit conversations about organic practices and cultivation methods. The farm gave us more land to cultivate so each intergenerational team now worked in three beds—two raised and one in-ground. This blessing came at a cost. Gardens and group friendships grew in the spring sunshine, but with more garden area, time for conversations about ecological relationships and environmental practices had to give way to serious weeding. The year ended in early June with an even larger harvest and a closing celebration for parents and friends that had a festival atmosphere.

Blossoming: Years Three and Four

In the first two years, we had developed a workable model of education for stewardship. We found additional funding and were now ready to work with more classes, and move the project from private to public school, to involve both boys and girls and children with more diverse social and economic backgrounds. We also sought to work with elementary classes where one teacher dealt with most school subjects, believing this would enable an easier integration of environmental concepts and conversations across the curriculum. In the third and fourth years, our young participants were 85 children in grades four to seven, from three different classes in two schools located in different socio-economic sectors of the city. The blossoming of our program required an increase in volunteer farm friends to work with the children at the farm. We retained 10 senior farm friends but were limited in our ability to identify enough older adults for all the children. However, interest in our project grew, and we were able to recruit an additional 20 volunteers from the local community and our university, to serve as a younger generation of farm friends for the children. The mix of adult participants now included community gardeners and university students with interests in environmental advocacy, intergenerational community building, and sustainable food growing.

Managing a larger project required additional planning and more structure. We developed themed lessons for each of the dozen farm days and began creating activities designed for before and after school-to-farm visits. We met with teachers outside of farm days to collaboratively plan for farm visits and provided them with resources and ideas for possible lessons to include in their classes. Working with the increased number of farm friends also required us to attune to students' learning needs. With some being more experienced with environmental concerns, educational practices, and gardening and others less so, we began partnering farm friends so they could support each other as well as the children. Farm friends took more ownership of the project, and some would spontaneously research problems such as methods of controlling the pest infestations in the garden beds and then share that with all the participants on the next visit.

Along with project growth came challenges. Our gardens grew merrily, our harvest was rich and tasty, and children and adults grew close through their time spent together. But we discovered the quiet, contemplative, and pastoral feel of the farm was compromised on those days when 60 children and 20 adults gardened together. We encouraged a meditative, slowed-down pace in the garden by having children write about hearing, smelling, tasting, seeing, and feeling all parts of the environment. Still, thoughtful conversations about the earth were difficult to foster and maintain.

Bearing Fruits: Five Years and Beyond

By the end of the fourth year, we had developed a solid understanding about attributes that worked, including enrollment and engagement practices, procedures, and resources that were needed on a continuing basis. Our intergenerational model was clearly powerful for building a learning community and creating opportunties for conversations about land, food, and environment. But we recognized that the quality and nature of learning, and the conversations and practices we sought to engender, required working with smaller numbers. We needed to create more space and opportunities in our program for small groups to experience and connect with nature—to contemplate, observe, and reflect on the food they were growing and its significance for the earth.

In the years that followed, we continued to support and maintain what was working, and added refinements to Intergenerational Landed Learning on the Farm. We have involved more schools and teachers, maintained a regimen of 10 to 12 visits per academic year, and have had participating schools bring a single class of students to the farm each year. Teachers apply to participate in the program and are asked to commit to meeting together on five or six occasions to share their ideas and classroom practices for integrating gardening activities with school curriculum. Other refinements include facilitating more focused conversations and lessons about plant health, local food issues, and healthy eating. These topics emerged naturally as we began to involve one group of children and their adult farm friends in preparing a 'healthy' snack each visit in an on-site kitchen. To better prepare our farm friends for their small group work with the children, we produced a volunteer handbook and provided workshops for new farm friends prior to the start of fall and winter programming. To support the integration of garden- and food-based activities across the curriculum, we have written and published a teacher resource book and a cookbook of garden-based recipes (Mayer-Smith & Peterat, 2010; Peterat & Hillis, 2011).

Learning from the Land

Each year we document the experiences of children and adults in Landed Learning to understand how intergenerational gardening influences care for the earth.

We have used a variety of approaches for the collection of assessment information, including formal and informal interviews with individual children and adults, focus groups with children and adults, still photography and video, qustionnaires, anecdotal reporting by teachers, parents, and volunteers, and reviews of children's journals and schoolwork. The information we collect has helped us review and revise our program, provided a picture of what children and adults learn through gardening, and taught us much about the practice of promoting connections to nature and dispositions of stewardship through gardening. In previous publications, we have written about the experiences of our multi-generational participants (see e.g., Mayer-Smith, Bartosh & Peterat, 2007; Peterat & Mayer-Smith, 2006). In this chapter, we focus on what we have learned over the years and provide advice for others interested in exploring environmental education in the garden.

Gardening can build environmental understanding and connections. We have seen that community gardening "on the farm" is powerful for promoting learning about the land and how to care for it. The primary experiences of touching soil and sowing seeds makes stewardship tangible and meaningful (see Figure 5.1).

Growing food teaches children *how* to care for the environment, as recycling, composting, and lifestyle choices become real and understandable. However, environment is a complex and abstract concept, difficult to grasp for many children. We find that the physical acts of digging, planting, harvesting, cooking, and eating need to be augmented by focused conversations about these activities. These conversations can help children understand that environment encompasses both the physical and biological world—including themselves.

FIGURE 5.1   Shoveling compost (photograph courtesy of Jolie Mayer-Smith).

[The environment] is definitely more clear now that we have gone to the farm, actually worked outside and seen how we could improve the environment. If you stop to think about what humans are doing to pollute the air, you realize it's not very good for the environment and being at the farm taught us.

(Sylvia, age 12)

It's very important to take care of the environment because we rely on it...like everything comes from our environment...and we should keep it healthy if we want to continue living because without the environment we cannot grow food.

(Sadie, age 12)

Last time [we talked] about environment I just thought we should not have any more buildings and I did not really have a reason. Now I have a reason and I think more about environment. If we have garbage at our farm, the garbage will go inside our soil and the bad stuff [gets] in there. I think I really care about environment now. And I pick up garbage that I see, even if it's not mine.

(Sam, age 9)

Children recognize the sensory experiences of planting seeds, caring for crops, harvesting, and tasting what they have grown provide important lessons, deep connections, and memorable understanding. They have told us that such learning will endure and guide them into their adult lives.

I'll end up remembering this because I actually did something for it. The farming stuff I am learning so when I have a garden when I'm older, I'll remember and be able to take care of it. I can apply it to other things.

(Jane, age 12)

It makes me want to garden more. It helps you enjoy many things in your life. You would know what plants you were eating.

(Jackie, age 12)

I never knew worms are really good for plants. I just saw they were eating the plant away and stuff. But they are actually really good to a plant... And I never knew there was so so [many] in the soil. I thought that it was just plain dirty old soil. But there is so much stuff you can find in the soil.

(Vick, age 10)

Gardening teaches responsibility and respect, builds self-esteem, and shapes new identities essential for stewardship. In the garden, children experience autonomy and control of their learning context, and become personally empowered as they engage in learning that is practical and self-directed. The decisions they make and actions they take have visible consequences and impact others. This is education that shapes new self-identities essential to taking responsibility for the environment.

> I really like being outside and like being able to be one with the ground. I like just being outside and being a part of nature.
>
> (Sam, age 12)

> At the farm I have more responsibility. We get to do our own thing and make our own decisions.
>
> (Joanne, age 12)

> I learned that you need to take care of the things or things will die. Because we need plants to live—they give oxygen and everything you eat.
>
> (Hope, age 9)

> Some people just go around cutting plants off and wrecking them...They (the plants) are more [important] than you think they are. Without plants and trees, we wouldn't have oxygen and all that. I watch out for plants now. Before when we used to play tag, I might run through gardens and stuff. Now I know it's way more important.
>
> (Gurjeet, age 11)

The garden provides a learning environment where children make personal discoveries and build understanding, independent of textbooks and lectures by experts (see Figure 5.2). Stinky compost, slimy worms and "stingy" bees, initially regarded tentatively, become respected and honoured for their ecological contributions. Children take pride in the hard work of planting and what they produce. While not every seed germinates, every child can experience success in the garden. This is inclusive education that builds self-esteem.

> At the farm, you can grow stuff and you can actually get to do it, but in the classroom we would be just drawing the tools. We wouldn't be actually using the tools.
>
> (Denise, age 12)

Gardening in intergenerational teams builds community and supports environmental care. A key lesson is that mentorship matters greatly. Bringing children and adults of all ages together in the garden creates a social–emotional network with environmental benefits. Human relationships, trust, and community grow along with the crops, and ageism and cultural stereotyping are diminished. By working side-by-side with adults who become their friends and role models, children gain

FIGURE 5.2 Sunflower discovery (photograph courtesy of Jolie Mayer-Smith).

the confidence to touch the soil, the caterpiller, and the compost, sample new foods, and take on healthy lifestyle practices. Some are moved to become environmental leaders and role models in their homes, schools, and communities. Children's comments illustrate the special relationship and understanding they gain from having an adult farm friend.

> They're kind of equal but...I think her role is a bit higher than ours. She is a role model to us. She shows us how you can involve having gardens as fun in your life.
>
> (Rene, age 12)

> It's kind of neat to have someone who spent part of their life farming, to be a guide. Normally, if you were just growing up in the city you'd have to grow stuff by yourself and read books. But (here) you have, like a primary source.
>
> (Anna, age 12)

> It was an experience of a lifetime! My garden friend was Jocelyne. She was so nice. I enjoyed spending my time with her very much! Jocelyne taught me so much about growing a garden. She taught me what I needed to know.
>
> (Sarah, age 9)

In the garden, *slow* environmental learning should be expected and embraced. Learning in gardens is slow and cannot be hurried (Mayer-Smith & Peterat, 2015). Building deep understanding about the connections among land, food, health, environment, community, and care requires time. Learning occurs over the cycle of the seasons, with the growth of plants. Understanding the significance of a flower and its ecology in the garden involves watching it break through the earth, unfurl over time, and develop into a fruit. This is very different from learning about a flower through a textbook or diagram where all parts are shown simultaneously (Williams & Brown, 2012). We also have found that learning-to-teach in the garden is slow and takes time. Teachers need time to discover how to embrace and enjoy the capricious elements of nature that can trump the best planned lesson. While at times challenging, teaching in the garden is also transformative. For teachers who are excited about learning alongside children, gardens are engaging, reinvigorting, non-repetitive, and emergent spaces that can inspire and stimulate new and creative educational practicies.

Digging In and Closing Words

Intergenerational Landed Learning allows us to have sustained converations with children about farming, farmers, and farms as well as model and practice care for soil, water, and land. But similar conversations and lessons can happen in smaller green spaces. Gardens have become abundant and popular on school grounds and community sites (see e.g., Gaylie, 2011). These are places where children can experience the wonder of tiny seeds sprouting from soil, feel the excitement and pride of eating something they grew themselves, and discover the connections among land, food, health, and environment.

Intergenerational food gardening, in school gardens or on a farm as described in this chapter, can foster deep commitment to environmental stewardship. Former participants tell us about lifestyle changes, including becoming more conscious consumers, recyclers, and gardeners. Others have gotten busy digging in and becoming leaders in new projects in community and school gardens. To date, we know of 15 garden-based environmental projects across the globe that have been initiated by former Landed Learning participants.

These projects along with our own indicate that gardens are inspiring and inclusive places for environmental learning. Many children today are challenged and unsuccessful in classrooms, where it is difficult to honor and support the rates of learning and energies of multiple, diverse learners. But *every student is successful in the garden*, for when multiple seeds are sown, the results are always positive. Garden learning provides space to move, activities that support bursts of energy, a place for peaceful contemplation, and ample opportunities for discoveries and learning about nature that happens at one's own pace. Our project provides one possible model for environmental education in a garden. To develop your own environmental education program in a garden, we have a few basic recommendations:

1. Start small.
2. Work with committed volunteers.

3. Create a simple, structured program.
4. Go slowly to build community, new identities, and new understandings.

References

Berry, W. (1987). *Home economics*. San Francisco: North Point Press.

Berry, W. (1990). *What are people for?* San Francisco: North Point Press.

Gaylie, V. (2011). *Roots and research: Urban school gardens*. New York: Peter Lang.

Gruenewald, D. A. (2003). The best of both worlds: A critical pedagogy of place. *Educational Researcher*, 32(4), 3–12.

Mayer-Smith, J., & Peterat, L. (Eds.) (2010). *Get growing! Food and gardening curriculum for elementary and middle grades*. Vernon, BC: Really Small Vernon Press.

Mayer-Smith, J., & Peterat, L. (2015). Slow pedagogy and slow research: New directions for understanding learning about food–environment relationships. *Of Land and Living Skies, A Community Journal on Place, Land and Learning*, 3, 15–22.

Mayer-Smith, J., Bartosh, O, & Peterat, L. (2007). Teaming children and elders to grow food and environmental consciousness. *Applied Environmental Education and Communication*, 6(1), 77–85.

McNamee, A. S. (1997). Ecological caring: A psychological perspective on the person environment relationship. In P. J. Thompson (Ed.), *Environmental education for the 21st Century* (pp. 259–267). New York: Peter Lang.

Morris, M. (2002). Ecological consciousness and curriculum. *Journal of Curriculum Studies*, 34(5), 571–587.

Peterat, L., & Hillis, J. (2011). *Garden eats and treats: A resource for parents, grandparents, teachers, children and anyone who gardens*. Vernon, BC: Really Small Vernon Press.

Peterat, L., & Mayer-Smith, J. (2006). Farm friends: Exploring intergenerational environmental learning. *Journal of Intergenerational Relationships*, 4(1), 107–116.

Pollan, M. (2006). *The omnivore's dilemma: A natural history of four meals*. New York: Penguin.

Williams, D. R., & Brown, J. D. (2012). *Learning gardens and sustainability education*. New York and London: Routledge.

Woodhouse, C. E., & Knapp, J. L. (2000). *Place-based curriculum and instruction*, ERIC Document Reproduction Service No. EDO-RC-00-6.

Acknowledgements

We acknowledge with appreciation major financial contributions to this project from the PromoScience Program of the Natural Sciences and Engineering Research Council of Canada, and support from many public and private organizations and donors. We also recognize and warmly thank the many volunteers who share their time, enthusiam, energy, and expertise with the children in our project.

Note

1 All names given to project participants are pseudonyms, in order to maintain confidentiality.

6

THE NATURALIST-IN-RESIDENCE

Learning with Students and Teachers in the Outdoors

Ted Watt

Vignette One

Our small group of fifth graders hiked quietly to the study site in the oak-pine forest across the street from our school. We sat down and got our equipment ready. All eyes were focused up into the trees. Sam got the boom-box ready and, at a signal from the timer, Destiny pushed the play button and the pre-recorded, black-throated blue warbler's call rang out into the quiet woods. Almost instantly an identical call echoed from the branches above our heads. The students were electrified. Abby almost forgot to note the number and timing of the calls on our data sheet. Excited smiles went around our circle! Next we tried scarlet tanager and, sure enough, same thing; and again with the eastern pewee. Wood thrush, no answer. As we schlepped through the poison ivy, brush, and partially buried rocks, the students shared their excitements. Every student was engaged! They tossed around the names of the birds like old friends, since we had been learning about them and their calls in class over the last several weeks. When we got out of the woods we checked each other for ticks and I reminded the students to do a full body check with their parents when they got home. We headed back to school to share our findings with the other teams who had been collecting similar data at other study points located throughout the forest preserve. (NGSS: Science & Engineering Practices: Planning and carrying out investigations & Analyzing and interpreting data)

I have worked as a naturalist-educator at the Hitchcock Center for the Environment in Amherst, Massachusetts, for the last 30 years. A big part of my job is to serve as

Naturalist-in-Residence (NIR) in local schools. Our work is closely coordinated with classroom teachers and with school curricula. We remain employees of our regional community nature and environmental center, but we spend full days at individual local schools leading field trips and classes to explore the school grounds and local natural areas.

Naturalists, in collaboration with teachers, fulfill a variety of purposes. They add a real-world dimension to classroom-based science study, lead field trips rich with interactions in nature to stimulate student creative and non-fiction writing, and provide positive learning experiences for students who may not learn best through traditional classroom methods. Importantly, naturalists can help schools and teachers build their own capacity to plan and implement nature experiences, thus becoming less dependent on outside experts. However you set up such a program, it promises to explore new approaches to student learning and in your teaching.

In this chapter, I describe my work as a Naturalist-in-Residence in elementary schools. While I believe strongly that all schools ought to have a NIR on staff, as they do for physical education, art, and music, I recognize that not all schools currently are able to fund such a position. In the absence of a funded NIR position, schools could foster relationships with volunteer naturalists in the community or students at local high schools or colleges to support teacher and student learning outdoors. Local bird clubs, nature centers, and state parks are all good resources for such contacts.

A Case Study

Pat, a local school principal, contacted our environmental center about embarking on an in-depth outdoor nature study program with her school. She already knew of our successful class field trips. Typically, students had visited our center for a two-hour exploration of some specific topic. After a field trip to our center, it was up to the individual classroom teacher to provide her students with opportunities for reflection and follow-up. Pat explained that one of her first grade teachers had come to her wanting to teach a unit on trees (NGSS: K-LS1-1, K-ESS3-1), but the teacher felt she didn't know enough about local trees to plan the unit. The school grounds had a rich assortment of tree species, some of them old and impressively tall. But this resource was largely unexplored because of teachers' lack of confidence about this science content. Pat contacted us, and we agreed to work in depth with the teachers at her school. Pat and a couple of her most motivated teachers wrote and submitted a grant to their city's local educational foundation to support our work. And the proposal was funded for three years!

Our NIR was funded to provide three field trips each year with each classroom in the school. The content focus of each field trip was coordinated with teachers' classroom curricula. Over the course of our eight-year NIR project, classroom teachers have become noticeably more confident outdoors. As individual teachers gained confidence, each at their own speed, they have taken more and more responsibility for leading the outdoor field trips themselves, with the NIR there for support and guidance if needed.

Additionally, the three-year grant funded our NIR to work with grade level teacher teams to tweak the district's science curriculum, developing an additional outdoor component to enrich existing classroom practice. The NIR met with teacher teams for three half-days each year over two years, and together we produced hands-on outdoor study units for each grade level. Teachers implemented the units in their classes. During the third year of funding, teachers from our school led workshops for their grade level colleagues from other schools in the district.

When I first started working with the fourth grades, they were studying life cycles and, in particular, the frog. Teachers were in the habit of ordering African clawed frogs from biological supply companies, raising them in aquaria in their classrooms, and observing mating, egg-laying, and tadpole hatching and development. It was all very neat. But what to do with the non-native frogs when the unit was over? Let them go? Send them home with students? Flush them down the *unthinkable*? Teachers had tried various solutions in the past but were uncomfortable with all the options. It was a problem. However, when the teachers learned that the native wood frog, living right outside their school, went through the full developmental cycle during the months of March through June every year, they were instantly on board. The teachers and our NIR worked together to revise the fourth grade life cycles unit, including information about the wood frog's vernal pool habitat and the timing of their annual cycle. Through our research, we learned that African clawed frogs can be carriers of a *chytrid* fungus that has been shown to kill native frog species, another reason to avoid them. The curricular changes we developed achieved the same educational goals, didn't cost anything for the living creatures, and at the same time helped students develop a deeper connection to their immediate environment. It has been a great success, with some glitches over the years, but a terrific connection between the teachers and the Naturalist-in-Residence (NGSS: 3-LS1-1, 3-LS4-2, 4-ESS3-2).

Vignette Two

As an integral part of an extended unit on rocks and the history of Earth, I accompanied the third grade class into the forest across the street from the school. Before we entered the forest, I gathered the group and set a tone by asking them to accompany me on a journey back in geologic time. We stepped into the woods and encountered a group of large gray boulders. Students were excited to examine the big chunks of rock, and they even attempted to climb on the biggest. Climbing was interrupted by the classroom teacher for reasons of safety. Students discovered that the gray color was actually made up of tiny crystals of white, gray, and black. We hadn't studied mineral identification yet, so I briefly explained what the minerals were and that the black was called mica, the white feldspar, and the gray was quartz. We were lucky to live in an area with granite, an igneous bedrock. I could see students getting attached to their own small piece of the bedrock, and I cautioned them, again, that we were in a public park and everything there, including the rocks, was protected. They could hold and examine the rocks but they couldn't take them home.

I asked the students to think of what they already knew about the formation of rocks. "How do you think these rocks were formed?" They immediately jumped in with lots of ideas. We reached the conclusion that it was igneous rock from an ancient underground bed of magma. I told the students that we would have been immediately vaporized if we had been there when the magma was molten! I asked the students if they noticed anything else. We spread out to explore the big outcrop, and soon I heard shrieks of discovery. "Here are some crystals!" "Wow, I found some too!" "Hey, look at this, there's a line of white going right through this rock!" After ten minutes of individual exploring, during which time there were very few behavioral "resets" by the teacher and me, we came together in our whole group and discussed the different sizes of the crystals. Students learned that the size of the crystal depends on the relative temperature of the rock as it cools—smaller crystals mean more rapid cooling....

I called everyone's attention to the white line running through the bedrock. I asked the students how they thought the line got there. All sorts of suggestions cropped up. Eventually Milagros got on the right track. "Yes, that's sort of right," I said. "It was molten when it squished in here." Students seemed to be visualizing the molten rock being forced into a crack in the solid parent bedrock and then cooling. I asked for student volunteers and all hands shot up. I arranged six volunteers in a tight group; they were the parent granite bedrock. I taught them to squeeze together tightly and be as solid a group as they could. Then two more volunteers became the molten quartz. Their job was to squeeze slowly but inexorably into the granite—to find a crack and then go for it, but slowly....

(NGSS: 4-ESS1-1, 4-ESS2-1)

Strategies for Success

We understand that implementing a Naturalist-in-Residence program presents a number of challenges. I describe several of challenges we have encountered over the years with suggested strategies for addressing them.

Administrative Support

It is critical that your principal be *on board* with this approach. Provide the principal with research-based information (Kellert, 2005; Kings College London, 2011) about the benefits of outdoor learning (e.g., increased student motivation for learning and active engagement, improved physical health, and participation by students with all learning styles). The book *Last Child in the Woods* by Richard Louv (2008) provides many powerful justifications for outdoor learning.

Connecting to the Standards

It is possible to design many exciting investigations in nature that address national education standards. To illustrate this, you will occasionally find, in the case studies and vignettes for this chapter, letters and numbers in parentheses. These refer to the Next Generation Science Standards (NGSS) and the Common Core State Standards for Literacy and Mathematics (CCSS). Letters and numbers refer to specific grade level standards and are included after descriptions of activities that address these specific learning standards.

Outdoor Education in Urban Environments

Urban environments provide a unique set of challenges for outdoor learning. Although the diversity of organisms available for study may be reduced, you can still plan detailed outdoor units. Mowed lawns, street trees, sidewalks, pigeons, and crows provide rich opportunities for study. We have studied dandelions blooming in the school lawn and insects in the dead autumn leaves that blow into corners of buildings, and even noises, natural and person-made, outside the school. We have walked to nearby parks, maintaining vigilance about hazards left in the grass, to study the trees growing there. We've brought frog eggs into urban schools for students to raise in their rooms. Urban students may well have different attitudes toward wild creatures so be prepared to take time to understand and discuss their concerns.

Another possibility is to enroll your class in weeklong residential outdoor education programs. These programs are designed for older elementary students and may expose urban dwellers to new environments. I have accompanied an urban, sixth grade class to the Cape Cod National Seashore for a week-long residential exploration that opened many eyes to new environments and engaging ways of getting dirty! We even rolled down some of the big blowing sand dunes in one of the public areas.

Parent and Community Support

Your parent volunteer group can be a tremendous ally for the program as has been the case in all of our schools. Have the NIR lead several parent or family nature programs, and invite your school community to participate. The excitement about learning from direct experience in nature is a powerful factor in building support for the program. Videos of students learning outdoors, possibly available from your local nature center, can provide more illustrative evidence of the value of the programs. Be prepared for questions about outdoor hazards, and don't minimize parents' concerns. Explain what you will do to reduce the hazards and explain what families will be asked to do as partners. Don't forget to clarify the links to the standards for parents, too!

Financial Support

You will need to find external funding to support your NIR program. Generating funding is not as difficult as you may think. Our programs in several districts were supported initially through local educational foundations. One budget included NIR time, salaries for substitutes so teachers could have release time from the classrooms to plan curriculum, nature study materials and trade books, and administrative time. Additional funding for our NIR programs has come from our state's cultural council, local community cultural councils, and significant contributions from individual schools' parent–teacher organizations. One of our residencies is focused on the water cycle and water conservation and has been funded for years by a local municipal water district. In one school district, we have partnered with a theater company, and our NIR works together with a teaching artist to integrate science and the arts, culminating in a final student presentation each school year. Arts funding has complemented our science and nature programming. Unfortunately, we have yet to be included in school district budgets as an integral part of staffing, like physical education, art, and music teachers. But we haven't given up.

Challenges to Student Participation

Most students will jump into the outdoor learning environment with both feet. We rarely encounter students who are deeply afraid of nature. Occasionally, students (and teachers) are grossed out by nature—both boys and girls. Gently encouraging exploration at their individual level can be helpful. Discussing proper clothing, including reassuring students that it is normal (and fun!) to get dirty, can relieve some students' concerns. Modeling enthusiasm and lively interest in the topic of investigation is another good technique to draw students in.

Orientation for both students and parents about proper clothing for inclement weather may be needed depending on your community. Our schools have an extensive supply of appropriately sized winter and rain gear for students to borrow. These will need to be laundered regularly. Hats especially need to be carefully laundered to avoid possibly spreading head lice.

Students with limited mobility are often very excited about getting out into nature. Accommodations can include choosing a shorter, more accessible route for exploring, including indoor study of nature, lining up adult helpers to support the student in traveling the uneven ground of the trail, and soliciting family assistance with the students' mobility challenges.

Eliciting Teacher Support of the NIR Program

Outdoor education poses significant hazards not present indoors, and teachers' fears of outdoor hazards should be taken seriously. A well-developed plan for knowing, responding to, and mitigating these hazards is important. Don't assume that teachers are equally knowledgeable about these hazards. You may have to educate staff about these issues. In one school, the school nurse was a key player in solving some of the outdoor hazard challenges. Home full-body checks for deer ticks (which often carry Lyme Disease) have worked well in our schools. The NIR's enthusiasm and comfort in the outdoors will go a long way to allaying staff fears.

Many teachers harbor fears about outdoor student behavior management. The outdoors is very different than the contained classroom. What if the students run wild? What if they don't listen? What if the management techniques that teachers use in the classroom don't work outdoors? Outdoor behavior management is different than when indoors. There will be considerably more physical activity and teachers need to welcome this, within certain clearly identified limits. There will be more noise. These are all real concerns. One of our NIRs uses a loud crow call, available for purchase from hunting supply outlets, to signal that she needs students to listen. Giving clear directions and expectations indoors before going out will go a long way toward helping students understand what you want when your class is outdoors. Discuss with your class how outdoor learning is different from recess. In most schools, being outdoors means recess, with its associated behaviors. Students are very capable of understanding the difference between the two. Planning outdoor activities within the context of a larger unit of study can set students up to focus on the tasks you have planned.

On occasion, student energy is just too high for them to focus on the activity you have planned. In this case it might make sense to temporarily scrap the lesson you had planned and instead instigate a running game, if possible one that reinforces the topic you had planned to investigate.

Vignette Three

The vernal pool was about a 20-minute walk from school. The students carried long-handled nets and plastic dishpans along with two one-gallon buckets with lids. When we reached the shore of the vernal pool, we gathered before dispersing to explore. I reviewed the proper methods of using the net and tubs and reminded students that the pool was a fragile ecosystem and not a place to horse around. The students then exploded down to the pool edge. "Hey, look at the little tadpoles!" "There's tons of 'em!" "Look, there's a frog!" "What kind is it?" "Is it a wood frog?" "I don't think so!" "Wow, I caught a little, wiggly, red worm!" "Here's a little tube made out of pine needles and it's moving all by itself!" Excitement filled the air.

The teacher, parent volunteers, and I checked in with groups and encouraged them to look carefully at what they had in their tubs. "See that bug there? Watch how it moves—it uses its six legs, right? Well, if I take this pine needle and touch it gently at the tail, watch what happens?" "Oh, wow!" "How does it do that?" "It swims but its legs just hang by its side!" "Watch its butt, see the little grains of mud shooting away?" "What does that?" "Air?" "No." "Water!" "Yes, it has a built-in jet pack that it uses to make a quick get-away if a predator gets too close." "It's a dragonfly nymph, you know, those big flying bugs with the four wings?"

After about 30 minutes of high-energy exploring, frog catching, and wet feet, we transferred the creatures into the buckets, leaving most of the water in the pool—bringing with us just enough water to support the animals back at school for the afternoon. After lunch, we observed the tadpoles, insect larvae, and other invertebrates through simple microscopes, drawing and writing about what students observed. Several of the writing prompts encouraged the fourth graders to consider their creatures' physical and behavioral adaptations to the aquatic environment. Explaining animal and plant adaptations is one of our science standards; therefore, we addressed one of our science standards through exploration of the students' own neighborhood and offered them an opportunity to understand and care about the organisms in their backyards. (NGSS: 3-LS1-1, 3-LS3-2, CCSS: ELA.LITERACY.W.4.2)

Benefits of NIR and Outdoor Education

Naturalists, in collaboration with teachers, could serve a variety of purposes and benefits. They add a real-world dimension to classroom-based science study, stimulate creative and non-fiction writing about nature, and provide positive learning experiences for students who may not learn best through traditional classroom methods. Importantly, NIRs can help schools and teachers build their own capacity to plan and implement nature experiences, thus becoming less dependent on outside experts. Furthermore, students have opportunities to use science skills that come naturally when in the outdoors, such as observing, asking questions, constructing explanations, gathering data, and refining explanations. Students also have myriad occasions to exercise their natural curiosity when in nature. Importantly, in the context of outdoor-based science inquiry, students show a greater openness to learning science content about the subjects of their investigations.

Much formal research has documented benefits to students: e.g., improved large body motor functions (Fjortoft, 2001); increased motivation for learning resulting in higher scores on standardized tests (Lieberman & Hoody, 2005); improved cognitive abilities (Berman, Jonides & Kaplan, 2008); greater respect for plants and animals (Collado & Corraliza, 2015); and improved focus of students identified as having attention challenges (Kuo & Taylor, 2004).

Conclusion

We envision a Naturalist-in-Residence in every school, just as most elementary schools have physical education, music, and art teachers. Naturalists-in-Residence help to remind students and teachers of the wonders and excitements of the natural world waiting outside the doors of the school. NIRs connect students to local nature with the idea that they will develop a sense of belonging and a sense of stewardship for the creatures and plants that they have come to know. It is our hope that they will, in developmentally appropriate ways, generalize these attitudes to the Earth and the planetary systems that support all life.

The future holds daunting challenges and our young people will be called upon to do their best to solve these problems. With a significant deepening of human understanding and connection to the natural world, I believe people will be better prepared and more inclined to defend a diverse and beautiful biosphere, one that supports life for all creatures. We envision our Naturalist-in-Residence programs making a difference as we all look toward the future together.

Vignette Four

It was a cold February day and the fifth and sixth grade class was scheduled to put into practice some of the animal tracking skills we had been learning. Students in this small rural school were well equipped to spend time outdoors. In small groups, we hiked down into the maple-hemlock forest right outside the school. Students were leading, and the classroom teacher, parent volunteers, and I encouraged students to notice any animal signs. The snow was deep and it had been cold for weeks! We weren't finding many signs of animal life. What a disappointment! I was puzzled and, in addition, felt a responsibility to 'produce' tracks in the forest. After about a half hour of minimal discoveries, my cell phone rang. One of the other groups had left the forest and headed over to the neighboring farm (we had asked permission ahead). They called to say they had discovered some fascinating tracks near the barn. We all headed over to join them.

All around the barnyard were smallish tracks and tunnels in the soft snow. I was puzzled at first. It could be several creatures. Then one of the students peered into one of the tunnels and saw blood! So we were tracking a carnivore! As we continued to explore, the tracks indicated a very agile, active, and curious animal, exploring every nook and cranny, even tunneling in and around rock walls. As we ranged further from the barn, we approached the steep bank heading down to the local North River.

Here came the set of tracks up the bank. I assembled the clues and honed in on the animal's identity. I challenged the students to notice as much as they could about the tracks and signs (and one group measured the diameter of the snow tunnels). Heading back to school, discussion was animated. We checked in field guides once back in the classroom and found illustrations of different species' snow tunnels. Students became more and more convinced that we had been tracking a mink! Students researched the mink's life history, gaining a deeper understanding of its unique adaptations to life in these hills. Students then wrote fictional stories about the life of a mink incorporating what they had learned. What a fun integrated unit—life science, animal adaptations, measuring, recording data, researching, and creative writing. (NGSS: 5-LS2-1, 5-PS3-1, CCSS: ELA.LITERACY.RI.5.7, ELA.LITERACY.W.5.2, ELA.LITERACY.W.5.3)

References

Berman, M. G., Jonides, J., & Kaplan, S. (2008). The cognitive benefits of interacting with nature. *Psychological Science, 19*(12), 1207–1212.

Collado, S., & Corraliza, J. A. (2015). Children's restorative experiences and self-reported environmental behaviors. *Environment and Behavior 47*(1), 38–56.

Common Core State Standards Initiative. Retrieved June 25, 2015, from www.corestandards.org.

Fjortoft, I. (2001). The natural environment as a playground for children: The impact of outdoor play activities in pre-primary school children. *Early Childhood Education Journal, 29*(2), 111–117.

Kellert, S. R. (2005). *Building for Life: Designing and Understanding the Human-Nature Connection.* Washington, DC: Island Press.

Kings College London (2011). Understanding the diverse benefits of learning in natural environments. Retrieved June 2, 2015, from www.lotc.org.uk/wp-content/uploads/2011/09/KCL-LINE-beneftis-final-version.pdf.

Kuo, F. E., & Taylor, A. F. (2004). A potential natural treatment for attention-deficit/hyperactivity disorder: Evidence from a national study. *American Journal of Public Health, 94*(9), 1580–1586.

Lieberman, G., A., & Hoody, L. (2005). *The effects of environment-based education on student achievement.* California Student Assessment Project, Phase II, California Department of Education, Sacramento, CA.

Louv, R. 2008. *Last child in the woods: Saving our children from nature-deficit disorder.* Chapel Hill, NC: Algonquin Books.

Next Generation Science Standards. Retrieved June 25, 2015, from www.nextgenscience.org/next-generation-science-standards.

7

A-HA! ANIMAL HABITAT ART

Creating Connections In, About, and Through Art and Nature

Geraldine Burke

I saw ... flashing, red and blue, right over my head—a rosella!
 Good Morning! You have brightened my day.
(Campus sighting by pre-service teacher)

I noticed ... There used to be more native birds here but they cut down a whole lot of trees to make the car park and you don't see so many now.
(Pre-service teacher comment)

I wonder ... why does the rosella have so many colours when the cockatoo is mostly white with just a bit of yellow?
(Child participant observation)

I saw ... a lorikeet nest in the lemon-scented gum tree near the garage. The nest is a hollow, originally excavated by a galah. Now the lorikeets have taken over. They are really bossy birds.
(Staff sighting of a bird hollow)

Using art to forge understandings of nature and culture is key to this chapter, as is the idea that we can forge creative connections across communities of learners (Wenger, 1998) when we engage in projects like the *A-ha!* art project. *A-ha!* began as an innovative learning/teaching experience for pre-service teachers at Monash University in Melbourne, Australia, when they used their campus surrounds as a subject-matter portal to engage with local wildlife. In turn, these pre-service

FIGURE 7.1 Children create images of eastern rosella, parakeets, and their habitats on wooden panels that will be formed into nest boxes to place in their school grounds (photograph courtesy of Geraldine Burke).

teachers guided local school children through explorations of their schoolyards (see Figure 7.1) to prompt art possibilities, wildlife awareness, and cultural links to artists and the NGV (National Gallery of Victoria). These experiences connected participants to wildlife habitats in their immediate locale in a way that led to protective action for animals such as cockatoos, possums, wood ducks, parakeets, eastern rosella, and microbats. Participants developed sensitive and responsible knowledge of the ways Indigenous and non-Indigenous people connect to animals, land, and country through their art. The project led to construction, decoration, and installation of wildlife nest boxes and to the development of a repertoire of ecologically responsible art skills and practices. The *A-ha!* project employed an immersive approach to art pedagogy (Burke, 2013) that is retold here through narrative (Clandinin & Connelly, 2000; Heo, 2004), and a/r/tographic renderings (Irwin and de Cosson, 2004) that reveal ways in which art education can forge deep understandings and a greater sense of care for our local wildlife and environs.

This account of the *A-ha!* project includes a subjective narrative from the vantage point of a participant university lecturer and researcher. Included are my observations and understandings of the *A-ha!* project in relation to my experiences; participants' experiences; the cultural and environmental context; and participants' roles as a/r/tographers (*artists*, *researchers* and *teachers*; see Irwin & Springgay, 2008). I also relate these understandings to the wider world of art, education, creativity, culture, context, and critical ways of knowing. This fits with the definition of autoethnography given by Ellis (2004) in which "research, writing, and method ... connect the autobiographical and personal to the cultural and social" (p. xix), as well as the environmental (Burke and Cutter-Mackenzie, 2010).

Creating Communities of Practice In, About, and Through Art *and* Nature

The newly proposed Australian curriculum for the arts (ACARA, 2013) gives primary teachers and students the opportunity to explore art alongside big concerns such as sustainability and intercultural understanding. These vital issues of our time can potentially connect us to environment, place, culture, and each other through creative experiences. To explore these learning possibilities, I developed the *A-ha!* project for pre-service teachers to explore in their Studio Arts subject, and then teach as an 'Art Reach' experience in a local primary school. Our Art Reach program links pre-service students and staff to local community, children, and teachers through exciting arts experiences. It positions art teaching and learning as a living inquiry where art experiences are shared events and situations that occur across time and space to involve us in "being" and "being with" others (Springgay, 2008, p. 160).

Through the Art Reach experience we come together as a community of practice (Wenger, 1998) forming a creative dynamic across individual participants, the teaching/learning process, the school, and the community. We soften institutional divides as we learn from and teach each other through art. The pre-service teachers' *A-ha!* investigations and the Art Reach initiative tested aspects of the curriculum by embracing a shared purpose. The outcome was discovery as we found different ways of expressing and understanding ourselves and others through art making and art appreciation. This approach aligns with UNESCO's *Goals for the Development of Arts Education*, which advocates for "systems of lifelong and intergenerational learning in, about and through arts education" (2010, p. 4). Importantly the *A-ha!* project explores local culture alongside learning in, through, and about nature. My aim was to make the *A-ha!* experiences as immersive as possible so that deep learning could take place within our local environment, thereby reflecting UNESCO's art education directive that "visual arts learning can commence from the local culture, and progressively introduce learners to other world cultures" (Teaero et al., 2004, p. 43).

The following narrative tracks the pre-service a/r/tographers as they first explore the animal habitat theme as *artists*, then take on the role of *teachers* working in schools through the university's Art Reach program, and ultimately become *researchers* forging expansive opportunities when they analyse their *A-ha!* teaching and learning.

Immersed in Art and Nature: Elementary Pre-Service Teachers Become *A-ha!* A/r/tographers

Our university studio space is buzzing with creative activity. One group of pre-service teachers draws, cuts, and stencils images of sulphur-crested cockatoos onto a large canvas. They have seen cockatoos at lunchtime pecking away on the nearby lawn and flying off to adjacent trees. But what trees? The students google 'cockatoo habitats' and discover that cockatoos forage for seeds in grassy areas as well as in the canopy of eucalyptus, banksia, and hakea trees. In fact, the cockatoos' strong bills allow them to crack open gumnuts and cones to access seeds. The students go outside to identify the trees using Internet images as their reference. They come back into the studio and are excited to add hakea and banksia images to their cockatoo artwork. They go on to create a screensaver design of cockatoos and banksia plants with the woody fruit of the banksia featured throughout. Later, a suite of screensavers is made available to other students in the class to help build familiarity with the biodiversity of our campus.

Meanwhile, other pre-service teachers create an array of artworks based on eastern rosellas, kookaburras, rainbow lorikeets, and wood ducks. Many of these birds traditionally nest in hollow branches on living and dead trees. However, development has diminished the number of hollow trees on campus, and old forests and trees are increasingly scarce in the surrounding area. We decide to join our university's biodiversity initiative and acquire nest boxes for the wildlife we have observed on campus. Along with making *A-ha!* mosaics, fabric designs, etchings, and murals, we decide to decorate *A-ha!* nest boxes to place in the campus trees. We learn that hollow tree habitats take 120 to 220 years to form (Gibbons, McElhinny & Lindenmayer, 2010). Our specially designed nest boxes target specific native species so that wildlife communities can nest without competing with introduced species. Our nest boxes provide us with an art and design project that has a multi-dimensional environmental purpose: to sustain wildlife on campus, to create images of observed animals and their habitats, and to learn about biodiversity and the ecosystem around us. Figure 7.2 shows children exploring biodiversity through *A-ha! Animal Habitat Art*. Figure 7.3 showcases examples of pre-service teachers' decorated nest box panels featuring local wildlife and surroundings.

In making our *A-ha!* artworks, we notice it seems much easier to depict animals than to know their habitats. Why is this? Are we really connected to the life of these animals or the land on which they live? We explore botanical illustrations and notice how species are studied in accomplished detail to aid scientific ways of understanding animals and plants, and yet these studies are decontextualized from their environment. In contrast, we look at artworks by Indigenous artist Bronwyn Bancroft. Her picture book *Patterns of Australia* (2005) is filled with images that celebrate the inter-relationship between animals, seasons, and country. Each page seems to pulsate with the energetic interplay of water, tide, and sea life, or desert, sky, meeting place, and wildlife. We look further through Internet searches and find the artwork of Lin Onus (1991, 1994). *Garkman* and

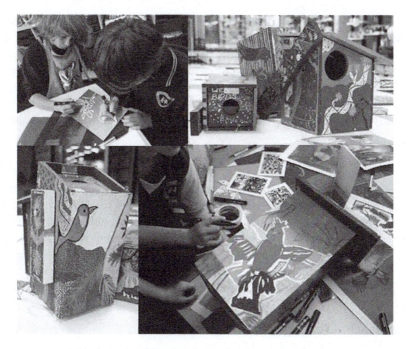

FIGURE 7.2 Children work collaboratively on nest boxes (photograph courtesy of Geraldine Burke and Kristian Lofhelm).

FIGURE 7.3 Pre-service teachers depict a common ringtail possum with grevillea background onto wooden sections of their possum nest box; a silver crested cockatoo is featured against gumleaves and gumnuts for a custom designed nest box for large parrots.

24 Hours by the Billabong Late Afternoon take our interest. While investigating these artworks, we notice how his layering of Western and Indigenous art styles conveys a connected view of animals and their environment. His images seem to capture the dynamics of frogs and stingrays along with the living entity of place and culture all at once. We start to get a sense of Indigenous ways of knowing; these artworks show the connection to homeland is deeply felt. As Mick Dodson (1997) (former Aboriginal and Torres Strait Islander Social Justice Commissioner) powerfully expressed:

> To understand our law, our culture and our relationship to the physical and spiritual world, you must begin with land. Everything about aboriginal society is inextricably woven with, and connected to, land. Culture is the land, the land and spirituality of aboriginal people, our cultural beliefs or reason for existence is the land. You take that away and you take away our reason for existence. We have grown that land up. We are dancing, singing, and painting for the land. We are celebrating the land. Removed from our lands, we are literally removed from ourselves.

Art Reach: Creating *A-ha!* Connections

The pre-service teachers head off to a local primary school to run an Art Reach program. They share their *A-ha!* artwork with the children and teach an art lesson they have prepared where children immerse in their school habitats and then paint *A-ha!* nest boxes for their schoolyard. Everyone seems excited. The children are thrilled their visiting teachers are artists as well as teachers. Together they discuss the solution nest boxes offer for native animals, and they explore which animals are present in their schoolyard or need to be encouraged back. Meanwhile, each group explores art making and art appreciation to make further links into the nest box themes of sustainability and intercultural understanding.

One group explores whether the brush-tailed possum should be given a nest box or not. Is it a pest? Should it be nurtured? The pre-service teachers show a YouTube clip by contemporary Indigenous artist Vickie Couzens called *My Grandmother's Country* (2010). In the video, Couzens tells her story through reclamation of the possum-skin cloak tradition. The motifs and designs she uses to adorn the inside of the possum-skin cloak explore her connection to land, threatened species, totems, and marriage customs in the Gunditjmara tribe.

Meanwhile, another group of pre-service teachers, children and schoolteachers investigate artworks by Australian artist Fiona Hall, who explores the political interface between nature and culture. Through artworks from *Big Game Hunting* [Exhibition] (2013) and *Shot Through* [Exhibition] (2011), they explore her artworks of endangered species from the *2011 IUCN Red List of Threatened Species*. These animals are adorned in military camouflage and decorated with trash and throwaways from contemporary culture. The children and pre-service teachers discuss these artworks and the reasons why animals become endangered. They understand that, although their artworks are very different from Fiona Hall's, they have a shared purpose to preserve and protect animals through art.

The pre-service teachers, schoolteachers and children are engaged and productive throughout the Art Reach program. One of the teachers has just received a grant for the school to undertake a project with an Indigenous Community School elsewhere in Australia, and a primary school in Indonesia. Together, we brainstorm how the *A-ha!* project could adapt across art forms, states, and countries; could facilitate connection through a shared focus on sustainability and intercultural understanding; and could protect and preserve animal habitats *and* share different ways of exploring art across cultures.

Excited, we start looking at Indonesian sarongs that feature birds and plant tendrils reaching skywards; we access Indigenous art local to the area around the Community School and find bark paintings of fish, rivers, and meeting places depicted in ochre paint. A new phase of the *A-ha!* project begins. Already, the learning is building momentum as the project travels across new sites and new contexts.

The *A-ha!* Walk

Back at the university, the pre-service teachers create digital stories and PowerPoint presentations about their *A-ha!* artwork, teaching, and research. These presentations become part of their teaching portfolio and go with them to job interviews and the like. With signed permission from school parents and the school, these beginning teachers can share their *A-ha!* experience and start new projects at different sites.

Meanwhile, decorated nest boxes are installed on campus after work by an environmental education class to identify the most suitable sites in relation to sun, prevailing weather, and human traffic. These students created fact sheets for the animals and walked the campus to find the best trees. They researched how much shelter was required; how natural the surrounding habitat needed to be; whether the nest boxes should face north, south, east, or west to provide the right protection and conditions for raising young; the best height and position in the tree; what shade was needed for hot days; proximity to food sources; and whether chosen locations were accessible for a scissor-lift to install the boxes.

The nest boxes are selectively placed around the campus after further consultation with green volunteers and ground staff, and create a dual opportunity: for wildlife to flourish and for people to enjoy an *A-ha!* campus walk (see Figure 7.4). The *A-ha!* walk has become a common activity for students, staff, and visitors. It has been incorporated into a variety of units where place-based learning (Gruenewald, 2003; Gruenewald & Smith, 2008) informs subject content.

FIGURE 7.4 A series of *A-ha!* nest boxes have been installed high up in trees on campus (photograph courtesy of Geraldine Burke and Melanie Attard).

FIGURE 7.5 Pre-service teachers created street art skateboard decks based on the wildlife found on campus. Featured are images of a microbat, wood duck, parrots, lorikeets, and cockatoos (photograph courtesy of Geraldine Burke).

A-ha! on the Move

Most recently, we extended the *A-ha!* project into Orientation Week. We created 'A-ha! on the move,' a get-to-know-you activity that prompted 121 incoming students to build awareness of the biodiversity on campus while also delving into street art graphics. This time the incoming pre-service teachers explored the *A-ha!* walk with mentor students, and then worked collaboratively to stencil and draw images of campus wildlife and natural habitats onto skateboard decks (see Figure 7.5). As a consequence, sixty *A-ha!* skate decks are now displayed in the Education Building as a memento of the students' first day at Monash University. They are an internal reference to the external campus habitat, a prompt for all who enter our faculty to be aware of the wildlife and landscape that was here before us and now makes do in our midst.

Emergent and ongoing, *A-ha!* is spreading into other areas. The *A-ha!* walk has become an Open Day activity; Art and Wellbeing (a peer group for university employees) is conducting *A-ha!* pursuits; a new study unit called Art, Community and Environment (ACE) is becoming known for its *A-ha!* explorations of animals, plants, and habitats with various primary schools. In turn, *A-ha!* projects and artworks are re-making strong environmental connections in our community through arts–based discovery.

A-ha! Theories Informing Practice

The *A-ha!* project employed an immersive approach to art pedagogy (Burke, 2013). Immersive art pedagogy (IAP) enables deep material investigations to develop a range of skills across art genres. For the *A-ha!* project, participants looked at photos, prints, videos, and models of local wildlife; they explored relevant sites collecting plants for further investigation. Their investigations inspired drawing, painting, printing, photography, mosaics, and repousse. Participants were encouraged to reflect on their work as process, and consider what they could do to develop *A-ha!* themes.

IAP positions creative connections at the heart of learning as shown in Figure 7.6. At the core of this approach is the belief that creativity grows as

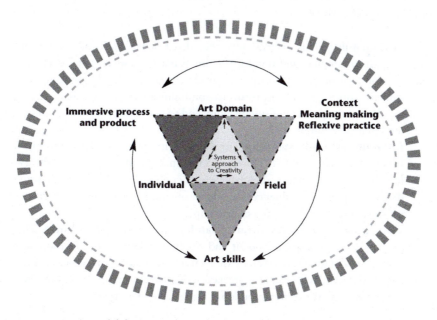

FIGURE 7.6 A model for immersive art pedagogy (Geraldine Burke, 2013). The light gray dotted line indicates the site in which IAP is enacted, and the dark gray radiating lines indicate the socio–ecological considerations that affect IAP as it plays out in each site of investigation.

the individual, field, and cultural domain dynamically interact with each other (Csikszentmihaly, 1988). For this project, pre-service teachers (the field) shared their art and learning with school children (individuals) and linked their local experiences to the cultural domain (artists and artworks in collections). Expansion continues as *A-ha!* continues to build momentum across more units, and as more groups dip into the project.

IAP encourages a context-dependent approach and deliberately relates to the specific characteristics of each site (see Figure 7.6). In addition, socio-ecological considerations inform the IAP approach; the *A-ha!* project considers that lived experience, place, experiential pedagogies, agency, and participation (Wattchow et al., 2014) are entangled with art experience. This leads to the perception that sustaining creativity (the individual's creative agency) creates sustainability—they are mutually sustaining.

Connections to Curriculum

The *A-ha!* project is in line with key concepts in the Australian curriculum for the arts, which positions art as a post-formal experience enabling connection to environment, place, culture, and each other. As a consequence, *A-ha!* objectives were developed with cross-curriculum priorities in mind, namely Sustainability, Intercultural Understanding, and Aboriginal and Torres Strait Islander histories and cultures (ACARA, 2013).

> **Sustainability**: This priority advocates that teachers and students explore how the arts reflect and transform cultural practices, social systems and the relationships of people to their environment (p. 24). In this learning area students choose suitable art forms to communicate their developing under-standing of the concept of sustainability and to persuade others to take action for sustainable futures (p. 25).
>
> **Intercultural understanding**: For this priority students are asked to move beyond known worlds to explore new ideas, media, and practices from diverse local, national, regional, and global cultural contexts (p. 22). This enables stu-dents to explore the influence and impact of cultural identities and traditions on the practices and thinking of artists (p. 22).
>
> **Aboriginal and Torres Strait Islander histories and cultures**: This priority seeks to expand student and teacher understandings of the many ways art making is undertaken by Indigenous Australians. It promotes cultur-ally sensitive and responsible appreciation of artworks, and recognition of the significance of art making in building Indigenous identity (p. 24).

This post-formal approach helped guide our art making and gave context to the teacher/learner discussions of *A-ha!* artwork and themes. It took us beyond art elements and principles to consider deep connections. As pre-service teachers created their own art and planned their teaching for the Art Reach session, we asked the following questions:

- **Meanings**: What meanings are intended when artists depict animals and habitats—together or apart? How are we to understand the intentions of Indigenous art, botanical art, or scientific diagrams of animals and their habitats?
- **Cultures**: What is the cultural context and its effects on this work?
- **Societies**: How does the *A-ha!* theme relate to *our* social context? Is it relevant to our lives?
- **Histories**: How does the *A-ha!* project reflect or contest the times in which we live?
- **Philosophies and ideologies**: What are the philosophical, ideological, and environmental perspectives guiding the nest box initiative?
- **Forms**: How can we move from aesthetically pleasing, two-dimensional depictions of animal habitats to well-placed images set on three-dimensional, functional art objects that will be installed and viewed high up in canopied trees?
- **Critical theories**: What theories are relevant to unified investigations of art, environment, and place?
- **Psychology**: What processes of the mind and emotions are involved in making animal habitat art? What inter/intra personal skills are developed as we make art together and across institutions?
- **Institutions**: What institutional factors support or constrain our work? How do we establish a successful process for installing nest boxes in campus/ school sites?
- **Evaluations**: How successful is the *A-ha!* theme in terms of awareness, action, and change? Do our images and designs present and promote biodiversity? (Adapted from ACARA, 2013)

What Does *A-ha!* Reveal?

As a participant university lecturer who worked across all sites of the *A-ha!* investigation, I applied Irwin and de Cosson's a/r/tographic renderings (2004) to the *A-ha!* narrative to uncover how art education and environmental awareness might work across communities of creative practice.

Living inquiry: Our physical experiences in local animal habitats resulted in deep and expansive learning relating to art, culture, and sustainability.

Openings: Participants became aware of art context and meaning through exposure to starkly different depictions of animal habitats. Although the nest box activity opened up many possibilities, it also closed off options by locking into a nest box theme. There was a lost opportunity to expand the children's *A-ha!* learning when one group spontaneously drew a series of cartoon predators such as foxes. This aspect of the animal habitat theme could be explored in future work.

Metaphor and metonym: The campus is a third teacher and the local birds and plants a lesson in biodiversity. They taught us that we are among them, and they depend on our custodial care.

Reverberations: The *A-ha!* project is an event rather than a unit of study. It uncouples curriculum from student/study cycles, morphing into a long-term project sustained through expanding communities of practice. The *A-ha!* project could extend in so many ways—into bird song and musical creativity, into mindful *A-ha!* walks, into digital art investigations open to multiple communities unbound by physical divides.

Excess: Sustainability and creativity are concepts that help unpack each other. The *A-ha!* project provokes transdisciplinary thinking in a way that rouses an "aesthetics of sustainability" (Kagan, 2011). Kagan suggests that this is based on a sensibility to "patterns that connect" enabling us to grasp a more complex view of aesthetics through interrelated concerns (p. 232).

Contiguity: The immersive and contiguous experience of pre-service teachers as a/r/tographers led to output rich with confident imagery, pedagogical information, and relevant research. In turn, they treated the primary school children as a/r/tographers who shared their rich art inquiries through the school community. The totality was more than art making. By developing a repertoire of practice, the participants built a sense of their own creative agency. They were involved in relational learning and material thinking (Barrett & Bolt, 2007). They connected to their surroundings through art images and place-related content. They walked and moved as part of the learning experience. They addressed biodiversity through their investigations and they worked together across their spaces and across time. They took up the challenge of transdisciplinary thinking by exploring art skills and techniques alongside environmental and intercultural understandings and notions of care.

So What and What Now?

The *A-ha!* project matters. It shows that the visual arts stimulate rich learning when directly linked to cross-curriculum priorities such as sustainability, intercultural understanding, and indigenous culture. Further, it fosters deep awareness of the wildlife we live amongst, and advocates for greater awareness of the biodiverse needs of animals and habitat. The immersive approach to teaching *A-ha!* freely engages multiple techniques and genres, and ensures participants explore their own art making through locally derived content while also linking into the cultural domain. It lights the way for pre-service teachers to reimagine themselves as artists, researchers, and teachers working in schools with primary-aged children. It demonstrates how a community of practice can form through professional engagement with groups who have different agendas but shared interests. And it shows how projects such as *A-ha!* can spread across institutional and age-specific boundaries to achieve insightful formal and informal learning.

We hope our *A-ha!* experience will be adapted by other intergenerational groups so they too can explore, discuss, create, and act on animal habitat themes in their part of the world. We hope they too share it with others and spread the word, *A-ha!*

References

ACARA. (2013). Australian curriculum: The arts foundation to year 10 – 2. Retrieved May 20, 2015, from www.acara.edu.au/verve/_resources/Australian_Curriculum_ The_Arts_2_July_2013.pdf.

Barrett, E., & Bolt, B. (2007). *Practice as research: Approaches to creative arts enquiry.* London: I.B. Tauris & Co Ltd.

Burke, G., (2013). *Immersive art pedagogy: (Re)connecting artist, researcher and teacher* (Unpublished doctoral dissertation). RMIT, Melbourne, Australia.

Burke, G., & Cutter-Mackenzie, A. (2010). What's there, what if, what then, and what can we do? *Environmental Education Research,* 16(3–4), 311–330.

Clandinin, J., & Connelly, F. M. (2000). *Narrative inquiry: Experience and story in qualitative research.* San Francisco, CA: Jossey-Bass Inc.

Csikszentmihalyi, M. (1988). Society, culture, and person: A systems view of creativity. In R. J. Sternberg (Ed.), *The nature of creativity: Contemporary psychological perspectives* (pp. 325–339). Cambridge: Cambridge University Press.

Dodson, M. (1997). Land rights and social justice. In Galarrwuy Yunupingu (Ed.), *Our land is our life: Land rights—past, present and future* (pp. 39–51). Australia: University of Queensland Press.

Ellis, C. (2004). The ethnographic I. In *The ethnographic I: A methodological novel about autoethnography.* Walnut Creek, CA: AltaMira Press.

Gibbons, P., McElhinny, C., & Lindenmayer, D. (2010). What strategies are effective for perpetuating structures provided by old trees in harvested forests? A case study on trees with hollows in south-eastern Australia. *Forest Ecology and Management, 260,* 975–982.

Gruenewald, D. A. (2003). The best of both worlds: A critical pedagogy of place. *Educational Researcher,* 32(4), 3–12. Retrieved March 3, 2012, from www.pieducators.com/files/ Critical-Pedagogy-of-Place.pdf.

Gruenewald, D. A., & Smith, G. A. (Eds.). (2008). *Place-based education in the global age.* New York, NY: Lawrence Erlbaum Associates.

Heo, H. (2004). Story telling and retelling as narrative inquiry in cyber learning environments. In R. Atkinson, C. McBeath, D. Jonas-Dwyer, & R. Phillips (Eds.), *Beyond the comfort zone: Proceedings of the 21st ASCILITE Conference* (374–378). Retrieved February 25, 2016, from www.ascilite.org.au/conferences/perth04/procs/heo.html.

Irwin, R. L., & de Cosson, A. (Eds.). (2004). *A/r/tography: Rendering self through arts-based living inquiry.* Vancouver, BC: Pacific Educational Press.

Irwin, R. L., & Springgay, S. (2008). A/r/tography as practice-based research. In S. Springgay, R. L. Irwin, C. Leggo & P. Gouzouasis (Eds.), *Being with a/r/tography* (pp. xix–xxxiii). Netherlands: Sense Publishers.

IUCN (2015). *The IUCN red list of threatened species.* Version 2015.1. Retrieved June 1, 2015, from www.iucnredlist.org.

Kagan, S. (2011). *Art and sustainability: Connecting patterns for a culture of complexity.* New Brunswick, NJ: Transaction Publishers.

Springgay, S. (2008). *Body knowledge and curriculum: Pedagogies of touch in youth and visual culture.* New York, NY: Peter Lang.

Teaero, T., Helu, F., Moore, H., Prasad, V., Barleyde, R., Katit, J., . . . Wagner, T. (2004). *UNESCO visual arts report in arts education in the Pacific region: Heritage and creativity.* Paris: UNESCO.

UNESCO. (2010). Seoul agenda: Goals for the Development of Arts Education. Second World Conference on Arts Education. Retrieved April 1, 2015, from www.unesco.org/new/en/culture/themes/creativity/arts-education/.

Wattchow, B., Jeanes, R., Alfrey, L.G., Brown, T.D., Cutter-Mackenzie, A., & O'Connor, J. (Eds.), (2014). *The socioecological educator: A 21st century renewal of physical, health, environment and outdoor education.* Netherlands: Springer.

Wenger, E. (1998) *Communities of practice: Learning, meaning, and identity.* Cambridge: Cambridge University Press.

Artworks

Bancroft, Bronwyn. (2005). *Patterns of Australia* [Picture book]. Victoria, Australia: Little Hare Books.

Couzens, Vickie. (June 10, 2010). *My grandmother's country* [Video file]. Retrieved February 2, 2015, from www.youtube.com/watch?v=CZwEB_fB3PU.

Hall, Fiona. (2011). *Shot through* [Exhibition]. Roslyn Oxley9 Gallery, Sydney, Australia. Retrieved June 5, 2015, from www.roslynoxley9.com.au/artists/17/Fiona_Hall/1324/.

Hall, Fiona. (2013). *Big Game Hunting* [Exhibition]. Heide Museum of Modern Art, Melbourne, Australia. Retrieved June 6, 2015, from www.roslynoxley9.com.au/artists/17/Fiona_Hall/1466/.

Onus, Lin. (1991). *Garkman* [Screen print on paper]. Retrieved January 18, 2015, from www.slideshare.net/Campbell_Jessie/lin-onus-images-7530289.

Onus, Lin. (1994). *24 hours by the billabong late afternoon* [Synthetic polymer paint on linen]. Retrieved May 20, 2015, from www.artnet.com/artists/lin-onus/24-hours-by-the-billabong-late-morning-t47s6XFgpFGIkSP54_1mtg2.

Acknowledgements

Thank you to pre-service teachers at Monash University and teachers and children from Bentleigh West Primary School who gave permission for their artwork and process to be photographed. Thanks also to Monash University staff and colleagues, especially Melanie Attard, Rosemary Bennett, Ruth Browne, Louise Broadbent, and Kristian Lofhelm, whose help in this project has been invaluable.

To know more about ART REACH or A-ha! please contact Geraldine.Burke@monash.edu.

8

HONORING THE SACRED LAND

Students in Conversation

Linda Wason-Ellam

A deep connectedness with all that surrounds humankind is a foundational concept of Indigenous teachings. This includes a reciprocal relationship to Mother Earth and all that the Universe contains including personal relationships, family, communities, the flora and fauna, and the Great Spirit that animates all. For too long, education has been viewed through a Eurocentric lens, which does not always harmonize with Indigenous needs. Increasingly, there has been a shift toward acknowledging and understanding Indigenous ways of learning as an effective educational perspective. For non-Indigenous students, learning of other cultures is crucial as it relates to our pluralistic democratic aspirations.

Connecting to "place" can be a starting point for elementary classrooms when integrating Indigenous ways of knowing with the school curriculum. Gruenewald (2003) advocates for a *critical* pedagogy of place in which students and teachers are challenged to reflect on "the kind of places we inhabit and leave behind for future generations" (p. 308). A critical pedagogy of place has a dual focus, a commitment to both social justice and ecological concerns. This learning begins with querying, "Where am I? Whose land are we on? What is the natural and social history of this place? How does this place fit into the global world? What can I do to care for the environment?"

Critical place-based education uses the local community and environment as a point of departure to teach concepts across the curriculum emphasizing hands-on, real-world learning experiences. Ideally, our prairie city is a focal place situated on the banks of the meandering South Saskatchewan River, a flyway for migratory birds and a habitat for fish and beavers. The river has provided an abundant source of fresh water that comes from the melt of the Rocky Mountains to the West that flows into a network of rivers. Water is drawn directly from the river through intakes upstream from the water treatment plant and pumped to homes, offices, schools, and industry. However, climate change, infrastructure water use, and dams producing hydroelectricity have combined to reduce the flow of the South Saskatchewan River by 70 percent. For this city, clean water is an ongoing concern.

In this chapter, I describe my work with a fourth-grade class in Saskatchewan as the students and teacher engaged in a study of water. This curricular unit was significantly shaped by Aboriginal perspectives and, in part, by dominant Euro-Canadian ideas about science and technology.

Mother Earth: Teaching from an Indigenous View

Education plays a critical role in raising awareness of environmental challenges and shaping the attitudes and behaviors of children so that they can make a difference. In this unit of study on water, learning resources included Elder talks, trade books, digital reading, and videos authored by Indigenous writers and others that "honor the land as a sacred place." As a university collaborator with the teacher, I did a case study of a grade four class of urban students many of whom are of Indigenous ancestry,[1] a unit that combined a variety of field experiences observing, responding, problematizing, and reporting on climate change, the fragility of clean water, and the increase in greenhouse gases within the contours of Saskatchewan, a Canadian prairie city.

In the beginning of this study on water use and its relationship to Mother Earth, three local Cree Elders, respected as knowledge keepers, storied the history of the local community and introduced how water was the lifeblood of their existence. Indigenous peoples regard water as a primal substance that is part of the creation stories (Friesen, 1999; Galeano, 1985), for it is the center of the web of the interconnections of life. The link to spirituality, healing, and cleansing is fundamental in the cultural practices that have been passed down from generation to generation (personal communication with three Elders, 2013). The class appreciated the legends on how plants, animals, and natural forces such as the wind, fire, and water are related to the sustainability of the land. The Indigenous peoples have a strong oral history and culture. The telling of stories is a tradition for the sharing of knowledge, values, skills, and histories. In viewing a video, *The Elders are Watching*, a poetic narrative (Vickers, 2011), the Elders give a remindful plea to respect the natural environment. They begin with the words, "They told me to tell you that they believed you, they thought you respected the land…they wanted you to know that they trusted you to care for the earth, the water and the air…." Illustrations accompanying the refrain show shadows of the Elders on a variety of landscapes as on earth, water, and air. Following the viewing of the video, the class discussed what the communities' obligation might be and it made recycling, responsibility for trash, and reusing more clearly. Caring for the earth, the water, and the land could be a "kid's job." Throughout the video, the Elders weave together respect for the land with critique about man-made environmental dangers such as mining, logging, polluted water, and industrial waste. The video and a response activity, and a creative art poster on water usage, were used to introduce students to ideas about resources, consumption, and conservation. Understanding the Indigenous relationship to the land creates a sense of kinship and community identity (Battiste, 1998). The land does not belong to individual peoples; it is a shared community. The nature of this tie is not so much one of ownership but one of stewardship. They are its custodians.

This inquiry unit was integrated in the cross-curricular strands of literacy and the provincial grade 4 science unit on Understanding Earth: Conservation of Energy and Resources. The school has a strong elementary science program that recognizes that modern science is not the only form of empirical knowledge about nature and aims to broaden student understanding of traditional Indigenous and local knowledge systems.

> [Indigenous knowledge is a] cumulative body of knowledge, know-how, practices, and representations [maintained and developed by peoples] who have long histories of interaction with the natural environment.... These sophisticated sets of understandings, interpretations, and meanings are part and parcel of a cultural complex that encompasses language, naming and classification systems, resource use practices, ritual, spirituality and world-view. (UNESCO, 2002)

The classroom teacher believes that families are rich in sociocultural resources and these funds of knowledge are defined as skills, abilities, ideas, and practices essential to a household's functioning and well-being (Moll & Greenberg, 1990). The underlying goal of this unit of study was that students develop their personal identities as they explored connections between their own understanding of the natural and constructed world and the perspectives of others, including both scientific and Indigenous perspectives, which inform individual and community decision-making.

Land-Based View

The land is not just soil or rocks or minerals. It is an environment that sustains and is sustained by people and culture. For Indigenous peoples, the land is the core of all spirituality, and this relationship is central to their identities and their existence in the world. Relationship with the natural world is integral to Indigenous teachings as many reservation schools are currently introducing programs such as "Miyo Pimatsowin" (based on the land, development of traditional skills, and critical thinking about Indigenous history). This mirrors the idea of an 'eco-pedagogy' that ties respect for the land, Mother Earth, with critical thinking about environmental degradation. In contrast to mainstream schools, local Elders speak of the traditional teaching process in which children figure things out for themselves rather than being told what to think as in the prevailing Euro-Canadian education system. Elder Wes Fineday (Cree) speaks about teaching:

> ...for our traditional teachers the process was critical, not so much the question or the answer but how you get there. That was for us the import-ant part and one of the biggest differences in the education philosophy.... In today's institutions teachers stand up and lecture to our children and then the children have to figure out...what do they want me to say back?... So what teachers are teaching is what to think....In the traditional perspec-tive, the important part of the process was how to use your own mind to think for yourself, so you can become [a] knowledgeable and wise decision [maker] about your own life, about the life of your own family, and the community. So, there is a whole different process and for different reasons.
>
> (Callele, 2010, p.10)

From the Elders, the class learned that on the local land, each clan had its own territory from which they "made their living." These traditional lands were defined by geographic boundaries such as rivers, lakes, and mountains. Tribes cared for their different environments and adapted to them. Spiritually, Mother Earth is an ancient central figure as Indigenous peoples feel that the earth *is* their mother, the sky the father, and all things are interconnected. In reading the picture book, *Mother Earth* (Luen, 1992), there is a strong message that all living creatures and elements exist as the bountiful products of a mother's generosity. The words encourage students to respect and replenish the planet. Similarly, *Dear Children of the Earth* (Schimmel, 1994) is a letter to all of earth's children to care about our animal brothers and sisters and our Mother Earth. The message is especially poignant now that the earth is challenged by pollution, water shortages, and the extinction of more and more species of flora and fauna. *Dear Children of the Earth* describes how Indigenous peoples cultivated land, but in a way different from the white settlers. They endeavored to live *with* the land to preserve, never to destroy; conversely, the settlers lived *off* the land and eventually parceled, fenced, and sold it when claiming the land as property. For the Indigenous peoples, earth cannot be called property for the land is their mother, nourishing the plants, animals, birds, and all peoples.

Indigenous peoples tend to live close to Mother Earth as subsistence farmers, herders, fishers, and hunters, with collective knowledge about the ecology of their surroundings. With that knowledge and experience, even small changes in water cycles, wildlife, soil, and weather are readily apparent. When talking to the class, one Elder reflected on how she had been intimately connected to the river, lake, and creek in her childhood community because they drank directly from these natural sources, drew the water for washing, bathed and swam in it, and caught their food there. Her land-based lifestyle allowed for a close relationship with water in all its forms. Another Elder, an indigenous farmer, noticed that a certain insect is slightly less abundant this year or a particular flower is blooming earlier. A third

FIGURE 8.1   Flooding on the reservation (photograph courtesy of Linda Wason-Ellam).

Elder stated that he saw a lot of damage to Mother Earth as water is taken from streams where water belongs *to animals*, not to mining companies. Unfortunately, the same closeness to the land that has provided Indigenous peoples early warning signs about global warming also means that they have suffered its negative consequences to a far greater degree than others. History and hegemony have left many Indigenous peoples living on land that is already degraded, so even relatively small changes in temperature or rainfall have an outsized consequence. As one student who shared a drawing of flooding at his reservation (see Figure 8.1) wrote, "Our land has changed when the dam was built and sometimes the river floods and we have to leave our homes until it is dry again."

Curriculum Making

An initial field trip to the river valley acquainted students with the pathways of clean water. They saw the weir, which blocks and stores a large amount of this water without adversely affecting communities downstream. Later, they toured a water treatment plant and participated in experiments on evaporation and condensation. Students observed a demonstration showing how seepage into the ground helps to replenish the water table. They learned that water is essential in their lives, and that their participation in the regulation of its use will affect the long-term sustainability of clean water. Earlier in the year, the class studied some basic climate change science, and students saw the conceptual linkage between the two inquiry units. Student #1 explained, "Like carbon, there is a fixed amount of water which is used and reused over again. Our daily habits of water waste threaten our environment."

As a class, the students were challenged to reflect on their own position in exploring the complex interrelationships between cultural and ecological environments and water usage. The heart of student inquiry in this unit meant collaborative conversations about the water usage, conversations that described the continuous movement of water on, above, and below the surface of Mother Earth. Students learned that over time, the mass of water on Mother Earth remains constant but the separation of water into the major reservoirs of ice, fresh water, saline water, and atmospheric water is variable depending on a wide range of climatic fluctuations.

The students used an array of embodied water experiments to learn about evaporation, condensation, precipitation, and measuring rainfall (e.g., Singleton, 2010), followed by response strategies such as student-generated photography, art, poetry, maps, learning logs, concept maps, graphs, posters, videos, song writing, and digital journals to document learning. Graham (2007) states, "Art making becomes part of a socially responsive process of reflection, critical thinking, and transformation. Blending place-based education with critical pedagogy generates an approach characterized by blurred boundaries between art making, social critique, scientific inquiry, and activism" (p. 379). Furthermore, Talking Circles, a turn-taking Indigenous pedagogy that allows all to voice an opinion, was utilized. Talking Circles afforded students with an opportunity to engage in a sharing of authentic personal reactions and feelings that are owned by each individual and acknowledged by others, without judgment or dismissal (Baldwin, 1998; Foy, 2009).

According to the classroom teacher, "Inquiry-based teaching is an approach to instruction that begins with exploring curriculum content and providing a framework for the students to ask their own questions which builds interest and curiosity." She believes that encouraging students to be active learners and following through on those issues, rather than passive learners simply receiving information, elicits greater student engagement and, in turn, creates greater student achievement. In preparation of this unit of study building understandings across differences, the teacher reflected on the words of Rachel Carson (1962):

> We stand now where two roads diverge. But unlike the roads in Robert Frost's familiar poem, they are not equally fair. The road we have long been traveling is deceptively easy, a smooth superhighway on which we progress with great speed, but at its end lies disaster (e.g., scripted rote learning). The other fork of the road—the one less traveled by—offers our last, our only chance to reach a destination that assures the preservation of the earth. (p. 277)

The teacher's goal was to have students think deeply and critically about Mother Earth as the dangers to her sustainability continue unabated. Student inquiry is not merely having students do a project. Rather, the teacher strives to nurture a deep, discipline-based way of thinking and agency with students.

Children in Conversation

Conversations were the central mediating factor in what learners came to understand about their lived experiences and texts, reflecting a social constructionist perspective on learning. This perspective has the potential to shift the focus on talk seeking unambiguous 'facts' or 'truths' toward constructing interpretation and offering justifications for interpretations from textual readings—whether print, oral, aural, visual, or digital. Critical questions invited students to interrogate the systems of meaning that operated both consciously and unconsciously about what they read, saw, or heard: e.g., *Whose story is this? Who benefits? What voices are not being heard?* From this perspective, the teacher's role shifted from asking literal questions with one correct answer to higher level thinking questions that encouraged students' exploratory talk:

Here I share evidence of student learning contained in their journals as well as reflected in some of their artwork.

> Student #13: I learned water does not disappear. It is always recycled as in evaporating to the clouds or draining deeper into the ground water of Mother Earth (see Figure 8.2).

> Student #19: When water freezes it expands and that can break water pipes.

> Student #17: We learned before that the atmosphere does not just have water vapor but it also contains gases, such as carbon dioxide that traps heat from the sun and keeps the planet warm as in greenhouse gases. However, people are using more energy with lights, televisions, cell phones, big trucks, and computers which affects the planet by making it warmer.

> Student #1: Water in the form of ice is found at the polar ice cap on the planet Mars.

> Student #3: Oil leaking from trucks and cars pollutes the water.

> Student #5: I found it is hard to believe that the water molecules in your body might have been recycled and part of a dinosaur a million years ago.

> Student #22: Water cannot be used up like oil. Water from the earth evaporates into the air, forms clouds, and falls back to Mother Earth as rain. There are some areas of the earth that receive little rainfall so water can be very scarce and on reservations, our cousins sometimes have to boil water for drinking.

> Student #19: Water pollution can lead to bacteria which makes people sick.

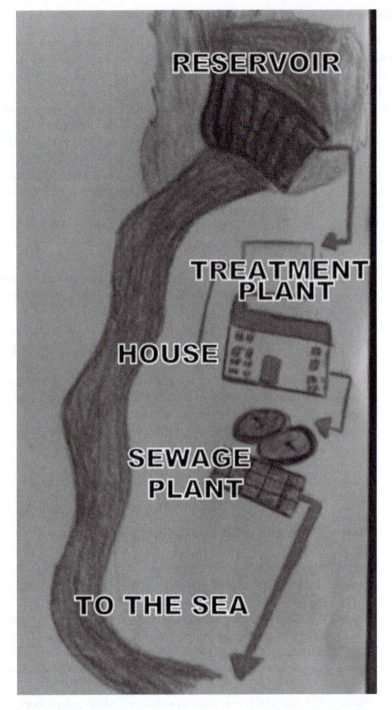

FIGURE 8.2 Water treatment plant (photograph courtesy of Linda Wason-Ellam).

As they learned that water was an important commodity:

Student #4: We water our gardens and lawns but some people waste water with overwatering. A lot of the water goes in watering the sidewalks and driveways where nothing grows. Someday, there may not be enough water.

Student #3 elaborated: If we had smaller grassy areas then you have a smaller use of water.

The city developed a water impact video, *The Importance of Water*, which outlined the water cycle in addition to being water wise. After viewing the video, students, in group conversations, commented on what they thought were the important messages.

Student #5: I viewed on the Internet that water vapor rising from plants, oceans, lakes, rivers, and the ground are carried over the Mother Earth by the wind. Eventually it makes its way back to the sea. I learned that in hot places like deserts, most of the rain that falls never makes it back to the ocean.

Student #6: I listened to the video and it said that some water takes a long time to flow back to the ocean because groundwater sinks into the ground and stays there a long, long time. Sometimes it gets locked into the rocks and it is called Fossil Water.

Student #2: Water use can double (the amount) during the growing season for outdoor watering. Plants, animals, and people share the planet, but it is people who use the most water because their lifestyle demands it.

Student #7 (In reference to the water treatment tour): I learned that showers and baths use the most water, followed by toilet flushing and laundry. Running water while brushing teeth, long showers, and small laundry loads waste water.

Student #11 (A special needs learner, see his picture on the water cycle in Figure 8.3): Water never disappears. We take water from underground sources as in rivers and lakes, and pump it into man-made reservoirs. Then this water goes to a water treatment plant to be cleaned. Then it is pumped to homes, schools, and offices through pipes buried in the ground. Our dirty water goes into sewers that carry the water to the sewage plant. Then the water is cleaned again and pumped back into rivers and goes back to Mother Earth through the water cycle again.

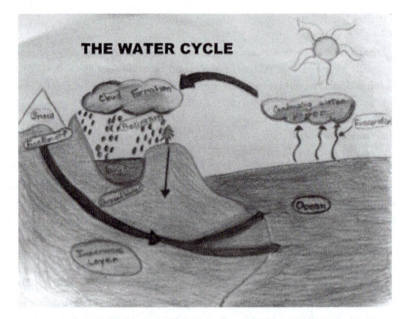

FIGURE 8.3 Water cycle (photograph courtesy of Linda Wason-Ellam).

Student #23: Water is always changing. It is always recycled as in evaporating to the clouds or draining deeper into the ground water of Mother Earth.

Student #16: When we drive big 4x4 trucks, they release harmful gases coming from the exhaust pipes which blows on windy days. This can make acid rain and damage the clean water in the environment.

Besides learning from children's literature and the story of Elders, students used the Internet to access sites such the US Geological Science School, which has an interactive water cycle map and a site for answering challenge questions, participating in opinion surveys about water issues, and taking true/false quizzes (US Geological Survey, http://water.usgs.gov/edu/watercycle-kids .html). The site has a strong conservation message, and its facts and figures show an uneven and inequitable international use of water as a life-giving resource. In today's world, print literacy is not enough. Millennium learners need to be literate in a multiplicity of communications channels and media, in which meanings are communicated not only through text but also through sound, lyrics, images, and a variety of digital media, thus redefining what it means to be literate in a changing world.

Lessons Learned

The success in this unit of study was due, in large part, to the teacher's conscious effort to make Indigenous perspectives central and to strive for equitable outcomes for all students. A second reason for the success of the unit was the teacher's conception of herself as learner, along with the students. The commitment to environmental responsibility and social justice requires a change in the role of teachers. Because action precedes the acquisition of new knowledge, teachers generally cannot plan a curriculum unit as a neat, predictable package. Therefore, teachers must become active learners, too, experimenting with their students, reflecting upon learning activities, and responding to students' reactions to the activities. In this way, teachers come to view themselves as more than just recipients of school district policy and curriculum decisions.

In this unit of study, much of students' explorations were through art, since "the arts offer opportunities for perspective, for perceiving alternative ways of transcending and of being in the world...and subvert our thoughtlessness and complacencies, our certainties" (Greene, 1991, pp. 32, 33). Students also expressed their thoughts through drumming, poetry, photovoice, and journaling. They contemplated how making alternative choices that were in spiritual harmony with Mother Earth requires critical thinkers who can connect their daily decisions to long-term consequences, not just for themselves but for their community as a whole. With damage to the global environment increasing, schools must play their part in preparing young people for this challenge.

References

Baldwin, C. (1998). *Calling the circle: The first and future culture*. New York: Bantam Books.

Battiste, M. (1998). Enabling the autumn seed: Toward a decolonized approach to aboriginal knowledge, language, and education. *Canadian Journal of Education, 22*(1), 16–27.

Callele, M. (2010). *Action plan on education in the context of treaty*. Elders' Gatherings: Foundational Wisdom of Traditional First Nations Education. Unpublished Document, Federation of Saskatchewan Indian Nations.

Carson, R. (1962). *Silent spring*. Boston, MA: Houghton Mifflin Company.

Foy, J. (2009). Incorporating talk story into the classroom. *First Nation Perspectives, 2*(1), 25–33.

Friesen, J.W. (1999). The functions of legends as a teaching tool in pre-colonial First Nations' societies. *Interchange, 30*(3), 305–322.

Galeano, E. (1985). *Memory of fire*: Genesis. New York, NY: Pantheon Books, Random House, Inc.

Graham, M. A. (2007). Art, ecology and art education: Locating art education in a critical place-based pedagogy. *Studies in Art Education, 48*(4), 375–391.

Greene, M. (1991). Texts and margins. *Harvard Educational Review, 61*(1), 27–39.

Gruenewald, D. (2003). The best of both worlds: A critical pedagogy of place. *Educational Researcher, 32*(4), 3–12.

Gruenewald, D., & Smith, G. (Eds.). (2008). *Place-based education in the global age: Local diversity.* Abingdon, UK: Routledge.

Luen, N. (1992). *Mother Earth.* Boston, MA: Athenaeum.

Moll, L. C., & Greenberg, J. (1990). Creating zones of possibilities: Combining social contexts for instruction. In L. C. Moll (Ed.), *Vygotsky and Education* (pp. 319–348). Cambridge: Cambridge University Press.

Schimmel, S. (1994). *Dear children of the earth.* New York: Cooper Square Publishing.

UNESCO (2002). Sustainable development. Retrieved May 20, 2015, from http://portal.unesco.org/en/ev.php-URL_ID=5065&URL_DO=DO_TOPIC&URL_SECTION=201.html.

US Geological Survey. The water cycle for schools. Retrieved May 11, 2015, from http://water.usgs.gov/edu/watercycle- kids.html.

Vickers, R. H. (2011). *The elders are watching.* Retrieved May 1, 2015, from www.youtube.com/watch?v=4VLBfOqS4j4.

Other Children's Books (used in the project but not referenced in the chapter)

Dorion, C. (2010). *How the world works.* Somerville, MA: Templar Books (Candlewick Press).

Hadley, E., & Hadley, T. (1985). *Legends of the Earth, air, and fire.* Cambridge, UK: Cambridge University Press.

Jackson, E., Dillion, L., & Dillon, J. (2005). *Mother Earth.* New York: Bloomsbury Publishing.

Kruger, L. F. (2009). *Taking care of Mother Earth.* Penticton, British Columbia: Theytus Books.

McKinney, B. S. (1998). *A drop around the world.* (M. S. Maydak, Ills.). Somerville, MA: Dawn Publications.

Singleton, G. (2010). *365 science experiments.* Heatherton Victoria, Australia: Hinkler Books Pty Ltd.

Strauss, R. (2007). *One well: The story of water on Earth.* Toronto: Kids Can Press.

Note

1   17 of 24 children in the class identified as having Indigenous ancestry.

9

CREATING MEANINGFUL OPPORTUNITIES FOR CHILDREN TO ENGAGE WITH CLIMATE EDUCATION

Candice Satchwell

Peter attended an 'eco' primary school—a school that had achieved recognition by fulfilling certain pro-environmental criteria as determined by the Eco-Schools framework.[1] Peter was proud of its eco status. He became secretary on the eco committee, and he watched with glee as the wind turbine was erected in the school playing field. This was a major achievement for the primary school, and the item was featured in the local newspaper. One day Peter heard of another school erecting their own wind turbine. Rather than celebrating the environmental success for the local community, Peter looked downcast and said, "That's not fair! That was OUR idea."

Peter's response raises many questions about values, attitudes, and human nature. We might feel heartened that Peter had taken ownership of the innovation, and that he felt protective of his school's reputation. But in this context, Peter's competitive edge is not as useful as it might be in other arenas; indeed, it is positively unhelpful. Peter's response is clearly a recognizable self-centered, child-like emotion, but how can we help children learn more other-centered, proactive, and collaborative values around environmental projects and community work, in general?

Any curricular initiative about the environment should have a sustained impact on behaviour. For example, when we teach arithmetic in the classroom, we expect children to be able to work out whether the school bus will get them home in time to watch their favourite TV show, or how much change to expect when they buy sweets in a shop. If education is situated solely in the classroom lesson, such that a child can successfully spell a list of words for a spelling test but cannot write a letter to their pen-friend, then our efforts to fully prepare our children to live in community have fallen short. It is important for literacy and numeracy to be seen by children as relevant and applicable to everyday life. I suggest the same applies to both social and ecological sustainability.

In this chapter I examine the relative merits of three different approaches to sustainability education, each of which aims to have a lasting impact on social behaviour:

1. Adopting a school ethos of sustainability, for example through becoming an Eco school—an international programme that awards schools 'eco status' if they fulfill certain conditions relating to sustainability.
2. One-off activities or visits from local authority or activist groups.
3. Engaging children as 'researchers' on a project relating to climate change.

I conclude by considering the notion of courage and the challenge of teaching about serious environmental issues in the context of institutional cultures (e.g., public education) that are politically conservative and averse to controversy.

Deep Dynamic versus Surface Learning

When teaching everything, not just concepts about the environment, our aim must be to develop deep rather than surface knowledge (Marton and Saljo, 1976). Rather than expecting children to memorize facts only to regurgitate them undigested on a test, we want the children to think deeply about new ideas and initiate related actions. Lublin (2003) summarizes characteristics of students who are engaged in deep learning: able to relate new ideas to previous knowledge; able to relate concepts to everyday experience; and able to interact vigorously with the content (p. 3). The emphasis is on making connections among prior knowledge, new knowledge, and future applications. So how do we promote deep learning about the environment? What is the best means of ensuring that what children learn in school is also useful and applicable in the context of life outside of the classroom? The notion of 'active' or 'dynamic' learning is helpful in this context, whereby the child is fully engaged in 'learning by doing,' and actively constructing their own understanding by being 'forced to think' (Petty, 2009). A statement from ten-year-old Ellie, collected while I was researching children's knowledge about climate change (Satchwell, 2013), summarizes the phenomenon of static learning—as opposed to dynamic learning—in relation to the carbon cycle:

> We just store it in our brains, and keep it there. We know it, but it just stays in there. We don't do anything about it. We forget about it until our next science lesson.

Ellie's view demonstrates the problem of children not being fully engaged with formal education. Ellie's learning is stuck inside the classroom, and it has characteristics we would associate with surface rather than deep learning.

Geoff Petty and others maintain that knowledge gained through active means is much better recalled, understood, and enjoyed (Petty, 2015). Further, many educators understand that knowledge cannot be transferred simply from one person to another in a straightforward way, like how we might think about a teacher 'delivering' lessons to children. Teachers who hold constructivist beliefs about learning are apt to set up learning experiences that give students 'space' to 'construct knowledge' for themselves and make sense of concepts and problems in their own way, which often also means allowing them to come to understandings in their own time.

School Ethos of Sustainability

The Eco-school Programme provides a 'checklist'[2] to consult when applying for a *Green Flag*, the designation for a school deemed exemplary in its sustainability practices. While this is a useful indication of what is required, there is a paradox in the implication that 'ticking boxes' against environmental initiatives is a satisfactory approach. It may be possible to positively answer the question 'Does your school have an Eco-Committee that meets at least once every half term?' or even 'Has sustainability been covered in at least three curriculum areas by most year groups?' But it is more difficult to claim with confidence that the children and staff hold values or display behaviours that are congruent with these responses. Rather, it is the school *ethos* that is reflected in these initiatives which is the real indicator of the school's credentials. The 'Note on Litter' at the bottom of the webpage is perhaps more telling in this respect: "During a Green Flag assessment, the assessors will be on the lookout for litter—and they will not recommend the school for its award if there is a litter problem."

The school attended by Peter had successfully received its Green Flag and has subsequently been awarded a prestigious International Eco-Schools Certificate for its "continued excellence in improving the environmental performance of the school and the wider community." This was partly a result of installing the wind turbine and fulfilling the requirements of eco-committees, recycling, and so on. But this school has taken a further step by embedding environmental education within the curriculum. The school's website describes the school's commitment to a holistic approach to the environment and combines this with invoking a belief in a dynamic learning approach: it aims to provide "a quality, investigative education, enriched by experiences gained from using the environment whenever appropriate."

The whole-school approach is also suggested in its belief in a link between attitudes and behaviour: From the school's website: *The teachers and support staff raise awareness of environmental issues, not just through delivery of the curriculum, but also through demonstrating good practice in their management of the classroom and the surroundings of the school. From this lead, the children are encouraged to act in an environmentally responsible way.* This expression of the interrelationship between the curriculum, the school ethos, and prosocial behaviour of staff and pupils implies a commitment to including the environment in everyday education. I suggest it also means that deep learning is more accessible, as the children are encouraged to make connections between what they learn in lessons and their experiences in the wider environment and the community.

Within the English school system, in which the National Curriculum has become increasingly prescriptive, such an approach is indicative of the school's confidence in itself. As an 'outstanding' school according to government inspectors, it has been able to, for example, incorporate literacy and numeracy within its curriculum through topic work, rather than devoting the statutory hour to each. In the same way, the school is in the position of being able to have the courage of its convictions and incorporate environmental issues and values in its teaching and curriculum. A school deemed as 'failing' would be under scrutiny to ensure improvement in results and would be more likely to resort to additional numeracy and literacy classes and increased testing. So while the eco school's investigative approach to the curriculum is one that is most likely to lead to deep learning, it is a luxury that not all schools feel they can afford. I will return to the notion of courage later in the chapter.

Clearly this school's efforts are laudable, and the school well deserves its eco status. However, even in this school where sustainability is embedded, Peter's comment indicates some lack of holistic understanding. Being able to erect your own wind turbine seems to be a highly dynamic as opposed to static example of learning—the children were involved in deciding how, where, and when the turbine would be installed, and engaged with the whole process at a deeper level by learning how it worked, watching its construction, and thereby contributing to their understanding of physics and geography as well as environmental issues. So what does Peter's protestation suggest is going wrong? Perhaps what is missing here is the understanding and transference of values relating to the project, not just within school, but beyond. When it comes to activities designed to improve our interaction with the environment, we need to subscribe to a set of values that places the interests of the planet above the interests of our own individual immediate gratification. If we don't work together—not only in our schools, but in our wider communities—we will make little difference.

Nonetheless, the Eco-Schools framework is one way of ensuring that this journey is at least begun, and from this initiative teachers and children can begin to make connections between school, community, and beyond.

One-off Environmental Activities

In a recent study (Satchwell, 2013), when I asked children in primary schools for memorable events relating to environmental education, they were quick to tell me about the day the council brought its recycling wagon to the playground. The main attraction for some of the children seemed to be that they were allowed to sit next to the driver, while another child gave me a list of statistics he had apparently memorized about how many tin cans or bags of textiles one would need to collect to earn £10. There is clearly novelty value in introducing someone from outside the school to talk about a topic; but there is also a value here in relating the children's learning in school to life in the community. Children were encouraged to take home the message that recycling at home was a good thing to do; and that these people driving the wagon would be the same people coming to their street to empty the recycling boxes. This is a neat demonstration of overlap between school, home, and community.

In our society, children are often construed as 'agents of change' in the context of the environment. They are seen as 'custodians of the earth' and 'ambassadors for the future.' But in reality, their agency and power is severely limited: they have little influence in relation to money, politics, or social systems. Even within their own schools, they have little say in how the school is run, how or what they learn, or even what they wear. While research has shown that children's 'pester power' is influential in terms of getting their parents to buy them expensive presents or unhealthy snack foods, children's insistence on recycling or walking instead of driving is less likely to be heeded. Nonetheless, they should not be dissuaded from trying, and one-off events can carry additional impact simply by being out of the ordinary.

Another example of the one-off activity occurred, again, during my study of children's understanding of climate change, but this time I was the initiator of the activity. I had collected a variety of websites and games relating to environmental issues, and I worked with teachers to engage students in exploration and play. Three weeks after one such day of activities using these climate-change related resources with a group of primary school children, I wrote individual letters to each of the children, asking what they could remember about the day. Inevitably perhaps, given the norms and expectations of children's behaviour when receiving visitors in school, I received a thorough reply from each child outlining the ways in which I had helped them to understand more about climate change. They told me how much they had learnt, and how, for example, they were now recycling, walking to school, and turning off lights at home. As delightful as it was to receive such positive responses, it is difficult to believe that I had really been the purveyor of such knowledge, or that the changes in their behaviour would be sustainable. One child wrote the following:

> Ever since I've been talking to you, I have been walking home from school a lot more than often and thanks to you I have been really thinking about and have started to recycle even.

Of course, influencing students' change in behaviour is not a straightforward and linear process. Without family support, it is unlikely that travel arrangements can be changed or household practices instigated that were not previously in place. For children to be effective in influencing the behaviour of others, there need also to be changes in households, communities, governments, and certainly global agreements. All the same, one-off activities are to be encouraged, particularly if children learn of the connections between the activities and their relationship to broader concepts at the local and global levels.

Involving Children in a Research Project

Engaging children in sustained long-term research is an example of dynamic learning and a good way of enhancing children's motivation. Here, I describe an example of a project that involved children in documenting their observations of the environment, part of my own research that examined children's understanding of climate change.

The project involved supplying 12 mobile camera-phones to children aged 10, 11, and 12, and creating a closed Twitter account for them to share their observations with their peers and me. The children were identified as co-researchers, and their role was to send a tweet or take a photograph whenever they encountered something that made them think about environmental issues. I was interested in how they would interpret this instruction, and how they would communicate with one another—and with me—about the topic. My research goal was to understand children's thinking about the environment in their out-of-school lives. As it happened, none of the children had their own mobile phones, so there was an added sense of novelty, especially their new identity as 'ecotalkers.' (For more on the advantages of learning with mobile technologies, see Galloway et al. (2014).)

The children were given the mobile phones to take home during the Spring half-term. The weather at this time was unusually hot, and was reflected in comments like the following:[3]

> I put an ice cube outside and it melted in 2 minutes
> Most of the flowers in my garden have lost there leaves but i dunno if thats with heat or my dads a rubbish gardener

Another topic was travelling on roads for the holiday week:

> Hi people a lot of cars that people buy are secod hand and most of the time those cars burn fuel less efficiently
> Read about tourism officials being mad as they lost millions cos the weather report said it would rain but it was hottest day of the year

The children took full advantage of their phones' inbuilt cameras and took photographs of a visit to the local tip, the countryside on a bicycle ride with their family, food compost, a wind turbine, recycling boxes, a rainstorm, and various other objects whose meaning was more ambiguous. For example, a blurred photograph of a patch of grass turned out to be a Frisbee, which had melted in the heat. These photographs were useful as discussion points for the group after the Twitter experiment had ended. The children had kept the photos on their cameras but had not Tweeted them—this technology being a little beyond them at the time—so we met to share and discuss these artefacts.

The topics of discussion, instigated by the children's own tweets and photos, include some of the following: the weather, the natural world, traffic, and energy sources (see Table 9.1). The fact that all of these topics arose spontaneously from the children indicated that they were piecing together their understanding of climate change: its causes (e.g., traffic), its effects (e.g., on weather, insects, earthquakes), and human adaptations (e.g., solar panels/energy sources). These relationships were specifically articulated when a boy who had taken photographs of a range of different artefacts and scenes was asked to explain them to a group of his peers and me. He explained that the photograph of a collection of plastic bags showed his understanding that plastic is undesirable for the environment; his photograph of a radio showed where he had heard the weather forecast, indicating the importance of communication in environmental issues; a picture of a rainswept scene taken from his house window showed a rainstorm that he thought could be a result of climate change; and a photograph of a joke relating to lawnmowers in the Arctic showed his understanding that the problem is global and not just local. By explaining each photograph and discussing its meaning with peers, children created narratives about the environment which helped them deepen their understanding of the all-encompassing nature of the topic.

By taking the mobile phones out of school—and even taking them away on holiday in some cases—the children integrated real experiences in their daily lives with school learning. They extended 'class time' into their own time. There was evidence of parental input in some of the tweets (detectable in some cases by a sudden standardization of spelling), and we could claim that the mobile phone acted as a bridge between home and school. In addition, the children worked

TABLE 9.1 Examples of children's tweets

I was on the motoway and I saw a soala powered lamppost
When we got back if you looked over the city all u could see was pollution
Cows prouduce a lot methane !
This morn barak Obama said that soler and wind are the way forward
The pope has a lot of solar panals in his cord yard!
Verey unusal whether here it is verey rainy
It dried up really quickly today after the rain today
Why does the weather keep doing this! Its really hot and them suddenly theres a really heavy downpour and even a storm!
Hi saved water from paddling pool we watered our plants with it. It's another hot day
We went to the park on Sunday I think the water is reused for the splash park it goes into a tank underground
Heat can affect the environment but the sun is usefel as it gives us resources like light
Hi its sunny today. I wonder if that affects the ice burgs in antarutica
Hi just been on net, read about an earthquake in Caribbean it was 7.1 magnitude it killed at least 1 person

collaboratively. After a school outing when they walked up a big hillside close to their school, their messages included the following Tweets (in a group of five children):

> Ecotalker 4: We saw lots of insects and things like that up [the local hill] that you don't usually see in your garden
>
> Ecotalker 5: Ye like the big green catipila
>
> Ecotalker 4: I've seen more wasps about and fewer butterflies and also there are less flies and other insects coming into our house
>
> Ecotalker 1: We seem to have a lot of clover in the garden this year and the bees are on it all the time
>
> Ecotalker 2: The weather is not settled, temps very mixed up. We should be having more sunny days with the odd day of rain

This Twitter exchange began from their observations on a school walk, observations that I suggest were heightened by their involvement in this mobile phone project. Children built on the previous comments of peers, indicating that they were thinking of ways in which the environment connected with nature and with the weather. As in the example relating to their photographs, the children's conversations became important 'sites' of learning. Facilitation by teachers at this stage can lead to children making connections between changing habitats and climate change. We can describe this as dynamic learning, reflecting a deep approach to constructing knowledge.

If this study were to be repeated or extended, I hope that the discussions provoked by children's tweets and photographs relating to their environment would develop into an action plan on some aspect of the local ecology that they deem problematic. This would comprise the final step from making meaning, creating collaborative understanding, and working together to do something about a problem they identify and define for and by themselves.

Courage in the Curriculum

In the UK currently, there is no requirement for children in primary school to consider causes and effects of climate change or, more generally, environmental education on sustainability. While the curriculum for 11 to 14 year olds includes aspects of climate change in science and geography, it is still not mandatory for children under 11 years. Instead, there is an ever-increasing emphasis on literacy and numeracy, with increasing numbers of assessments and tests so that records can be kept to prove it. (See children's poet Michael Rosen's (2015) 'Guide to Education' for an eloquent description.) The results of the 2012 Programme for International Student Assessment (PISA) tests showed the UK as 26th in maths out of 65 countries, and 23rd in reading, indicating no improvement since the last tests in 2009. The response has meant that in the UK, currently, there is even more pressure on schools to 'raise standards.' This, in turn, has led to more rigorous testing and focus on a narrower curriculum. I suggest that these two points combine to *reduce* environmental education in schools.

For a start, the over-emphasis on the 3Rs in schools results in less time for extra-curricular activities, which is where environmental education typically is situated. Second, one could argue that the ethos of constant assessment and testing in schools encourages a competitive attitude to education. The incessant testing of children inevitably involves some element of pitting them against one another; and the results of the tests lead to league tables which compare schools with one another, thereby inculcating an ethos of competition between schools. Such competitiveness is potentially detrimental in the cause of saving the planet. Klein (2014) declares:

> For any of this to change, a worldview will need to rise to the fore that sees nature, other nations, and our own neighbours not as adversaries, but rather as partners in a grand project of mutual reinvention. (p. 23)

The primary curriculum as it stands means that it is up to individual teachers— and only if they have the support of their headteachers—to make space in a crowded curriculum to provide children with the opportunity to understand the interaction of the natural world and human activity. Clearly, for teachers to help children *act* on this knowledge takes some courage.

A memorable event recalled by some children was an environmental group that visited primary schools to engage children in activities to help them to understand the carbon cycle, to recognize ways in which they and their families used energy, and to think about ways of adapting to climate change. Taking a full day of curriculum time to accommodate this visit was a brave decision for the school in a time when government targets have to be met. It also resulted in an experience that, perhaps, made a lasting impression on the children. The event was an example of dynamic learning, involving children in carefully constructed activities, which led to them making their own discoveries about energy and how it is used. At the end of this day, they were encouraged to go home and make a difference to the ways their families used energy. I have pointed out the complexities of such an assumption—transference from one context to another is not straightforward. However, crossing boundaries between school, home, and community is crucial if our actions in school are to have any long-lasting effect.

Therefore, it is crucial that schools take this leap of faith to devote school time to environmental education, which might include inviting out-of-school experts to collaborate, as above, or by making fundamental changes to the curriculum. But, as noted earlier, it is only the schools with the highest test scores that are likely to feel the confidence required to make changes. Additionally, Smith (2007) points out, "By and large, people who enter the field of education are those who are comfortable in schools *as they are* rather than people who wish to become agents of institutional or community change" (p. 204). Smith insists that the issue of courage is a critical and sadly often lacking element that is required for schools to embrace environmental education. Through having the courage of their convictions teachers can themselves become agents of change.

Teachers of young children are in a position to help their learners understand the benefits of collaboration, sharing, empathy, and compassion. The most effective way to learn, as many experts on education will testify, is by doing—not by being told about something or tested on something, but by doing it. If we can encourage a seismic shift in the way our children treat the earth, the way they treat one another, and the way they would wish to be treated themselves, then indeed we can help children themselves become agents of change.

> Because in the hot and stormy future we have already made inevitable through our past emissions, an unshakable belief in the equal rights of all people and a capacity for deep compassion will be the only things standing between civilization and barbarism.
>
> (Klein, 2014, p. 462)

I suggest that for it to be reasonable to think of children as 'agents of change,' *teachers* must first find the courage to make changes themselves. By engaging as activists in their communities and schools, teachers can show children, by example, what it means to be agents of change. And from their interaction with meaningful and holistic curricula, children learn habits and cultural practices characterized by empathy, compassion, and collaboration.

References

Galloway, J., Merlin, J., & McTaggart, M., (2014). *Learning with mobile and hand-held technologies: Inside and outside the classroom.* London: Routledge.

Klein, N. (2014). *This changes everything.* New York: Penguin Books.

Lublin, J. (2003) Centre for Teaching and Learning: Good practice in teaching and learning. Retrieved March 24, 2015, from http://www2.warwick.ac.uk/services/ldc/development/pga/introtandl/resources/2a_deep_surfacestrategic_approaches_to_learning.pdf.

Marton, F., & Saljo, R. (1976). On qualitative differences in learning – 1: Outcome and process. *British Journal of Educational Psychology, 46,* 4–11.

OECD PISA 2012 (2012). Retrieved March 29, 2015, from www.oecd.org/pisa/keyfindings/pisa-2012-results.htm.

Petty, G. (2009). Evidence-based teaching (2nd Edition). Cheltenham: Nelson Thornes.

Petty, G. (2015). Active learning. Retrieved April 13, 2015, from http://geoffpetty.com/for-teachers/active-learning/.

Rosen, M. (2015). Guide to education. Retrieved May 1, 2015, from http://michaelrosenblog.blogspot.co.uk/2015/04/guide-to-education.html.

Satchwell, C. (2013). Carbon literacy practices: Textual footprints between school and home in children's construction of knowledge about climate change. *Local Environment: The International Journal of Justice and Sustainability, 18*(3), 289–304.

Smith, G. (2007). Place-based education: Breaking through the constraining regularities of public school. *Environmental Education Research, 13*(2), 189–207.

Notes

1 www.eco-schools.org.uk/
2 www.eco-schools.org.uk/applyforanaward/greenflag/greenflagchecklist
3 Original spelling and punctuation in children's tweets are retained.

10

ACTS OF RESISTANCE

Decolonizing Classroom Practice through
Place-Based Education

Christy Radbourne

Educational progressives are calling for transformative schools that will create more engaged, democratically present citizens. To complicate matters, this call for critical thinkers and engaged citizens is echoed on both the political left and right. It would then follow that both, having the same goals, would be seeking similar reforms. The problem is that for the dominant market-centered perspective, the purpose of schools is to enhance the nation's competitive status within the global economy rather than transform the complex social structures that result in income inequality and environmental degradation. These structures perpetuate the individualistic consumerism that drives Western economies. The current market-based neo-liberal agenda for education is based on the logic that it can close achievement gaps between marginalized and privileged students through the use of standardized standards, curricula, pedagogy, and national assessments. However, as most educators who work in high-poverty schools understand, the accountability movement is an albatross around teachers' necks that tends to punish (and close) usually the poorest schools and, in the end, continue the screening/sorting function of public schools.

Place-based education, the focus of this chapter, offers a pedagogical and practical tool for transforming schools into democratic cultures and helping students learn to be 'agents of change.' Place-based education (PBE), in its simplest form, is an educational approach that centers the curricula in the local or regional community in which the school and students are located. With PBE, school and community members partner to redesign curricula to ground the school in community life, with a key goal being the development of students as engaged, activist members of the community. This process fosters a concept of community that organizes itself around the concept of the "acceptance of otherness and cooperation within difference" (Furman, 1998, p. 307). Place-based education offers classrooms and schools an opportunity to engage in democratic community practices (Freire, 1994) and socio-ecological justice pedagogy (Furman & Gruenewald, 2004) as a means to actively resist colonizing structures and pedagogy in schools (hooks, 1994).

This chapter examines the political context for the current situation in public schools, describes place-based education and its decolonizing potential, and offers teachers and school leaders practical ideas that can be implemented in the classroom as well as throughout the school.

Setting the Context

Schools tend to reflect the world outside their doors (e.g., the *haves* tend to do well and thrive in school and the *have nots* tend to struggle and fail), and the dominant voices within schools usually mirror the voices of power in the wider world (e.g., white, male, individualism, market-based). The purpose of education reflected in the standards movement, high stakes testing, charter schools, and teacher union busting, baldly stated, is *to produce students who will contribute to the economic prosperity of the nation* (Foster, 2004).

Though the term *globalization* is relatively new, the related concept *colonialism* has a long history, beginning with the Conquest of the Americas in the late 15th century (Bowers, 2001). Colonialism, a practice of domination, or subjugation, of one people over another, is a product of the Western Age of Enlightenment. Arising from *man's* need to examine, define, and ultimately control his surroundings, namely the earth and her processes, *colonialism* is the underlying belief system that the earth and its people could be exploited for its natural resources and labor for the benefit of 'man' (Eisler, 1987). This belief system has led to the conquering of Indigenous people and the appropriation and exploitation of natural resources worldwide. Colonialism relies on the belief system that the earth is an object to be dominated and used by men, positioning specifically white men at the top of human hierarchy.

Prior to the Age of Enlightenment, an Indigenous worldview of the earth as a *sacred mother* permeated belief systems across Europe. Indigenous communities, often matriarchal in nature, organized their governance around consensus, rather than hierarchy and majority. However, the colonial mindset not only condones the appropriation of the earth and her resources, but also positions white men as saviours and Indigenous people as savages (Eisler, 1987). Since Indigenous people and women have traditionally been associated with the earth, the colonial belief system included these peoples as subjects for domination and exploitation. This also has had ramifications for the types of people, knowledge, and ways of living that were viewed as valued or important. Other belief systems, cultures, knowledge, and ways of living were denigrated as *less than* their white European counterparts. This *colonial mindset* is the foundation on which today's Western economic system was built, in the United States, Canada, and recently, throughout the world.

Public schools in the early twenty-first century continue to reflect the colonial mindset through forms of pedagogy and curricula that seek to standardize curriculum and teaching as part of the accountability movement. For example, in Ontario, Canada, districts evaluate schools every three years. Schools are rated according to the Ontario School Effectiveness Framework, which contains specific *"look fors"* that include proscribed pedagogical practices such as *"balanced literacy instruction"* and *"assessment for learning practices."* Curriculum is still written by the dominant voices of power, reflecting what they recognize as valued and of value to the marketplace (e.g., Ontario's grade 6 biodiversity curriculum reflects only Western perspectives and is not inclusive of traditional ecological knowledge). Local cultural knowledge bases and local histories are conspicuously absent in today's increasingly standardized curricula.

Standards and limits are imposed on teachers and curricula by provinces or states through the imposition of rigorous, standardized, onerous lengthy curricula, and national standards, like the Common Core in the U.S. In Canada, Ontario's Grade 3 language curriculum alone has 15 overall expectations and 72 specific expectations. Pedagogy and teaching practices are expected to yield quantifiable results on standardized tests, such as the Education Quality and Accountability Office's (EQAO) literacy and numeracy tests in Ontario. Districts, schools, and teachers not producing acceptable results are often punished through increased scrutiny, decreased funding, or public censoring. By determining which knowledge is valued and enacted through curricula, and then controlling *how* knowledge is conveyed, government education policies tend to perpetuate the colonial mindset in schools, especially in schools serving historically marginalized communities. By limiting the purpose of school to economic prosperity and the needs of the market (Foster, 2004; Foucault, 1994), the school becomes more or less entrenched in the colonial belief system.

Place-Based Pedagogy

Place-based pedagogy is an educational approach that recognizes, values, and embraces the local context both as a knowledge base and as a connecting point for communities and schools. It is also a pedagogy of resistance (Pyle, 2008). It works to resist the consumptive, individualistic culture we've developed within the U.S. and Canada by connecting communities and schools in seeking social and ecological sustainability. Place-based education, in its simplest form, constitutes an educational method that centers the curricula in the local or regional community in which the school and students are located. Place-based education (PBE) connects school and community in the redesign of curricula to enable students to learn from their experience and activism in community. This process requires the recognition of local diversity and histories to address issues of race, class, gender, and socio-economic status in a concrete context (Gruenewald, 2008).

Place-based education can be a powerful educational response to community disintegration and ecological illiteracy within schools. Teachers' opportunities for resistance lie within the ability to experiment with pedagogies, such as PBE, that engage students in the critical analysis of problematic school and community structures *and*, simultaneously, provide opportunities for students to take action in response to this analysis. These acts of resistance also provide the foundation for the creation of a school culture that fosters the embracing of diversity, the safety and security for students and teachers to take risks, and harmony with nature and each other (Furman, 1998).

A well-known example of place-based education is the Antioch University New England CO-SEED program (Knapp, 2008). CO-SEED, a place-based school improvement and community development program, has supported and funded PBE projects throughout New England in both rural and urban settings. One of CO-SEED's more successful projects is on the island school of Vinalhaven off the coast of Maine. Vinalhaven served multiple boat access only island communities and the school was in rough shape. Students were disengaged and often left the island after graduation to pursue lucrative fishing careers elsewhere. In 1998, the incoming superintendent implemented changes that reflected place-based education. Emphasis was placed on creating a caring community of teachers, connecting community and families with the school, and redesigning the curriculum to reflect local contexts. The redesigned curriculum included a geology curriculum that was grounded in exploring local geologic formations and careers as well as a marine science unit that studied local marine life and the effects of red tides.

With the power to engage students in their communities as the teaching context for curriculum, living examples of PBE in action across schools and communities are abundant. Examples of PBE in schools include, but are not limited to, using local geographic and physical environments as teaching contexts. They also provide students with opportunities to connect and act on local issues, work with local businesses, and contribute to local economies (Smith & Sobel, 2010). I now describe four PBE projects with which I have been involved.

Reconnecting with the Ecological Community

During the 2011–2012 school year, three teachers and I, as vice principal, embarked on a research project to bring PBE into our classrooms. Our school was located in suburban Ontario, in a previously undeveloped area that now was being rapidly transformed by housing developments. The teachers and I set out to learn if reconnecting the students with their quickly disappearing natural environment would improve critical literacy skills. The project also addressed students' ecological literacy and attitudes.

After their engagement in several PBE activities such as nature excursions, a frog pond investigation, and a *'visualizing our place'* art investigation, a noticeable shift in students' ecological literacy and attitudes towards the environment occurred. An unexpected by-product of their attitudinal change toward the environment (from *fear of and disregard for* to *curiosity, respect, and caring for*) was a reshaping of their respect and caring for one another (Chambers & Radbourne, 2013). The most significant changes in children's attitudes towards the environment were found among Grade 2 students. Prior to the project, over 75 percent of the students' indicated that the natural environment was a place to be feared. One survey item asked second graders to respond to the prompt: *When out in the woods, one must be quiet because....* Here are the responses of four students:

(student one): Something will get you and kill you
(student two): So the predators won't hear you and chase after you
(student three): A wolf (bear) will get you and eat you
(student four): Something will eat you...

Students' attitudes by the end of the project appeared to show greater concern for animal life. Eighty-nine percent of students on the post-project survey reflected this concern.

(student one): You should be quiet so you can see animals
(student two): So you don't scare the creatures
(student three): Because if you are noisy and screaming you will miss lots of things
(student four): If you don't watch where you are going you might step on animal houses

The primary goal of the Ministry of Education, Teacher Learning and Leadership Program (TLLP) project was to improve student critical literacy skills, and the staff was particularly encouraged by the students' ability to discern multiple perspectives. For example, some of the Grade 2 children, without prompting, were able to identify both sides of a local issue (housing development) and provide arguments to support both, in writing and imagery. As one Grade 2 student wrote when asked about her thoughts on the new housing development adjacent to the school:

It is good because they are making homes for humans, but I don't think it's very nice and nature needs to live and they are kind of tearing down the trees and stuff, and there's some animals in there and they are losing their homes.

(Grade 2 student)

This response, as well as others by students in Grade 2, is noteworthy because the concept of identifying two sides of an argument and presenting both points of view is a skill that the Ontario language curriculum does not emphasize until Grade 6. Still, the most significant literacy gains were made by the students with special needs. The following is a response to the prompt, *"Describe what you see outside the school yard"* from a student identified 'significantly at risk' in reading and writing:

> I saw a tractor. I saw tiny pieces of ice connected to each other on the ground. I saw a tree and a broken branch on the ground. I saw a rock and snowflakes. I felt the wind that is swirling around and taking snow off the ground. I saw a footprint that looked like a paw. I saw a hole with a piece of ice around it and some grass in it. I saw the sky and it was blue. I found a cloud that was shaped like a choo-choo.
>
> (Grade 2 student)

This particular student response was interesting for two reasons. It demonstrated the student's interest and connection with the natural environment, and it also provided insight into how connecting children with their environments through place-based education (PBE) might motivate a student struggling with reading and writing within the confines of traditional pedagogy and curriculum. Through strategically designed interactions and experiences with their local environments and cultural places, students demonstrated their ability to interact with their environment, think critically about their place, and express that knowledge using multiple modes of communication (Comber, Nixon & Reid, 2007).

Finally, the construction of the outdoor classroom/school garden became a galvanizing focal point for the entire school (Chambers & Radbourne, 2013). The Grade 6 participating class created the garden design, which included several species of local perennials, a tribute garden to a student who passed away during the year, and space for an annual vegetable garden. Both Grade 2 and Grade 6 classes completed the garden construction. Unexpectedly, during the recess break, when the remainder of the school entered the schoolyard, dozens of students from every grade approached the participating students and asked to help, thus spending their recess digging, raking and moving straw, dirt, and plants. The outdoor classroom/garden has become a hub for learning across classes in the school, thus providing a starting point that students, and particularly students at risk, can use to generate new perspectives and create new understandings they can take back into the classroom (Koop, 2007).

Grounding Math in the Local

At Ogden Community School, a small urban elementary school in Thunder Bay, Ontario, teachers and students are practicing *active resistance* in math education. It began simply with a project designed by an arts and heritage community organization and a local pizza restaurant. Through the arts and heritage community partner, the school was introduced to the owner of a local pizzeria that uses only locally sourced ingredients. The Grade 4/5 class participated in three workshops with the community partner and the pizza owners to learn about the benefits of local businesses and the importance of buying local. After these sessions, the students were tasked with the job of designing original labels that would represent the restaurant's offerings and include 'buy local' messaging. Over 25 unique labels were created by students, and these were displayed publicly at the school's 2014 Math Night for parents. In a school of just under 200 students, an audience of 100 students, parents, grandparents, uncles, aunts, and siblings showed up to listen to students talk about real-world problem solving in math and, of course, to enjoy pizza and the student labels!

Math Night 2014 was just the beginning of the school's collaboration with the pizza restaurant. The kindergarten classes constructed a large raised bed herb garden on the school grounds. The school obtained a grant for the materials and the herbs grown were pizza friendly. The partnership continued in math classes throughout the school. Teachers, who had decided that the context for the teaching of mathematics had to be authentic and real world, designed open-ended rich math tasks related to real-world problems solved every day at the local pizza eatery. The Grade 6 classes studied problems, such as the relationship between delivery distance and the appropriate temperature of pizza bags to ensure the restaurant's guarantee to deliver the pizzas at a set temperature. The Grade 3 classes figured out how many pizzas their class would need for a party given a set number of slices per pizza, and then set about figuring out the cost. Even kindergartners got into the act determining how many pieces of pepperoni could fit on their favourite pizza! The result was engaged, enthusiastic students who persevered to solve difficult problems long beyond their usual time on task. Finally, at Math Night 2015, the students' pizza math work was displayed throughout the school and the local pizzeria owners gave presentations to parents, students, and staff all about the math used every day in their restaurants. Students explained their thinking and work to parents and both had an opportunity to learn together. The partnership continues today as the local pizzeria and the Grade 6 teacher explore ways in which the students can become involved in everything from feasibility studies to cost–benefit analysis.

Contributing to Community Sustainability

The Ogden Community School Grade 6 class regularly examines their classroom community every day through their daily Circle of Power and Respect (CPR). The Circle of Power and Respect is part of Ogden School's commitment to using restorative practices to build community within the school. Based in Indigenous worldviews, restorative practice encourages the use of talking circles to build and support community. The CPR is also about connecting with each other and collaborative problem solving around issues which arise in the classroom. As they work through the problems and challenges in their classroom and school, students also investigate issues in the larger community as well as the national and international contexts. After the Bangladesh factory fire of 2012, the Grade 6 class explored the root causes of sweatshops and child labour. Through their inquiry, students determined that supporting Fair Trade commerce and goods was one way that they as consumers could influence unfair labour practices, even in places as far away as Bangladesh. The project evolved from a Mother's Day Fair Trade Tea to a full deputation to the local city council requesting that their local community become a Fair Trade city, committed to purchasing and offering of goods that could be verified as fair trade commodities. The Grade 6 class has since graduated and left the school, but the current class has continued this project and has asked the school board to become a Fair Trade school board.

Following the path of fair trade, the current Grade 6 class began to investigate the notion of local food security. With help from local community partners and the local district health unit, the class identified the availability of fresh and local food as a significant problem for low-income families in the community. Students determined that significant factors in food scarcity and poor diets included cost, transportation, and availability. After investigation with various community partners, and the production of a Pop Up Food Fair (PUFF) at the school, the students decided to host an experimental Good Food Market (GFM). The idea of the GFM is to bring in low-cost fresh, preferably local produce, to a location centrally located within the neighbourhood and sell bundles of this food at cost. The students obtained food from a local grocer for the trial run. They then determined the price of an assorted bundle of fresh produce and took orders on a Monday from school families. The food bundles were packed and distributed by the students at the school that Wednesday. The GFM was a resounding success, with all 30 bundles sold out in the first round of orders. Further student research indicated that there would be a market for a regular GFM. Now conducting pricing research, students are bargaining with local grocers to obtain the best price for the best produce. Hopefully, the GFM will run monthly, alleviating some food security issues in the low-income families and contributing to the sustainability of the overall community.

Leading the Place-Connected Community School

Redefining the school as a community, nested within and connected to the surrounding community, is my goal as a transformative school leader. As the principal of Ogden Community School, my mission is to influence the structural conditions and culture that bring to life the vision of a diverse, sustainable community. Our community suffers from high rates of poverty, low parent education rates, and high crime and substance abuse rates. Therefore, reconnecting the school and community and building a school culture that embraces diversity and local histories has become a key leadership goal. Foster (2004) and Brown (2004) make it clear that the transformative leader's role in education is that of a social justice activist. As such, even as school leaders grapple with the challenges of accountability frameworks that dictate curriculum and practice, they must help create spaces for teachers to become change agents as well. This begins with relationship building with staff, students, and parents. Providing autonomy to staff so they are empowered to take risks in teaching and connecting with students and introducing challenging pedagogy are critical to making space. In addition to making space and growing teacher efficacy, democratic dialogue (Freire, 1994) and collaborative leadership foster teacher risk taking and transformative ownership. Finally, the transformative principal must also shelter staff from the accountability regime as much as possible, not by relaxing rigor or expectations, but by allowing teachers to focus on the job of teaching and inspiring their students. At the core of every effort must be a communally agreed-upon core of values around which the community can be organized. Engaging parents and the larger community are the final cornerstones for creating the transformative community school.

We began by working as a community to develop and agree to four core values. Building on an already strong school culture that had a deep ethic of care and love, the school needed to connect with the larger community in a meaningful way. A deeper understanding of the local context, as seen through the eyes of parents, students, and community members, was necessary. Surveys asked parents about their engagement with the school, the barriers they experienced, and their hopes for their children's school. Data was taken from a previous survey of students' thoughts on their school's welcoming environment, safety, and well-being. Similarly, community partners, local not-for-profits and support agencies were asked for their view of the school's overall environment and engagement. Staff worked collaboratively to analyze the data, added their own ideas, and finally decided on four core statements that enshrined the values of the school and community:

I Can
I Hope
I Trust
I am Valued

These value statements were introduced to the students at an assembly and were posted throughout the school. Each class created their own multimedia presentations of what the values meant to them.

Next came building more connections with community. Community partnerships in schools have traditionally been about obtaining goods and services that severely cash-strapped schools often find difficult to obtain on their own (Sanders & Harvey, 2002). The goal at Ogden was to create partnerships that would deepen the local connections and understanding for students and staff. We reached out to locally owned businesses, neighbourhood action groups, and local NGOs that had social and ecological justice as a key part of their mission. The partnerships formed in the first year opened space for teachers to explore PBE in creative ways. Staff engaged in finding new partnerships and ideas for bringing together students, parents, and community in the development of rich, engaging curricula. Students, staff, parents, and partners alike refer to the *Ogden Community* when speaking of the school. Perhaps the highest compliment to all our work has been our nomination for the Ontario Premier's Safe and Accepting Schools award for the year 2014–2015. Though the award selection process is underway, the recognition of the efforts to create a community school where the "acceptance of otherness and the cooperation with differences" creates a harmony with nature and each other (Furman, 1998) is an affirmation that small acts of resistance to the colonial narrative can indeed generate communities of change and hope.

Conclusion

On every front, there is a recognition that schools, indeed education itself, needs to do things very differently if we are to produce learners who are democratically engaged agents of change in their communities. While the recognition may be there, mainstream educational reform is still firmly enmeshed in the colonial narrative, though creatively disguised today as 'best practices' and 'world class standards.' Without addressing the deeply embedded colonial structures inherent in the school system, school reform will fall crucially short of altering the community crises that define the problem: fragmented communities, isolated groups of color, and ecological illiteracy. In response to these community crises, place-based pedagogy engages community inter-generationally, connects environments and people, and provides students with the skills to recognize oppressive structures and the tools take action to improve the quality of community life. Place-based education infuses the local context into teaching and learning. Above all, it expresses the relevance of real-world community problems coupled with the strategic knowledge to solve them. Students, teachers, and school leaders can engage, through PBE, in small acts of resistance, which, when taken collectively, can transform schools into communities of hope and activism.

References

Bowers, C. A. (2001). Toward an eco-justice pedagogy. *Educational Studies, 32*(4), 401–416.

Brown, K. M. (2004). Leadership for social justice and equity: Weaving a transformative framework and pedagogy. *Educational Administration Quarterly, 40*(1), 77–108.

Chambers, J., & Radbourne, C. L. (2013). *Teaching critical literacy through the natural environment as text.* Paper presented at the annual meeting of the American Educational Research Association, San Francisco, April 8, 2013.

Comber, B., Nixon, H., & Reid, J. (Eds.). (2007). *Literacies in place: Teaching environmental communications.* Newtown, NSW. Primary English Teaching Association.

Eisler, R. (1987). *The chalice and the blade: Our history, our future.* San Francisco: Harper-Collins.

Foster, W. P. (2004). The decline of the local: A challenge to educational leadership. *Educational Administration Quarterly, 40*(2), 176–191.

Foucault, M. (1994). Omnes et singulatim: Toward a critique of political reason, 1979 lecture. In P. Rainbow & N. Rose (Eds.), *The essential Foucault* (pp. 180–201). New York: The New Press.

Freire, P. (1994). *Pedagogy of the oppressed* (Rev. ed.). New York: Continuum. (Original work published 1970)

Furman, G. (1998). Postmodernism and community in schools: Unravelling the paradox. *Educational Administration Quarterly, 34*(3), 298–328.

Furman, G. C. & Gruenewald, D. A. (2004). Expanding the landscape of social justice: A critical ecological analysis. *Educational Administration Quarterly, 40*(1), 47–76.

Gruenewald, D.A. (2008). Place-based education: Grounding culturally responsive teaching in geographical diversity. In D.A. Gruenewald & G.A. Smith (Eds.), *Local diversity: Place-based education in the global age* (pp. 137–154). New York: Routledge.

hooks, b. (1994). *Teaching to transgress: Education as the practice of freedom.* New York: Routledge.

Knapp, C. E. (2008). Place-based curricular and pedagogical models: My adventures in teaching through community contexts. In D.A. Gruenewald & G.A. Smith (Eds.), *Local diversity: Place-based education in the global age* (pp. 5–28). New York: Routledge.

Koop, C. E. (2007). Starting small. In B. Comber, H. Nixon & J. Reid (Eds.), *Literacies in place: Teaching environmental communications.* Newtown, NSW: Primary English Teaching Association.

Pyle, R. M. (2008). No child left inside: Nature study as a radical act. In D.A. Gruenewald & Smith, G.A. (Eds.), *Local diversity: Place-based education in the global age* (pp. 153–172). New York: Routledge.

Sanders, M. G., & Harvey, A. (2002). Beyond the school walls: A case study of principal leadership for school-community collaboration. *Teachers College Record, 104*(7), 1345–1368.

Smith, G. A., & Sobel, D. (2010). *Place- and community-based education in schools.* New York: Routledge.

11

"DAPTO DREAMING"

A Place-Based Environmental Education Project Supporting Children to Be Agents of Change

Karen Malone

This chapter describes a place-based participatory research project conducted in a primary school near Sydney, Australia. In this project, elementary-school aged children came to develop a strong sense of place attachment, place identity, and environmental knowing. I will argue that by allowing children opportunities to engage in place-based encounters with humans and the *more-than-human* world, children can begin to comprehend and have sensitivities to such concepts as interdependence and sustainability. These new ways of knowing, including indigenous, socially critical, and new materialities, are embedded in 'multiple ecologies of place and knowing.' These may well be critical attributes for young people to take on the role of environmental change agents in order to support a sustainable future.

Children's Encounters of Place

Around the world, research on children's encounters with place has shown that, regardless of the type, quality, and diversity of the place within which children live, it has a direct effect on the children's life experiences (Chawla, 2002; Jack, 2010), their forming of an ecological identity (Stone, 2005) and their potential for environmental learning (Malone & Tranter, 2003a; Malone & Tranter, 2003b). Local neighbourhoods and villages, outside or within a city environment, are important places for children to develop their emerging ecological self (Chawla, 2002; Driskell, 2002). Places found close to a child's home, for instance, can offer a set of local affordances in relation to the child's place encounters and their developing sense of self. The affordance of an environment is the measure of a place's capacity to respond and complement the child's identity building. Heft (1988, 1989) and Kytta (2004) argue that the affordances found in a local environment offer *scaffolds* to support children to engage in place-making activities by themselves or with others. These ecological 'objects,' the 'things' that children encounter that make up a 'place,' are often viewed spontaneously by children from both a functional and relational point of view. As children's ecological place identity evolves (physically, emotionally, and socially), how objects or affordances in the environment shape the children's encounters of and relations to place also evolve.

Chawla (2007) introduced her model of environmental knowledge development as shown in Figure 11.1.

This model illustrates that for children to gain environmental knowledge and competence, they needed mobility and accessibility: that is, the freedom to explore the environment, to have 'place-based educational encounters.' They also need a selection of responsive affordances (objects) in the environment they could encounter and re-encounter over time. The argument articulated by Chawla draws on an important thesis: the important role that childhood experiences of *nature and community* have for building children's environmental and social competence, and indirectly their capacity and desire to be active agents of change.

There has been growing debate in environmental education circles around the relevance of what children are 'learning' about their place in schools. Some researchers have called for a balance between what children learn and do in classrooms, for example, and what they are exposed to and experience outside the classroom. Michael Stone (2009) in his book *Smart by Nature* supports this idea.

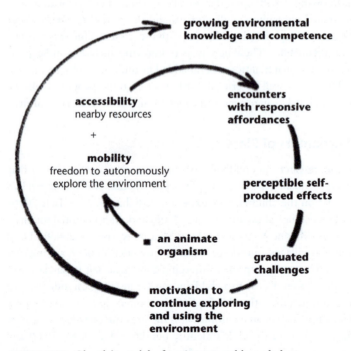

FIGURE 11.1 Chawla's model of environmental knowledge development (Chawla, 2007).

> When people acquire a deep knowledge of a particular place, they begin
> to care about what happens to the landscape, creatures, and people in it …
> Place-based education is fundamental to schooling for sustainability. Places
> known deeply are deeply loved, and well-loved places have the best chance
> to be protected and preserved, to be cherished and cared for by future gen-
> erations. (p. 13)

Smith (2002) believes that when schooling seeps into the realm of the real
world, *learning outside the classroom*, and students and educators become creators of
a place-based curriculum,

> …the wall between the school and the community becomes much more
> permeable and is crossed with frequency.…The primary value of place-
> based education lies in the way that it serves to strengthen children's con-
> nections to others and to the regions in which they live. (pp. 593–594)

Smith (2007) and Gruenewald and Smith (2008) argued that place-based
education could alter the conventional societal function of school. That is, it has
the capacity to provide young people with the skills needed to regenerate and
sustain their own communities and contribute to global calls for a more sustainable future. This was also supported by Jensen and Schnack (1997) who argued
that while definitions of environmental actions in schools often focus on environmental outcomes (i.e., planting trees, building school vegetable gardens), the
aim of environmental action should also be about children connecting to place. As
citizens of their community, children come to believe they are capable of making
a difference now and in their future lives:

> The fundamental assumption is that environmental problems are structur-
> ally anchored in society and our ways of living. For this reason it is necessary
> to find solutions to these problems through changes at both the societal and
> individual level … to make present and future citizens capable of acting on
> a societal as well as a personal level. (p. 164)

In a case study of the children in Dapto Primary School, I will illustrate how
the children in this particular neighbourhood on the south coast of Sydney in
Australia have developed a sense of efficacy and agency through their individual
and collective place-based educational encounters with the environment. These
encounters have promoted a strong sense of place attachment, a foundation for
their capacity to take up and be open to a role as environmental stewards and
change agents. I am reminded here of the words of David Sobel (1996): "If we
want children to flourish, to become truly empowered, then let us allow them to
love the earth before we ask them to save it" (p. 39).

Dapto Dreaming: A Place-Based Educational Project

The Dapto Dreaming Project was implemented from April to July of 2011. The aim of the project was to provide an opportunity for primary age children to have input in the design of the new development by Stockland urban developers. This study utilised the framework of the global Child Friendly Cities Initiative (UNICEF, 2001), and it replicated a number of studies, particularly in Australia, that have been conducted by the author, who has implemented a similar research design focusing on the *child friendliness tool kit* and children's independent mobility (Malone, 2008; Malone, 2011; Rudner & Malone, 2011). The methods and tools of the child friendliness tool kit had grown out of the author's involvement in the ten-year UNESCO Growing Up in Cities Project (Chawla, 2002; Driskell, 2002). The project was located in a suburban community on the outskirts of the urban sprawl of the city of Sydney.

The Children's Place

Horsley is a neighbourhood in the small town of Dapto, located on the outskirts of the City of Wollongong in the Illawarra region of New South Wales, Australia. The area around Dapto was originally inhabited by the Dharawal (or Thurawal) Indigenous Australians. The name Dapto means 'water plenty' in aboriginal dialectic, as the area was known for its rich environmental land and aquatic resources and was a significant meeting point for different aboriginal tribes. The neighbourhood boasts a number of large and smaller playgrounds and parks, with every child having a playground or park within walking distance of their home. Dapto Public School is a large school with a population of around 700 children enrolled from kindergarten to grade 6. The gray outlined areas in Figure 11.2 illustrate the new urban development sites with the community of Horsley where the school is located in the top right-hand corner (see Figure 11.2).

In the research brief, the development company stated, "Stockland is committed to the adoption of child-friendly principles to create a nurturing, supportive and stimulating environment for the children of Brooks Reach and surrounding communities."

The Research and Educational Activities

The role of the place-based participatory research and educational workshops was to support children to collect data about their experiences of their neighbourhood and, then, evaluate the child friendly qualities of the community. The team conducted two research workshops with 150 children, 30 from the kindergarten classroom (5–6 years old) and 120 grade 5 children (9–10 years old).

Kindergarten Children

One grade of kindergarten children were engaged in two sessions—the first explored how they experience the local area; the second session focused on their

FIGURE 11.2 Aerial view of Brooks Reach Development (photograph courtesy of Stockland).

dreams of what a child-friendly community in Dapto would look like. Children had the opportunity to share and discuss their opinions and explain their drawings to the researchers. Adult researchers using a storytelling strategy conducted individual interviews with each child and completed the survey of child friendliness of a neighbourhood on their behalf.

Grade 5 Children

All grade 5 children were engaged in three sessions. In the first session, students explored their mobility around the neighbourhood using a predetermined children's independent mobility survey (CIM survey; Hillman et al., 1990) that had been conducted in a number of locations around the world. The second class session explored how children felt and experienced the local area. This included filling in the child friendliness survey (CFC survey; UNICEF, 2008), drawing their neighbourhood, and giving each child a disposable camera for a weekend so they can take images of their local community. The third session focused on their dreams of what a child-friendly community in Dapto would look like and their ideas of child friendliness that could be applied in the new urban design.

On completion of the in-class place-based educational studies workshops, a smaller group of 12 children worked with the adult research team to collate and analyse the children's data and develop a children's report. This group also developed a list of child-friendliness indicators from the data to be used as the foundation of the design recommendations to the developers. Opportunities were given through the reporting process for children to speak to other children as 'shared producers' of the report on the research and also the design of the play space. A play consultant and artist, local Indigenous advisors, Stockland staff, and the Stockland landscape architect worked alongside the children as supporting adults. The project culminated in a celebration of the children's designs and the opportunity for children and local community members to discuss their visions with Stockland and city council staff.

Children Dreaming and Designing Child Friendliness

When evaluating the potential child friendliness of the urban environment, there were two key place-based elements considered: *place affordance* and *place accessibility*. Place affordances are the environmental features and settings that have the potential to be perceived, discovered, shaped, and used by children (Heft, 2001). Place accessibility is the opportunity for children to be able to access these physical affordances (Kytta, 2004) in terms of time and the physical capacities inherent in the place itself. In the Dapto Dreaming Project, the CIM survey provided data on place accessibility, and the CFC survey, children's drawings, photographs, and guided tours provided data about how place affordances were identified. This data obtained through the research with the children in and out of the classroom was then organised in order to inform a play space design, the urban attributes of the new development, and the capacity for children to access these two elements.

Environmental Affordances

"Big, big, big, big playgrounds." Brendan & Zane, age 6

Children's survey results indicated the elements that children liked most about their neighbourhood: it was quiet with friendly people; there were accessible parks and playgrounds; and there was lots of nature. Children's favourite activities in the neighbourhood in order of preference were sport, physical activity, playing with other people, and interacting with animals and nature. Interestingly, watching television and DVDs and using computers were very low among their favourite activities. The data revealed that children, especially the older children, played structured sports on a regular basis, and the favourite non-sporting pastime was to play with friends in the local parks and wild natural spaces on the neighbourhood boundaries.

Lachlan's photograph, taken at a point in the park where it leads into the wooded forests on the edge of the neighbourhood, provides a wonderful perspective of the real and potential affordances these spaces provide for children (see Figure 11.3).

Fishing, catching frogs, going for walks, riding bikes, and generally hanging around the creeks and woodlands were common activities for the older boys on the weekends and after school. Corey's photograph (see Figure 11.4) of his weekend play place suggests that the open paddocks of the countryside that butt onto the periphery of the neighbourhood area are important play spaces for children.

FIGURE 11.3 Natural places to play, Lachlan, age 11.

FIGURE 11.4 Play places, the old farmhouse trees, Corey, age 11.

The large old trees that were planted as a wind break for the farmhouse now provide a haven for animals and children alike. Corey explained this is a place for engaging in rough and tumble play and building because there is an abundance of loose materials for cubby building.

This drawing by Logan (see Figure 11.5) of her neighbourhood illustrates how natural elements of the environment, rocks, bushes, trees, and the pathways to get to them are central and interwoven to his experience and perception of the neighbourhood.

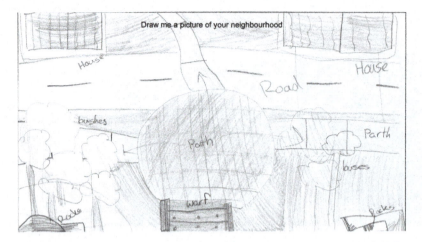

FIGURE 11.5   My neighbourhood, Logan, age 10 (photograph courtesy of Karen Malone).

Some of the younger children also made reference to activities in nature: "My favourite activity is fishing with my family" (Tyler, age 5); he also spoke of how his parents took him to these wild spaces on the edges of the neighbourhood. This neighbourhood experience of nature was also relayed through a strong sentiment for protecting and valuing existing natural and indigenous elements of the landscape. Children in workshops discussed the important stewardship role they had to play in protecting nature, including plants and animals. They included it as one of their child friendliness indicators: "If the flora dies it wont be beautiful anymore" (Kimberley, 11); "It can let the animals have freedom and feel safe" (Jason, 11); "We need to protect nature so no animals die and become extinct" (Olivia, 10).

Being active and 'playing' was also an important issue discussed by children. The availability of parks, playgrounds, and a variety of play settings allowed for a diversity of play and leisure opportunities to exist: "We need lots of places to ride bikes" (Brad, age 10). "Exercise keeps everyone fit and healthy, as well as living a long life" (Tiegan, 11); "Let kids run free" (Jack, 10); "It is fun" (Logan, 10); "I like to ride on my scooter around the block" (Zane, 6). These photographs taken by Georgia and Jye, both age 10, illustrate the varied play spaces available to children in the neighbourhood (see Figures 11.6 and 11.7).

Accessibility and Mobility

> "My neighbourhood is safe, not many strangers and my neighbours are friends." Jaida, age 5

Although less than half the children do not walk home from school, more are allowed to cross the main road alone and around a quarter of the boys are allowed

FIGURE 11.6 Local playground, Georgia, age 10.

FIGURE 11.7 Local playground, Jye, age 10.

to ride their bikes around the neighbourhood. In our statistics regarding children's independence, boys tended to benefit from more freedoms than their girl counterparts. Survey data from parents indicated that *stranger danger* was a more significant issue for children's accessibility than traffic dangers, fast drivers, litter, and bullying by older teens.

As illustrated clearly by their comments, children in this neighbourhood have a strong connection to their community and especially their neighbours with whom they share the space: "I have lots of neighbours, I know all of their names" (Kate, age 5). Children in the workshops identified a child-friendly neighbourhood as a place for *creating communities*: "Safe communities are communities we can trust" (Tiegan, age 11); "So we can share ideas and we can make more friends" (Olivia, 10); "Create good atmosphere, socialise and make new friends" (Lachlan, 11). Parents appreciated the role neighbours had in supporting their children's safety. A majority of parents agreed that there were other adults in the community who would care for their children when they were outside in the neighbourhood (without parent supervision).

Indicators of Child Friendliness

Once the survey, photographic, and drawing data were collated, children were then asked to analyse the data for key themes that would become the basis for the indicators. Table 11.1 provides an overview of the final list of child-friendliness indicators, an icon that represented it, and the comments from the children as to why these indicators were important.

TABLE 11.1 Child-friendly neighbourhood themes

Icon	Indicator/theme	Comments from children why these indicators are important
	A place supporting play and has playgrounds	To let children have fun – Jason; So children don't just sit on the lounge and get unfit, so they could be running around – Kimberley; So people can develop their climbing skills and have fun – Logan; To have safe playgrounds – Paul.
	A place that keeps and protects nature	Saves old trees, keeps our heritage and your families future – Aaron; Keep scar trees and indigenous things – Jack; To keep animals and plants from extinction and let animals have freedom and feel safe – Jason.
	A place where we create communities	Have street parties, where people can get together, be nice to neighbours, share ideas – Aaron; So other people meet people and make more friends – Georgia; Groups or parties to get to know your neighbourhood, create a good atmosphere, socialize and make new friends – communal gardens – LA; So we can share our ideas and make friends – Olivia.

Icon	Indicator/theme	Comments from children why these indicators are important
	A place that allows you to be active	It can be fun and children will be healthy and a good weight – Georgia; Let kids run free – Jack; It can be fun and you can run and play – Kimberley; So we can be healthy and fit – Olivia; Exercise keeps everyone fit and healthy and living a long life – Tiegan; It can be fun – Logan.
	A place that promotes learning	People don't throw rubbish, play safe and learn to look after the environment – Jason; Important to teach children about the environment – Aaron; To teach kids to respect the environment, like at out school we have a green team – LA.
	A place that is safe and clean	No pollution keeps us, animals and plants safe so there should be no litter – Connor; So no animals or people step on needles or pins and other sharp objects – Georgia; Keep us healthy and nature healthy – LA; Prevents animals, plants and ourselves from injury – Tiegan.
	A place that values children	The future lies in our hands, so if you don't educate us the future generation, to look after the community it will be a bad place – Connor; Because the future is in our hands – Paul; Valuing children is important because we can pass on our education to future generations - Tiegan.
	A place that has pathways	Have pathways so you don't have to be worried about being hurt or run over by cars and motorbikes – Connor; Keep safe and so you don't step on nature - Jack; Keep safe so you're not walking on the road – Paul; So you don't tramp on plants – Logan.

Once the indicators were identified, in small groups, children designed the children's report, 'Dapto Dreaming,' that was produced *for* children and *by* children. Children wrote in the introduction:

> Our Dapto dreaming report is about the things we like about our neighbourhood and the things we think could be changed to make it even better. It's about making sure adults listen and value us and include our dreams in

their designs for our place. The report is organised around the eight things children told us help make this neighbourhood child friendly.

A play space and pathway design were developed by the children and presented to the developers. Three months later, the developers presented the playground design with all the children's ideas to children, parents, and staff of the school at a school assembly. On May 4, 2012, a number of children who participated in the project were bussed up to the Brooks Reach site to perform a 'turning of the soil' for the development of the playground. After the playground was completed and opened in late 2012, Stockland Developers and the research team were awarded the prestigious 2013 *Planning Institute of Australia* project of the year Presidential Award and Child and Youth Planning Award for the entire Dapto Dreaming Project. This was the first time ever a collaboration among a university, school, *and* developer won such an award.

Conclusion

"Valuing children is important because we can pass on our education to future generations." Tiegan, age 11

This chapter has described children's local environmental knowledge and competence by focusing on children's place-based encounters of their neighbourhood through everyday engagement and a school-based educational research project. When supported by collaborating adults, it appears that children can learn to recognise their sense of connectedness and stewardship for the local environment as well as a sense of responsibility to the planet: "The process of building a sense of agency through seeing the effects of one's action is integral to mastery of experiences, when people undertake an activity that they consider significant and succeed" (Chawla, 2009, p. 16).

Three months after the project's completion, we interviewed the children about their experience. Here are some representative comments:

Being able to help, proud that we're part of the design of the playground.

Doing stuff on the interactive board, going out onto the site, working with James. Looking forward to seeing it finished.

I got to be part of it with my friends.

I liked that I got to help design it—now it feels like I own it somehow.

We will make sure our friends go down to the playground and make sure Stocklands built the way they said they would.

I liked everything of the project and especially being creative. No one really questioned why I spent my Friday afternoons doing it. I talked to lots of my friends about it.

I liked it because we got to get out of the classroom and go to the site, it was more interesting than sitting in a classroom. I would do it or something similar again. It's good kids get to be part of it and make a difference.

Beyond the opportunities for the children to practice and learn agency, another equally significant aspect about this project was the decision by the urban developers to create an ongoing relationship between themselves and the children. With the children taking on the role as development 'advisers,' the project has continued to take on a whole-school focus. As a consequence many teachers are considering new ways to incorporate learning outside of the classroom as part of their everyday classroom curriculum. A representative from Stockland stated:

We loved working with the children and the school. The school has been 100% supportive and we look forward to working with them more as the development moves forward. Ongoing plans to keep in contact with the school involve getting some of the kids being part of the tree re-generation project up on the site, educating them on the construction point of view, showing them how a construction site works possibly so they can generate future employment ideas for themselves. It is about bringing them on the journey with us.

It was seen as a brave and unique initiative for an urban developer to value children's insights and to allow them to participate fully in a genuine pre-development process. Therefore, this project was testimony to a new way forward in a reciprocal relationship between children and urban developers and reinforced the important role children could play as key social agents in community planning. Beyond the design process, the project was also a valuable model for teachers on the role of place-based learning in empowering children to be active change agents. The children continually gave feedback to the teachers and research staff that being involved in the project has allowed them to express many of their ideas and views that didn't have an outlet in other areas of their life.

I have argued in this chapter and in other places (Malone, 2012) that children's understanding of what a quality environment is for children is the direct result of deeply felt encounters with the human and more-than-human entities and the shared relations they adopted as a consequence. The children's engagement in the project reflected high levels of place attachment and place identity which, in turn, shaped a strong personal commitment and motivation to protect and nurture those place-based relations (Malone, 2012). Reflecting the research findings of 'Dapto Dreaming,' I have added two stages to Chawla's original model (see Figure 11.8).

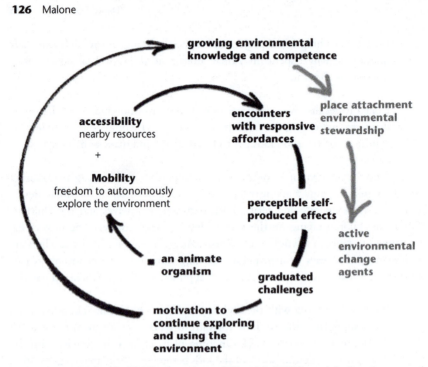

FIGURE 11.8 Malone's (2012) adaptation of Chawla's (2007) model of environmental knowledge development.

These two additional stages recognize *place attachment and motivation* and the capacity to take up the role as an *active environmental change agent* (Malone, 2012).

The challenge for teachers who are encouraging children's active participation as environmental change agents is to come to the realisation that this work does not or cannot just be supported in classroom-based environmental education curriculum or even in programs that offer *occasional* place-based learning outside the classroom. This project revealed very strongly the important role that children's encounters with their environment in the everydayness of play and being in community had in enhancing their place attachment and ongoing sense of connection to the objects and relations within it. A final recommendation for teachers who are supporting children as environmental change agents in the classroom is to consider ways to encourage children's everyday encounters in the natural environment during school *and* when they are out of school in their local neighbourhoods.

References

Chawla, L. (Ed.). (2002). *Growing up in an urbanizing world*. London: Earthscan/UNESCO.
Chawla, L. (2007). Childhood experiences associated with care for the natural world: A theoretical framework for empirical results. *Children, Youth and Environments*, *17*(4), 145–170.
Chawla, L. (2009). Growing up green: Becoming an agent of care for the natural World. *The Journal of Developmental Processes*, *4*(1), 6–23.

Driskell, D. (2002). *Creating better cities with children and youth: A manual for participation*. London: Earthscan/UNESCO.

Gruenewald, D., & Smith, G. (2008). Creating a movement to ground learning in place. In D. Gruenewald & G. Smith (Eds.), *Place-based education in the global age*. New York: Taylor & Francis Group.

Heft, H. (1988). Affordances of children's environments: A functional approach to environmental description. *Children Environmental Quarterly, 5*, 29–37.

Heft, H. (1989). Affordances and the body: An intentional analysis of Gibson's ecological approach to visual perception. *Journal for the Theory of Social Behaviour, 19*, 1–30.

Heft, H. (2001). *Ecological psychology in context: James Gibson, Roger Barker, and the legacy of William James's radical empiricism*. Mahwah, NJ: L. Erlbaum.

Hillman, M., Adams, J., & Whitelegg, J. (1990). *One false move: A study of children's independent mobility*. London: PSI.

Jack, G. (2010). Place matters: The significance of place attachment for children's well-being. *British Journal of Social Work, 40*, 755–771.

Jensen, B. B., & Schnack, K. (1997). The action competence approach in environmental education. *Environmental Education Researcher, 3*(2), 163–178.

Kytta, M. (2004). The extent of children's independent mobility and the number of actualized affordances as criteria for child-friendly environments. *Journal of Environmental Psychology, 24*(2), 179–198.

Malone, K. (2008). *How child-friendly is my community? A study of the child friendliness of the City of Brimbank*. Research report for the Smith Family and the City of Brimbank, University of Wollongong, New South Wales.

Malone, K. (2011). Changing global childhoods: The impact on children's independent mobility. *Global Studies of Childhood, 1*(3), 161–166.

Malone, K. (2012). "The future lies in our hands": Children as researchers and environmental change agents in designing a child friendly neighbourhood. *Local Environment: The International Journal of Justice and Sustainability, 18*(3), 372–395.

Malone K., & Tranter, P. (2003a). Schoolgrounds as sites for learning: Making the most of environmental opportunities. *Environmental Education Researcher, 9*(4), 283–303.

Malone, K., & Tranter, P. (2003b). Children's environmental learning and use, design and management of school grounds. *Children, Youth and Environments, 13*(2). Retrieved January 23, 2015, from www.colorado.edu/journals/cye/13_2/Malone_Tranter/ChildrensEnvLearning.htm.

Rudner, J., & Malone, K. (2011). Childhood in the suburbs and the Australian dream: How has it impacted children's independent mobility? *Global Studies of Childhood, 1*(3), 202–233.

Smith, G. (2002). Place-based education: Learning to be where we are. *Phi Delta Kappan, 83*, 584–594.

Smith, G. (2007). Place-based education: Breaking through the constraining regularities of public school. *Environmental Education Research, 13*(2), 189–207.

Sobel, D. (1996). *Beyond ecophobia: Reclaiming the heart in nature education*. Great Barrington, MA: The Orion Society.

Stone, M. (2005). "It changed everything we thought we could do": The STRAW Project. In M. Stone & Z. Barlow (Eds.), *Ecological literacy: Educating our children for a sustainable world*. San Francisco: Sierra Club Books.

Stone, M. (2009). *Smart by nature*. Berkeley, CA: Center for Ecoliteracy.

UNICEF (2001). *Partnerships to create child-friendly cities: Programming for child rights with local authorities*. New York: UNICEF/IULA.

UNICEF (2008). *The child friendly cities research program*. New York: UNICEF.

SECTION III
Teaching Peace

Section III examines peace education. The rationale for a section on peace reflects our assumption regarding the inextricable link between peaceful relations among humans (social justice) and peaceful relations between humans and non-human life (eco-justice). Injustice that is done to both human and non-human life reflects unequal power relations and the violence done by the more powerful to the less powerful: e.g., human violence to the natural world, the violence of richer nations to poorer nations, the violence of men done to women, the violence done by white people to people of color. These three chapters on peace education are a modest reminder to teachers that peaceful relations should permeate humans' relations with all life—animals, insects, plants, the air, water and land, and, of course, each other.

Rhys Kelly (Chapter 12) focuses on humans' relationship with each other, addressing explicit strategies for teaching children to resolve conflict, engage cooperatively in learning activities, and do restorative justice in the classroom and school setting. Kelly argues that strategies focused on collaboration and cooperation, if taught well, promote peace and a problem-solving orientation to conflict. Ben Paxton, Ingrid Hakala, and Sahtiya Hammell (Chapter 13) use the discipline of philosophy to ground the engagement of children in ethical discussions of their relations with people *and* non-human life. The authors believe that ethical actions, which are the subject of ethics-centered conversations, must be grounded in the following responsibilities: do no harm, help others, engage in caring relationships, and show respect for living beings. Finally, environmental ethicist Allen Thompson, in the third chapter in this section, maps out a teaching script that invites children to reflect on the 'right' relation between humans and nature. Children are invited to use logic to make sense of the human–nature relationship, and the teacher functions from a more Socratic position, as facilitator and guide.

12

NURTURING SOCIAL AND ECOLOGICAL RELATIONSHIPS

The Contribution of Conflict Resolution Education

Rhys Kelly

Peace education and environmental education have many affinities. At the heart of both, arguably, is a concern with transforming violent or unpeaceful relationships (those that are oppressive, exploitative, or destructive) into peaceful ones (relationships that are nurturing, enabling, cooperative, and caring). Many peace educators would argue that peaceful relationships among people are not imaginable without also understanding and addressing our violent relationship to the natural world; environmental concerns are integral to any comprehensive vision of peace, and therefore to peace education (see for example Amster, 2014; Andrzejewski, 2009). Likewise, it is difficult to imagine any meaningful environmental education that did not also express, even implicitly, the value of peaceful relationships. To nurture health and resilience within ecological systems is to emphasise interdependence, connectedness, and care.

Peace education is a broad field, encompassing many different objectives and contexts of practice, from dealing with legacies of war in post-conflict societies to educating about world affairs in relatively affluent, peaceful schools (Soloman and Cairns, 2010). It is therefore difficult to speak of it as one 'thing.' This chapter will focus on one important dimension of peace education: the effort to foster qualities and skills for engaging constructively with conflict. The idea of 'engaging constructively with conflict' (as opposed to avoiding, limiting, or managing conflict) recognises that conflict is a natural and often productive part of human relationships; it is not always 'bad' (Lederach, 2003, 2005). Most of what we consider as progressive social change, such as increasing gender equality, has been achieved through social conflict and struggle. It is often through conflict that we, as individuals or cultures, learn and grow. The challenge, then, is not to avoid conflict, but to find appropriate, creative, and non-violent approaches to conflict, so that we can harness its constructive energy and limit its destructive potential.

Skills for engaging with conflict might initially seem tangential to environmental education. However, the nature of the changes happening in our world—the 'crises' in this book's title—will only strengthen the need for those skills and qualities that enable people to imagine and maintain positive relationships in the face of change and/or adversity. I suggest there are at least three reasons for this.

Firstly, if there is to be an effective effort to de-carbonise the economy and address the wider threats to ecological systems, citizens everywhere will probably be faced with some hard choices. At the most general level, this is a question about whether we continue with 'business-as-usual' or make a serious effort to change course. Do we continue to consume energy and resources at the current rate, with all that implies, or do we commit to changing our relationship to the natural world? Even if there is a commitment to change, there will be conflicts to manage in the process. For example, do we prioritise using land for 'green' energy production (biofuels, wind, and solar), for food, or for protecting biodiversity? Do we prioritise initiatives to 'green the economy' over the protection of existing jobs and industries? Might there be a need to consider some forms of rationing or redistribution, to ensure that limited resources are used fairly and efficiently, and that carbon reduction targets are met? Will it become necessary to restrict some personal freedoms (i.e., through limiting the amount we travel) in order that broader, longer-term goals are achieved? Resolving these and related questions in a fair and equitable way will require advanced democratic skills: an ability to deliberate with others about complex issues, to reach informed and responsible decisions, and to resolve conflicts constructively (Few, Brown & Tompkins, 2006). It will require other things as well—democratic institutions and processes, and an independent, honest media. But the qualities needed for active, responsible citizenship will be crucial.

Secondly, the environmental crisis creates a need for greater solidarity and cooperation at different levels of society, with people working together to build a more resilient and sustainable way of life. This will be challenging in those cultures that have celebrated competition over cooperation and individualism over community, and which have undermined the possibility of meaningful interdependence among people. It will be complicated by actual or perceived conflicts of interest—for example, over declining resources, jobs, or other social goods. A renewed and more resilient form of community will require much effort to understand and communicate across different worldviews, to build relationships that can withstand the pressures of political and economic change, and to maintain space for dialogue and social learning (Wilson, 2012).

Thirdly, active citizenship sometimes requires that we engage in conflict, to seek social change through what Adam Curle (1971) called 'constructive escalation.' Curle's point is that the suppression or avoidance of conflict can be problematic, especially where this is linked to the operation of power. Challenging inequality or injustice—or the continuation of a system that is violent—sometimes requires an effort to make conflict manifest, to engage in protest and challenge. The nature of the environmental crisis means that change is unlikely to happen without some conflict. The challenge is to avoid destructive, violent forms of conflict, whilst engaging in meaningful action.

These points may seem quite distant from the everyday lives of elementary school children and their teachers. Yet, children at school often experience analogous challenges—moral choices (e.g., relating to friendship preferences); choices that imply trade-offs (e.g., how time is spent); dealing with children from different, unfamiliar cultures and backgrounds; negotiating the complexities of social comparisons and hierarchies; experiencing conflict with their peers or teachers; and sometimes dealing with situations or rules that are, or feel, unjust. In other words, the very nature of schools as communities and institutions means that children will be learning—consciously or not—about civic, relational life. The challenge for educators is to help children develop good habits and appropriate skills, not only to help make the school a caring and functional environment, but as part of a wider civic mission. As Deborah Meier suggests:

> Students learn from us; the robustness of our school community, its capacity to exercise judgment on important matters, and its inclusiveness are all part of young people's education. Where else might kids learn about the trade-offs, critical judgments, and responsibilities inherent in democratic life—including when and how to resist? If educating young people to make judgements based on credible evidence, reasoning, and collaboration with others is essential to our task, then we must create schools that have the intention of practicing these arts and the time to do so.
>
> (Meier, 2006)

The remainder of this chapter examines several strategies for supporting these aspects of education in elementary schools (much of which may be applicable in other educational settings too). I will introduce three areas of practice within Conflict Resolution Education—cooperative learning, peer mediation, and restorative justice—before offering a brief comment on some wider issues that educators might consider in this area of work.

Conflict Resolution Education

Conflict Resolution Education (CRE) is an umbrella term for a range of initiatives broadly concerned with developing students' social and emotional competencies. Although most obviously associated with specific skills or processes for handling conflict, in reality CRE initiatives tend to have a range of overlapping objectives. Jones (2006) gives a helpful summary of the core goals that CRE initiatives might seek to address. These are:

1. To create a safe learning environment. CRE initiatives, such as peer mediation and restorative justice schemes (discussed below), can help schools address conflicts and behavioural issues when they arise. In contexts where school violence is a problem (Harber & Sakade, 2009), this can help to reduce tensions and contribute to culture change.
2. To create a constructive learning environment. Linked to the above, CRE can support the creation of positive school and classroom cultures, in which children and teachers are able to communicate, cooperate, and collaborate effectively.
3. To enhance students' social and emotional development. Conflict Resolution has a clear normative orientation. Processes like mediation and teaching methods like cooperative learning communicate core values of fairness, respect for others, justice, and nonviolence. They encourage better communication, awareness of self and others (including emotional awareness), critical thinking, and creative problem solving—all key elements for more peaceful social relationships.
4. To create a constructive conflict community. Finally, CRE aims to establish habits, skills, and processes that enable students and teachers to deal constructively with conflict when it arises.

As I will show, different approaches to CRE may pursue some or all of these goals, in different ways. It is worth noting that CRE is often both a means and an end in learning situations; it aims to foster certain skills and qualities in students, but in contributing to the creation of a positive, peaceful learning environment for learning, it can support learning more generally. This reflects a relational understanding of the learning process itself. Learning is understood not as an individual activity, but a profoundly social one, taking place through interaction and using the shared social tools of language and culture. In short, people learn in and through relationships (Wetz, 2011). CRE, in its different forms, nurtures beneficial relationships within and beyond the school.

Cooperative Learning

Cooperative learning is a good example of a broad and integrated approach to CRE. As developed by Johnson and Johnson (2004, 2009), cooperative learning involves the use of collaborative group work to teach simultaneously about curriculum content *and* interpersonal skills. That is, structured, cooperative group work is used as a pedagogic strategy for engaging students with their core curriculum, whilst explicitly developing students' social, interpersonal skills. Many teachers use small groups for teaching, of course, but cooperative learning has a number of distinctive features:

- Long-term working groups and relationships: Students are often assigned to fixed groups for a long period—a term or semester—rather than being in ad hoc groups for specific activities. This can be a more demanding approach for both staff and students, as any difficult interpersonal dynamics will not be easily avoided (Kelly and Fetherston, 2008). Yet, this 'shared fate' can motivate students to invest in their relationships, to address conflicts if they arise, and work at developing an effective collaborative relationship. Thus, a key element of cooperative learning is 'processing'—spending time reflecting purposefully on how well the group is working, and what they can do to work together better. This can help students become more attuned to their own behaviour and its influence on others, and with a teacher's support, develop good habits in their social interaction.

- Design for independence: Johnson and Johnson understand that for genuine cooperation to happen in group work, there must be what they term 'positive interdependence.' Group members must genuinely need each other for the successful completion of a task, otherwise there is little incentive for collaboration. As such, the cooperative learning involves careful design of learning activities in order to create such positive interdependence. The classic example of a cooperative learning activity is the jigsaw exercise. Here students are given different pieces of information relating to a task or topic. Because each student has only one piece of the jigsaw and need all the pieces for completion of the task, they are dependent upon and accountable to each other; they must be effective in their preparation and contributions to the group. In addition, the cooperative situation requires and promotes certain skills and attributes—being able to summarise and explain information clearly, being able to listen effectively, or eliciting information through questioning. Again, not all forms of group work necessarily promote cooperative behaviour. Rather, it can be common for students to work quite individually in supposed group work situations. The appeal of cooperative learning (and other similar methods, like team-based learning) is the consideration given to task design, with the aim of creating a need for genuine cooperation.

- Constructive conflict: Cooperative learning activities sometimes deliberately create conflict situations within or between groups to teach good ways to deal with it. For example, Johnson and Johnson advocate the use of 'constructive controversy' exercises, a process that models the steps in deliberative, democratic decision-making. This centres on a chosen controversy, an issue around which there are clear areas of disagreement (for example, wind farms). Students are divided into pairs or groups and asked to research one side of the issue, to prepare the best possible case for their position, and to plan how to put their case across effectively. Students then make their presentations and engage in open discussion, exploring areas of disagreement, refuting attacks, etc. The next steps are the crucial ones. After debating, students then reverse positions, making the best case for the opposing side based on what they have heard. In a final step they collaborate to synthesise all the arguments and evidence, working towards a conclusion on which they can all agree. Although students first experience the common adversarial approach to political discussion, the deliberative element at the end reinforces the value of cooperative inquiry and addresses a number of skill areas. In order to produce a synthesis, the students must listen to each other effectively, they must ensure that discussion is inclusive and resolve differences consensually, and so on. This teaches a number of useful lessons—conflict and disagreement are not bad, but there are more or less constructive ways to handle it; active listening can improve mutual understanding; systematic, collaborative inquiry can lead to more robust outcomes.

The attraction (and perhaps challenge) of cooperative learning is that it can be integrated into everyday classroom work, providing a vehicle for collaborative projects on a range of subjects, whilst making the learning *from* and *about* collaboration an explicit focus of teaching. According to the four goals of CRE mentioned above, it can contribute to the establishment of a constructive learning environment as well as, or through, fostering social and emotional learning.

Peer Mediation

Mediation is commonly defined as an informal, voluntary process in which a 'third party' (someone who is not directly involved in a dispute) helps the disputants (those who are experiencing conflict) find a solution to their problem. Mediation usually aims to help disputants improve their communication about what has happened, their needs or interests, and ideas for solving conflict in ways that are acceptable to all. The mediator has no power and the disputants are only bound by what they agree to voluntarily.

Peer mediation schemes create opportunities for children to act as mediators in common, everyday disputes among children in school. Such schemes became popular in the United States during the 1980s, and have since been adopted in thousands of schools worldwide (Cremin, 2003, 2007). There are different models of peer mediation, but they usually include provision of training for volunteer mediators, and the establishment of a mediation service at specific times and/ or locations in the school run by children. For example, peer mediators (usually working in pairs) may be available during lunchtimes and break times, so that disputes in the playground can be addressed quickly and without the need for teacher intervention.

Peer mediation schemes obviously need adult support (Cohen, 2005). Teachers may be involved in arranging or providing initial training, and working out procedures and policies so that the scheme runs effectively. Teachers responsible for coordinating the scheme are often on hand during mediation sessions, in case there is a need for additional support or to assist with difficult cases. They also facilitate de-briefing sessions afterwards, to help children process their experience of mediating and draw out any learning.

As noted earlier, the value of peer mediation schemes arguably goes beyond the existence of a procedure for handling conflict in schools. Mediation expresses or embodies a particular ethos, a set of values and ideas about conflict and how it can be handled. The establishment of a peer mediation scheme is therefore a means for establishing or reinforcing a particular culture in the school, as well as teaching values and skills to children in an experiential manner. According to Liebmann (2000, pp. 12–13, in Cremin, 2007) mediation implicitly emphasises:

- Listening to others, for feelings as well as facts;
- Cooperation with others, valuing their contributions;
- Looking for common ground rather than differences;
- Affirmation of self and others as a necessary basis for resolving conflict;
- Speaking for oneself rather than accusing others;
- Separating the problem from the person;
- Trying to understand alternative points of view;
- Using a creative problem-solving approach to work on conflicts;
- Looking at what people want for the future rather than allocating blame for the past;
- Looking at all the options before selecting one to try; and
- Looking for a 'win-win' solution, where everyone's interests are satisfied, rather than the adversarial 'win-lose' approach where one person wins and the other person loses.

Mediation schemes enable children to experience what can be termed 'non-violent communication.' The presence and intervention of a third person can help to diffuse strong feelings, slow down and channel communication, and help disputants to properly hear what the other is saying. Perhaps most crucially, peer mediation schemes can empower children within a context where adults usually set and enforce rules and punishments. As Hilary Cremin (2007) writes, "People are more likely to change their actions if they hear how their behaviour is affecting the other person and if they have been involved in reaching a solution—rather than being subjected to an imposed solution (p. 16). Her research suggests that the more equal power relationship among children, and their closer understanding of how it feels to be a child, makes peer mediation effective, and more empowering than more traditional processes for dealing with pupils' disputes.

Johnson and Johnson's (2004) 'Teaching Students to Be Peacemakers' (TSP) programme is an example of a more integrative programme. It combines teaching about conflict theory (what conflict is, what causes it), different strategies for response (from withdrawal to compromise), and techniques for negotiation (resolving conflicts without help) and mediation (helping others resolve conflicts). Once students have been trained, teachers set up a peer mediation scheme, as described above.

The TSP programme is intended to be progressive and developmental. It is taught over 12 years, with students attending training each year. The training becomes more complex and sophisticated as students progress, and the opportunity to practice skills year-on-year helps students to achieve meaningful competence. The idea here is that skilful conflict resolution requires mastery, and mastery requires core skills to become habitual or second-nature. Only through repeated practice, in a supportive environment, is this possible. While this is a more ambitious and demanding approach than a stand-alone peer mediation scheme, there are potential benefits in having a clear and developmental curriculum centred on increasing skills and understanding throughout the school years.

Restorative Justice

Restorative Justice (RJ) programmes have some similarities to peer mediation, particularly in terms of a focus on empowering pupils to deal with situations of conflict in a constructive way. RJ processes usually come into play when some harm has been caused, but as an alternative to more traditional (punitive) mechanisms for dealing with misconduct. Morrison and Vaandering (2012) argue that standard school disciplinary processes often "rob students of a rich opportunity for collective problem solving, learning, and growth. Instead they (students) learn that other 'people of power' solve problems" (p. 140).

By contrast, the focus of RJ is dialogue about what happened between those involved and those affected by the incident, with an emphasis on empowering students to find solutions to problems and to learn from mistakes. Where traditional disciplinary processes in schools focus on which rules or laws were broken and what punishment is deserved, RJ focuses on who has been hurt, what their needs are, and the obligations of the wrongdoer to address these needs and rectify the harm. The aim here is to foster reflection, understanding, and empathy, primarily in relation to the victim's experience, but allowing exploration of the motives and intent of the 'wrongdoer.' This reflects a contention "that socially responsible actions and responses are best learned in a relationship culture where individuals are respected and well integrated into a social network" (Morrison, 2001, p. 196).

There are different practices associated with RJ in schools. However, the use of 'classroom circles' are considered a foundation for developing a restorative culture. As the name suggests, this involves classroom dialogue with students sitting in a

Three Shifts Toward Restorative Schools and Classrooms

From...	To...
Efforts to suppress misbehavior based on the view that misbehavior is evidence of failing students or classrooms.	Recognizing and using the inherent value of misbehavior as an opportunity for social and emotional learning.
Authority-driven disciplinary actions that focus only on the identified misbehaving students.	Restorative circles that bring together everyone who is most immediately affected by the incident.
Punishment and exclusion used to control misbehavior and motivate positive behavior changes.	Dialogue leading to understanding and action to set things right and repair and restore relationships.

(From: Clifford, 2013)

circle, sharing thoughts and addressing shared issues in an inclusive, participatory, and consensual process. The circle arrangement may seem obvious or unimportant, but it both symbolises and encourages a different set of expectations. Compared with the usual classroom arrangement—children in rows, teacher at the front— the circle approach fosters a sense of equality and accountability; everyone can be seen and heard. Amos Clifford (2013) describes two types of classroom circles: 'community-building circles,' which focus on building relationships within the class, and 'responsive circles,' focused on addressing a specific issue or problem. However, the two are related: community-building circles are used to build a relationship, trust, and familiarity with dialogue, which in turn supports the use of circles to deal with more controversial issues. A responsive process usually involves some guiding questions designed to elicit information about what happened and encourage exploration of both effects and possible responses. For example:

- What happened and what were you thinking at the time of the incident?
- What have you thought about since?
- Who has been affected by what happened and how?
- What about this has been hardest for you?
- What do you think needs to be done to make things as right as possible?

A teacher/facilitator might use various techniques to encourage full, but safe participation, including agreed-upon ground rules and the use of a 'talking stick.' The important thing is that processes are open and honest, focused on inquiry and discovery, rather than leading students to specific, pre-determined conclusions.

There is emerging evidence that restorative justice practices can have numerous beneficial effects in schools, ranging from improved behaviour and participation to noticeable effects on students social and emotional learning (Clifford, 2013). Because different sides of a story are listened to, pupils tend to see the process as being 'fair' and equitable. Likewise, the focus on restoration as opposed to punishment helps to maintain community within the school, preventing the harm that can arise from exclusion or stigmatisation of a wrongdoer (McClusky, 2008). There is much more to discuss here, but there are many resources available online, including detailed lesson plans and activities (see resources below).

Commentary on Small School Configurations

There is clearly value in these and other efforts to teach young people how to engage more constructively with conflict (see Akgun & Arzu, 2014). At the same time, however, it is important to keep asking some broader questions about the need for such initiatives within schools, and about their limitations in addressing the prevailing culture of education. For example, the Human Scale Education movement has argued persuasively that many problems in contemporary schools—including poor discipline and unpeaceful relationships—are linked to the size of educational institutions. As we know, the tendency in most state education systems has been to favour larger schools. This is often in the belief that these offer 'economies of scale,' and a richer experience for children—arguments for which there is some support. However, there is growing recognition that it is difficult in big schools "to establish the kind of human relationships that lead to good educational outcomes" ('good educational outcomes' here meaning not just academic achievement, but the well-being and flourishing of the individual student) (Haimendorf & Kestner, 2009). The sheer size and anonymity of large schools make it harder for children to know one another other well and, crucially, to be known properly by their teachers. In turn, problems of discipline and conflict become both more likely and more difficult to manage when relationships within the school are weaker. By looking at the relationship between scale and the culture of the school, we might gain a more a critical perspective on the taken-for-granted structures and systems of discipline and control in schools (Vaandering, 2013).

It is worth noting here that making schools smaller is not necessarily the best focus for change; there can be very poor small schools and very good larger schools. Rather, Haimendorf and Kestner (2009) suggest that the most important thing is to 'adopt the *characteristics* of smallness'; to adapt the size and culture of learning communities *within* a school so that they enable the same kinds of relationships that good small schools can achieve. There might be any number of ways to ensure that students feel part of a defined peer group, and have a sense of continuity and regularity in their relationships with each other (such as classroom circles or cooperative learning); the point is to understand what conditions make good relationships more likely.

There are also different ways to teach the values and skills that are the focus on conflict resolution education, and indeed there can be advantages to embedding these in everyday classroom activities rather than labelling them as a 'special' activity. For example, the foundational skill of 'active listening'—being able to listen attentively and respectfully to others, to notice body language and other aspects of communication, to ask questions to elicit more information, etc.—can be practiced within many classroom processes. It can obviously be modelled by a teacher in their interactions with students. It can also be integrated into peer feedback processes or small group discussions, through explicit instructions to take turns, to summarise what others have said, to give and receive feedback in appropriate ways—such activities can help develop good habits in social interaction.

Conclusion

If there is a central theme in this chapter, it is about relationship. I started by discussing the connection between peace education and environmental education via a shared concern with violent, unpeaceful relationships—including our relationship with the natural world—and the necessary effort to establish more peaceful, nurturing relationships. I then discussed some different approaches to conflict resolution education all of which are concerned with encouraging or restoring positive relationships, through better communication, cooperative learning, through social and emotional awareness, and through processes like mediation and dialogue. I also suggested that conflict resolution education is informed by a relational pedagogy, an understanding of learning as a social, interactive process.

Clearly, if we are to address the environmental problems that are the concern of this book—climate change, biodiversity loss, soil erosion, etc.—there is a need to critically re-examine our relationship with nature. There are many ways to approach this, including through nature-based learning and other approaches to environmental education. I would like to end by suggesting that the experience of cooperative, nurturing, respectful, and restorative human relationships might enable and encourage the same in relation to nature. Conflict resolution education can help to create school communities where such qualities can flourish and be part of children's experience. In turn, this might encourage a capacity for the necessary restorative work so urgently needed in our often unpeaceful world.

References

Akgun, S., & Arzu, A. (2014). The effects of conflict resolution education on conflict resolution skills, social competence, and aggression in Turkish elementary school students. *Journal of Peace Education, 11*(1), 30–45.

Amster, R. (2014). *Peace ecology*. London: Paradigm Publishers.

Andrzejewski, J. (2009). Education for peace and non-violence. In J. Andrzejewski, M. P. M. P. Baltodano & L. Symcox (Eds.), *Social justice, peace and environmental education* (pp. 99–120). London: Routledge.

Clifford, A. (2013). Teaching restorative practices with classroom circles. Centre for Restorative Processes. Retrieved March 3, 2015, from www.centerforrestorativeprocess.com/.

Cohen, R. (2005). *Students resolving conflict: Peer mediation in schools.* Culver City, CA: Good Year Books.

Cremin, H. (2003). Pupils resolving disputes: Peer mediation schemes share their secrets. *Support for Learning, 17*(3), 138–143.

Cremin, H. (2007). *Peer mediation: Citizenship in social inclusion revisited.* Maidenhead: McGraw Hill/Open University Press.

Curle, A. (1971). *Making peace.* London: Tavistock Press.

Few, R., Brown. K., & Tompkins, E. L. (2006). *Public participation and climate change adaptation.* Tyndall Centre for Climate Change Research.

Haimendorf, M., & Kestner, J. (2009). *School structures—Size matters: Transforming large urban comprehensive schools into small learning communities.* Bristol: Human Scale Education. Retrieved February 13. 2015, from www.hse.org.uk/research_and_resources-occasional_papers.html.

Harber, C. R., & Sakade, N. (2009). Schooling for violence and peace: How does peace education differ from 'normal' schooling? *Journal of Peace Education, 6*(2), 171–187.

Johnson, D. W., & Johnson, R. T. (2004). Implementing the "Teaching Students To Be Peacemakers Program." *Theory Into Practice, 43*(1), 68–79.

Johnson, D. W., & Johnson, F. (2009). *Joining together: Group theory and group skills* (10th ed.). Boston: Allyn & Bacon.

Jones, T. S. (2006). Combining conflict resolution education and human rights education: Thoughts for school-based peace education. *Journal of Peace Education, 3*(2), 187–208.

Kelly, R., & Fetherston, B. (2008). Productive contradictions: Dissonance, resistance, and change in an experiment with cooperative learning. *Journal of Peace Education, 5*(1), 97–111.

Lederach, J. P. (2003). *The little book of conflict transformation.* Intercourse, PA: Good Books.

Lederach, J. P. (2005). *The moral imagination.* Oxford, UK: Oxford University Press.

McCluskey, G., Lloyd, G., Kane, J., Riddell, S., Stead. J., & Weedon, E. (2008). Can restorative practices in schools make a difference? *Educational Review, 60*(4), 405–417.

Meier, D. (2006). 'As Though They Owned the Place': Small schools as membership communities. *The Phi Delta Kappan, 87*(9), 657–662.

Morrison, B. (2001). The school system: Developing its capacity in the regulation of a civil society. In H. Strang & J. Braithwaite (Eds.), *Restorative justice and civil society.* Cambridge, UK: Cambridge University Press.

Morrison, B., & Vaandering, D. (2012). Restorative justice: Pedagogy, praxis, and discipline. *Journal of School Violence, 11*(2), 138–155.

Soloman, G., & Cairns, E. (2010). *Handbook of peace education.* New York: Taylor and Francis.

Vaandering, D. (2014). Implementing restorative justice practice in schools: What pedagogy reveals. *Journal of Peace Education, 11*(1), 64–80.

Wetz, J. (2011). *Relationships as a springboard for learning.* Human Scale Education. Retrieved May 1, 2015, from www.stanleyparkhigh.org.uk/uploads/asset_file/HSE88_Relationships-as-a-Springboard.pdf.

Wilson, G. A. (2012). *Community resilience and environmental transitions.* London: Routledge.

Selected Resources

Centre for Restorative Process: www.centerforrestorativeprocess.com

Cooperative Learning: www.co-operation.org

Human Scale Education: www.hse.org.uk

International Institute of Restorative Practices: www.iirp.org

Peer Mediation: www.schoolmediation.com

13

AN ETHICS-BASED PEDAGOGY

Ben Paxton, Ingrid Hakala, and Sahtiya Hammell

Though it can be distressing to acknowledge, we live in a deeply troubled world. Environmental crises, wars, violence, poverty, and social injustice fill headlines across the globe. Most of these problems are of our own making. Fortunately, just as we are responsible for their creation, we also hold the key to their resolution. As educators, we play a pivotal role in addressing and ameliorating global social and environmental crises by promoting ethical behavior through ethics-based pedagogies. Ethics and ethics-based pedagogies enable us not only to solve existing problems, but also to proactively anticipate and avoid future crises. They accomplish this by helping us to learn how to think and act ethically, individually and together, in order to promote human flourishing and the well-being of the planet.

As Socrates said over two thousand years ago, ethics is a formal discipline that asks questions concerning "how we ought to live" (Plato, 1968). An ethics-based pedagogy offers a framework for educators to integrate ethical concepts and principles into lessons of any type or level, and across disciplines and activities. This approach invites educators and students alike to explore fundamental questions about who we are as individuals living in community with others; what kind of society and world we want for ourselves and our children; and what kind of relationships we need to have with other forms of life and the planet. In taking the time to encourage our students' and ourselves to think intelligently about goals, values, actions, and principles, we can make significant progress towards advancing the common good.

The nature and scope of environmental crises now facing our planet are well documented. But sadly, environmental crises are not the only serious problems confronting humanity. We must also deal with pressing social issues. Violence and war are leading causes of unnecessary injury, death, and environmental degradation. In 2014, there were 42 active armed conflicts around the world, causing

180,000 fatalities and creating 12,181,000 refugees (IISS, 2015). As egregious as war and violence are, humans are even more likely to suffer and die simply because they are poor. According to UNICEF, approximately 29,000 children under the age of five die *every day* due to easily preventable causes (e.g., malnutrition and diarrhea) which are the direct result of living in poverty (UNICEF, 2015).

Over the past few decades, we have become increasingly aware of the ways in which social and environmental problems are interrelated. For example, leading intelligence reports predict that within a decade impending global water short-ages and environmental degradation are likely to spur terrorism, violent con-flicts, and regional wars (ICA, 2012). Complex interrelated problems such as these require comprehensive educational solutions that target the heart of the problem—human behavior. Moral philosophers and other educational theorists have long believed that the ultimate solution to these issues is to educate people to be good human beings and citizens of the planet. Ethics and ethics education are central to this mission. In order to introduce the idea of an ethics-based pedagogy and illustrate its applications, we have divided this chapter into two sections. In the first, we present an ethical framework that can serve as the basis for ethical conver-sations and learning across the curriculum. In the second, we introduce the idea of the "ethical conversation" as a pedagogical approach to group problem-solving.

An Ethical Framework for Educators

We offer a basic ethical framework that can be taught to diverse groups of students at all levels of education. It can also constitute a basis for ethical and ethics-based classroom practices and school policies. These principles provide a foundation for good education across a spectrum of subjects, including but not limited to environmental stewardship, peace and non-violence, anti-bullying, drug and alco-hol abuse, gender and sexuality, character, and multiculturalism. But they're also important for every other subject and school-based activity, and can be used in non-school settings as well. Math class, afterschool programs, and soccer practice should be ethical spaces where ethical learning takes place, too.

Ethics—often called moral philosophy—has existed as a discipline in the Western world for over 2,500 years, going back at least as far as ancient Greece and the works of great philosophers like Plato and Aristotle. Ethics is *prescriptive* (tells us what we should do) and *proscriptive* (tells us what we should not do), whereas most physical and social sciences are *descriptive* (and we hope, predictive). The long history of rigorous inquiry and study in ethics has brought us to the point where we are today—a time when ethical knowledge generally leads to what ethicists have called "convergence" (Beauchamp & Childress, 1994). While ethical theories and principles differ and sometimes conflict, they tend to point in the same general direction and lead to similar conclusions.

We pause to note that, historically speaking, Western ethics has tended to focus almost exclusively on the welfare of human beings. In the Judeo-Christian tradition, humans were long thought to have been created in the very image of God, which made them special. Animals and plants were thought to have little moral value, being created merely for human use and consumption. In moral philosophy, ethics has been closely associated with the capacity to make decisions based on reasons that could be articulated through language. Because reason and language were thought to be uniquely human attributes, animals and other life forms were thought to have little or no moral standing.

It has only been within the last couple hundred years that Western views concerning the moral worth of non-humans have begun to change. The suffering or pleasure of all life, not just humans, has become a matter of moral concern. As we learn more about the intelligence of various animals, it has become more difficult to draw sharp distinctions between ourselves and our non-human co-inhabitants. Crows, parrots, dolphins, whales, elephants, chimpanzees, gorillas, and dogs—to name just a few—are proving to be much more intelligent and social than we once thought. And the more we learn about the way human beings think and act, from fields like moral psychology, the less intelligent our own behavior appears to be. And of course, our growing knowledge about the complex ecological interdependence of species means that even from an anthropocentric perspective, the well-being of non-humans matters.

The following guiding principles have been derived in part from conversations that originated within the Critical Perspectives on Early Childhood Education (CPECE) special interest group (SIG), part of the American Educational Research Association (AERA), which culminated in a statement of ethical principles developed by Beth Swadener and Leigh O'Brien (2009). They were designed in concert with a vision for education that recognizes that "living in harmony with each other and the natural world have to become our collective priorities" (Swadener & O'Brien, 2009, p. 122). Our primary ethical responsibilities are as follows: *do no harm, help others, engage in caring relationships, and show respect for living beings.* By "others," we mean people, animals, plants, and, by extension, the entire biosphere upon which we all depend.

Do No Harm (Non-Maleficence)

The *principle of do no harm*, or *non-maleficence*, is one of the oldest and most basic principles in Western ethics. It is known to most of us through the *Hippocratic Oath*, which doctors and other healthcare practitioners are required to take before receiving their licenses to practice. It is also a basic concept in environmental ethics (e.g., "leave the forest in the same pristine condition in which you found it"). The principle requires us to act in such a way that we leave others at least as well-off as we found them.

When we say "do no harm," we are referring specifically to *unnecessary* harm. Some forms of harm may be deemed necessary if they are done in order to advance another greater good. For example, a dentist may extract a diseased tooth, thus causing the patient some pain and discomfort, in order to prevent the infection from spreading throughout the rest of the mouth. Likewise, we may kill and consume certain animals and plants in order to provide the sustenance necessary for human beings to survive. In cases where harm is considered necessary, we are still required to limit it as much as possible. And the good achieved must always outweigh the harm inflicted.

In practice, the principle of *do no harm* proscribes certain kinds of behaviors. First, it prohibits unwarranted violence and abuse; e.g., battering or bullying another human being or animal. These actions clearly cause harm and are barred except in rare circumstances, such as self-defense. Second, it prohibits economic exploitation and neglect, which are often but not always associated with living in poverty. And third, it prohibits social and political oppression.

Help Others (Beneficence)

The *principle of helping others*, or *beneficence*, is also a very old and fundamental principle in Western ethics. It goes a bit farther than the principle to "do no harm," as it instructs us to act in such a way that we advance the interests and well-being of others (people and other forms of life). Whereas the principle to do no harm asks us only to refrain from causing unnecessary pain and suffering, the principle of helping others asks us to make the extra effort to make the lives of others better, wherever possible. It thus serves as a check against our more self-interested tendencies and invites us to empathize and act altruistically.

In practice, the principle of helping others may manifest itself in innumerable ways. At its most basic level, it prescribes certain behaviors. First, we must help others meet their basic needs (food, water, shelter, security, etc.) whenever possible. For example, we currently have the capacity to adequately feed every human being on the planet without significant sacrifice to anyone, so we are morally obligated to do it. And we must do the same for the environment, by passing laws that help to promote and sustain healthy environments. Second, we must make every effort to fully include all human beings in the activities of civil society. Humans are a social species, and their flourishing requires inclusion. And we must also remain considerate of the ongoing well-being of non-humans, and be mindful of their welfare in our decision-making.

Engage in Caring Relationships (Caring)

Caring, of course, has been a human quality for as long as there have been human beings. The *principle of caring*, however, has been formally developed by feminist philosophers Carol Gilligan (1982), Nel Noddings (1984), and others over the past fifty years and has had a unique impact on the ethics of education. The principle of caring emphasizes the importance of relationships, and our ethical responsibilities to attend to the welfare and well-being of others with whom we

are in relationship. It draws a distinction between the more abstract ethical obligations we have to people (and life) with which we may never have any immediate
contact, and the more distinct and visceral ethical obligations we have to people
(and life) with which we engage on a regular basis. It is similar, in a sense, to the
environmental slogan, "Think globally, act locally."

In practice, the principle of caring asks us to pay attention to social and environmental interdependence. We may be individuals, but we require others to help
us survive and thrive. And they need us, too. Life is a team sport, and like the old
saying goes, there is no "I" in team. When we fully recognize our interdependence, and see others as an extension of ourselves (and vice versa), our obligation
to care for others becomes clearer. For example, we ought to take special care of
our aging populations who depend upon us, as we once depended upon them
and one day will depend upon the younger generations for our own care. And
we should make decisions that are environmentally friendly, like reducing carbon
emissions and conserving water, because we require a healthy earth for our own
well-being, just as the earth requires a healthy human population for the prosperity of all life.

Respect Living Beings (Autonomy)

The *principle of respect*, or *autonomy*, is one of the most important and influential
modern concepts in Western ethics. It expresses the important idea that each
and every human being enjoys the very same basic dignity and worth as every
other. This impartiality is grounded in the recognition that all human beings are
endowed with the power to make rational, ethical decisions—to decide for themselves how to live their own lives (within reason). The principle of respect reminds
us to treat other persons as we ourselves would like to be treated, like the so-called
Golden Rule, because the interests and aspirations of others are just as valuable as
our own. Other human beings are *like us* in the most important and fundamental
sense—they have the *capacity* to think intelligently and to act ethically (even if this
capacity is yet unrealized, or takes a form different from our own).

While respect for persons has traditionally been associated with the treatment
of human beings, we extend it here to apply to non-humans as well. Although
non-human animals have long been thought to lack the intelligence and rational
capacity of humans, it is nevertheless becoming increasingly clear that many if not
most of them have a remarkable ability to think and to act, as well as the capacity
for suffering and for pleasure. Thus, while humans and non-humans are clearly
not the same and should not be treated as such, we do share some very important characteristics. So just as we ought to treat other human beings with respect,
including those with very significant cognitive impairments or other severe disabilities, we ought to do the same for other forms of life.

In practice, the principle of respect entails three more principles. The first,
equality, tells us that the interests and well-being of each individual are as important

and legitimate as every other. For example, the interests of the wealthy are no more important than the interests of the poor, and the interests of U.S. citizens are no more important than the interests of Brazilians. The health and well-being of everyone matters equally. If, for example, we should decide that it is a good idea to build wind turbines in order to generate power, the principle of respect prohibits us from placing them in someone else's "backyard" if we are not willing to have them placed in our own. The benefits and burdens must be shared equally, and the interests of no individual or group should be privileged over another.[1] Likewise, we should treat non-humans and the environment as if they too have a legitimate stake in the future, because they do. We should not build factories in unique wildlife habitats, for example, just as we would not want the same factories built in our own neighborhoods. The interests of non-humans may not count the same as the interests of humans, but they still matter and should be taken into consideration.

The second principle, *freedom of expression*, reminds us that every individual has an equal right to communicate her thoughts and ideas. The only way we can communicate our interests to others is through the process of free expression, and when it is limited or curtailed, it robs us of our ability to direct our own lives and to participate in the democratic life of the community. Children and adults alike have the right to express themselves, and as educators we ought to encourage open and fair communication whenever and wherever possible, for ourselves, our colleagues, and our students.

And third, all human beings have the *right to political enfranchisement and social empowerment*. Every individual has the right to full and equal participation in democratic association with every other individual. When persons are oppressed or marginalized, their autonomy is violated because their capacity to direct their own lives is restricted. They become mere pawns in a game directed by others. Similarly, when the welfare and interests of animals and the environment are ignored, they too become nothing more than means—or objects—to be used for someone else's selfish purposes. Of course, non-human life cannot advocate for itself the way humans can, so we must do it on their behalf.

Altogether, these principles provide the basis for modern conceptions of justice and democracy. Of course, you have likely already noticed that even these very basic and nearly universal principles are routinely ignored or violated—by governments, businesses, special interests groups, and individuals. But rather than despairing about this fact, we ought to work to change it. What kind of world would we live in if humans did live their lives in accordance with ethical principles? We believe in a much better world than the one we currently inhabit—a better world for everyone. But the change must start somewhere, and we believe that the best and most effective place to begin is in formal and informal education settings. In the following section, we provide examples of some of the diverse ways and contexts in which educators can engage with ethics-based learning in classrooms and schools.

Conversations as an Ethics-Based Learning Context

Paulo Freire, the great Brazilian educator and advocate for social justice, believed that the best way to begin the process of empowering the poor and disenfranchised was to engage them in conversations about their own lived experience (Freire, 2003). It was through dialogue, he believed, that critical consciousness—the ability to think intelligently about solutions to social and environmental problems—could be developed. Marietta McCarty, the well-known philosopher of education, has successfully engaged young people in conversations about philosophical subjects and issues long thought too mature and difficult for children (McCarty, 2006). The message is clear: *good* conversations are essential in education and they should begin early. Lessons and activities are important, but in many ways their value and effectiveness will be determined by the quality and longevity of the conversations they help to facilitate. *How we talk to each other, and what we talk to each other about, has a profound impact on how we live.*

One of the most important and effective ways to teach young people (or people of any age) to think and act ethically is to invite them to participate in conversations about their values and moral ideals, and how these can be put into practice. The basic questions for all of us to consider are these: What kind of people do we want to be, and in what kind of world do we want to live? Many teachers and educators are reluctant to engage in conversations like these—conversations about ethics—because they feel ill-prepared to discuss topics they perceive to be controversial. An ethical framework, grounded in rigorous studies from fields like moral philosophy and moral psychology, can provide us the basic knowledge base and vocabulary we need to begin to feel comfortable initiating these fundamentally important conversations, as well as providing lessons, guiding activities, and formulating school policies and practices.

Starting Ethical Conversations

The following exercise is something we have seen practiced in many different contexts over the years, and when it is done well, it can be phenomenally effective. We'll call it *starting ethical conversations.* Whether you're teaching in a traditional classroom, an enrichment program, or coaching a soccer team, this exercise can be invaluable. It begins with a facilitator(s) who is familiar and comfortable with the ethical framework presented in the previous section—or some equivalent. The framework provides the basics for ethical dialogue, both in form and content.

The facilitator invites participants into a conversation about ethics by first preparing a physical space conducive to constructive civil dialogue. Being seated comfortably in a circle usually works best, and the facilitator(s) should be part of, rather than outside or above, the circle. Whatever materials are necessary should be ready in advance. You'll want some kind of record of your conversation, so that you may refer back to it later and keep track of your progress. This can be done in a variety of creative ways—a large piece of paper upon which everyone can write or draw is a good option, as are individual journals. There are many possibilities, and the more fun and engaging the process, the better the outcomes are likely to be.

The next step is to ask open-ended questions based on the principles provided in the ethical framework. It is often best to begin by asking the group what it is that brings us all together. What are we doing here and what do we aim to achieve? Answers may vary, and at first participants are likely to be a bit tentative. When working with younger children, the responses may be silly at times, or even inappropriate. It is important for the facilitator(s) to remain respectful and compassionate whatever is said. Try not to be judgmental. Conversations can be awkward and a bit uncomfortable, especially at the beginning, so patience is a must. Remember that this is only the beginning of a conversation that is to last as long as the group remains together. It will always be work in progress, and perfection is not the goal.

How might this work in practice? Let's imagine for a moment that you're leading a discussion with a group of elementary school students concerning expectations for the upcoming school year. It's the first day of class, and after making sure everyone is in the right classroom, appropriately situated, and properly introduced, you invite your students to participate in an ethical conversation. While seated in a circle, you ask the group, "Why are we here?" and "What are our goals?" The conversation begins, and the group starts to engage in a lively and constructive dialogue. As you talk, you ask students to make note of important milestones by writing them down on the large piece of paper you've placed in the center. Milestones should consist of simple and clear statements about the group's expectations concerning specific ethical behaviors and interactions. When they are proposed, you should help the group think and talk about why they are important, what they might look like in practice, and how they can be implemented.

For example, let's imagine that a student named Olivia raises her hand and says, "I think it's important that we be kind to each other." You respond, "Thank you Olivia, that certainly does sound important." And then turning to the group ask, "What does it mean to treat someone with kindness?" and "Why is it important to be kind to others?" After some discussion, you might ask, "Can we come up with some examples of people treating each other with kindness?" and "What happens when people don't treat each other kindly?" And after yet more discussion, you might conclude with, "How might we treat each other with kindness here in this classroom—can we think of some examples?" and "How might we respond when someone makes a mistake and does not treat another with kindness?" The more concrete and relevant you can make the conversation, the better.

Of course, not every comment the students make will be constructive, and some may even be inappropriate. But these contributions can be opportunities for ethical learning too. Simply talk about why the statement under consideration is or is not helpful. You're likely to be surprised, after a little practice, at how intelligent even quite young children can be talking about ethical issues and human interactions. And when and where one or more students go astray, you and the other participants can help redirect them in a more positive direction.

When the activity is close to completion, you should invite everyone to review the progress you've made and to decorate the paper so that it might be hung with pride in a prominent place in the classroom. On it is a list of ethical guidelines, e.g., "Speak positively to each other and about others," "Support and encourage each other," "Be mindful about how our behavior is impacting our environment," "Treat each other with respect." The emphasis here is on promoting positive behaviors and interactions through mutually agreed upon expectations (rules or guidelines) grounded in ethics.

The "contract" you've made now hangs on the wall. So is the conversation over? No, it's only just begun. As frequently as necessary, you may revisit the conversation to check in with how you're doing, both individually and as a group. This may be done in a variety of ways and in different contexts. You might ask students at some later date to write a short personal reflection on how they think they're doing living up to the expectations set by the group. You may revisit the document with an entire class in order to handle a "problem" that arises, as we describe in the next section. And from time to time, you may make revisions as the situation requires. You may want to ask ongoing questions, such as, "How are we doing living up to our goals?"; "Is there anything we're doing particularly well or not-so-well?"; "Do we need to change or add anything to our list?" These are just suggestions, but by keeping the conversation going, you'll ensure that the ethical conversation you started continues to inform learning and growth for everyone.

Continuing Ethical Conversations

The ethical framework discussed in the previous sections can serve as a guide for ongoing ethical conversations, and the "contract" you've now developed with your students can help keep those conversations grounded. Simple yet important questions based on the framework and contract will help prompt further conversation. At first, you might make a list of questions to help you facilitate dialogue, but as you become more practiced the questions should come more easily. Here are some examples of situations that are common in elementary school settings, followed by sample questions that relate directly back to the four principles covered in our ethical framework.

Doing No Harm

A teacher takes his or her fifth grade classroom on a field trip to a nearby stream to learn about the scientific method, waterways, and the local wildlife. One student begins to throw stones at some fish congregating in a small pool. She is laughing and several of her classmates move to join her. The teacher notices and asks the student what she is doing, and the student responds that she is trying to hit the fish. The teacher asks the students to think about the contract they made together, and whether or not throwing rocks at the fish lives up to their agreed upon expectations not to cause unnecessary harm.

- *Sample Questions*: What does it mean to cause harm? What are some of the kinds of things we do that might harm others? Why is harming another a bad thing? What does it feel like when someone else harms you? How do you feel when you harm another? How do you think we might be better off if we refrain from causing harm? What steps do we need to take, individually and as a group, to prevent harm? Are there any rules of practices we might think of that could help us prevent harm? How should we handle situations when someone is harmed by another?

Helping Others

A student is asked to read aloud and has trouble pronouncing several words. Some students nearby begin snickering and teasing their classmate. The teacher takes the opportunity to engage the students in a discussion about helping each other when they experience challenges. The teacher notes that everyone faces challenges—one student may stumble over words while another may stumble over a soccer ball. In each case, there are ways we can help others to learn and grow that may be as simple as offering a few words of encouragement.

- *Sample Questions*: What does it mean to help someone else? How is helping different from harming? How do you feel when someone helps you? What are some examples of helping? How do you feel when you are able to help someone else? How might you help a friend? How might we help a class-mate? Are there ways we could help out animals? How might we help the environment as a whole? What can we do as a group to help each other?

Engaging in Caring Relationships

A first grade teacher notices several students standing around a student who is lying on the playground crying. The teacher quickly approaches the students and asks what has happened, and the crying child says she fell and hurt her leg. The teacher asks one student to fetch the school nurse while he and the remaining students work together to comfort the injured girl. The teacher initiates a conversation later in the day about what it means to take care of one another.

- *Sample Questions*: What does it mean to care for another human being? What does it mean to care for an animal? What does it mean to care for the environment? Why is caring important? What does a caring relationship look like? Can you describe a caring relationship? How does it feel when you know someone cares about you? How does it feel to care for someone else? What are some of the things we might do to encourage caring relationships? How might we care for the environment?

Respect for Living Beings

A fourth grade class is participating in a year-long classroom garden project. The students are assigned to groups with responsibilities to tend a particular portion of the garden. In one group, a student bullies her classmates with mild threats and belittling comments. Her group complains to their teacher, who facilitates a discussion about what it means to treat one another fairly and with respect.

- *Sample Questions*: What does it mean to treat another living being with respect? What does it mean to treat another with a lack of respect? How does it make you feel when someone treats you with respect? What are some of the ways in which we can show someone you respect them? Can you think of behaviors that might indicate a lack of respect? What does it mean to treat animals with respect? Is respect for human and nonhuman animals different, and if so in what ways? What can we do as a group or class to promote respect for one another?

As participants (teachers and students) become more relaxed and comfortable with the ethical framework, conversations will begin to flow more easily. Ask follow-up questions for more depth and clarification. Encourage participants to ask each other questions when they arise, reminding them that they also need to be respectful of one another. Remember that the conversation is meant to further a goal—for individuals and the group to think and act ethically in order to promote the common good. It may sound a bit idealistic at first, but we've found students and others take to this approach quite quickly and find the benefits very rewarding.

Conclusion

In this chapter we have proposed a simple yet important idea—that an essential component of any reasonable response to the myriad social and environmental crises that plague our planet is to teach human beings to think and act ethically. To that end, we presented a basic ethical framework consisting of four universal ethical principles: (1) *Do No Harm*, (2) *Help Others*, (3) *Engage in Caring Relationships*, and (4) *Respect Living Beings*. We then provided some examples of how to use the framework to construct an ethical contract and engage students in ongoing ethical conversations.

The chapter reminds us of the instructions passengers receive upon boarding an aircraft: "In the event of an emergency, place the oxygen mask on yourself before assisting others." Ethics-based education is the oxygen mask humans need in order for us to be able to systemically save ourselves and our fellow passengers on "Spaceship Earth." What kinds of beings we choose to be and how we choose to live will have a profound impact on our future and the future of all life on earth. We should choose wisely.

References

Beauchamp, T., & Childress, J. (1994). *Principles of biomedical ethics*. Oxford: Oxford University Press.

Freire, P. (2003). *Pedagogy of the oppressed*. New York: Continuum International Publishing Group.

Gilligan, C. (1982). *In a different voice: Psychological theory and women's development*. Cambridge, MA: Harvard University Press.

IISS Armed Conflict Database: Monitoring Conflicts Worldwide (2015). Retrieved July 30, 2014, from https://acd.iiss.org/.

Intelligence Community Assessment on Global Water (ICA). (2012). Global water security. Washington, DC: US Department of State. Retrieved February 16, 2016, from www.state.gov/e/oes/water/ica/.

McCarty, M. (2006). *Little big minds*. New York: Penguin Group.

Noddings, N. (1984). *Caring: A feminine approach to ethics and moral education*. California: University of California Press.

Plato (1968). *The republic of Plato*. New York: Basic Books.

Swadener, B., & O'Brien, L. (2009). Social responsibility and teaching young children: An education for living in ethical and caring ways. In J. Andrzejewski, M. Baltodano, & L. Symcox (Eds.), *Social justice, peace, and environmental education* (pp. 121–135). New York: Routledge.

UNICEF (2015). UNICEF millennium goals. Retrieved March 20, 2015, from www.unicef.org/mdg/childmortality.html.

Note

1 There may be ethical exceptions, e.g., when steps must be taken to address past or ongoing inequalities or injustices. In these circumstances—like privileging the interests of the poor who are most in need and have suffered the greatest from social and economic inequality—such remedies may be justified until the problem is resolved and justice restored.

14

ENVIRONMENTAL ETHICS
Reflections on Valuing Nature Rightly

Allen Thompson

Many people think that environmental problems are essentially ethical problems, and much of ethics can be understood as concerned with responding rightly to value in the world. So environmental ethics involves asking important questions about how and why we value nature and the nature of value in the world. I encourage elementary teachers to explore these questions with their students. Remember, we want to help children think clearly and consistently, not tell them what to think. We begin with a distinction between two different ways something could be good or valuable.

Many things are valuable because they are useful. For example, a favorite toy is valuable to a child because it's fun to play with. If you want to have fun and a particular toy is fun to play with, then that toy is valued because with it, you can get what you want. In general, money is valuable because you can use it to get other things that you value. Philosophers call the value that something has because of its usefulness *instrumental value*. You may think of it this way: something has instrumental value because it operates as a means (i.e., as a tool or instrument) to get something *else* that you value.

At the same time it seems that some things are valued, or perhaps *should* be valued, independently of being useful. Many people have the strong intuition that some things are valuable simply in virtue of their very existence, not their usefulness. For example, it seems that happiness or pleasure is valuable for its own sake and not for the sake of something else. Philosophers call this kind of value *intrinsic value*.

Some things may have only instrumental value, perhaps money for most people, while other things may be both instrumentally and intrinsically valuable, perhaps like health. The classical Greek philosopher, Aristotle, believed that the well-lived human life was always intrinsically valuable and never instrumentally valuable.

Beyond any usefulness, we believe that each and every human person is valuable in and of themselves. The Enlightenment philosopher Immanuel Kant concluded that we should never treat any human person merely as a means only but always also as an end in themselves, that is, as intrinsically valuable. Consider asking your students these two questions:

- What properties or qualities could make a person intrinsically valuable?
- Are people intrinsically valuable even if I or we don't value them intrinsically?

In the early 1970s philosophers who were concerned about deteriorating environmental conditions and the deplorable treatment of non-human animals began thinking about how they could contribute to social movements concerned with such things. Their philosophical diagnosis of the cause of environmental problems led to a theory of value called *anthropocentrism* (i.e., human-centeredness), which asserts that all and *only* human persons are intrinsically valuable. From an anthropocentric perspective, it follows that everything in the non-human world of nature has only *instrumental value*, valuable only insofar as it can be useful to human beings.

If the dominant theory of value in the dominant global culture is anthropocentric, then this would explain why human beings were, in general, respecting nature only to the extent that it could be useful to them. According to anthropocentrism, when nature is not useful to humans, it has no value. Therefore, degrading ecosystems and harming animals are not, considered by themselves, morally problematic behaviors.

But is anthropocentrism *true*? Do you agree that humans and only humans have intrinsic value? Philosopher Richard Routley posed a thought experiment that seems to provide evidence that anthropocentrism is mistaken. We can call this the "Last Person" thought experiment. (And you can pose this question to your elementary students, perhaps starting around third grade, if you feel they are developmentally ready to consider this make-believe scenario.)

Imagine there is only one person left on Earth, the very last human. There will never be more human people nor will other, human-like extraterrestrial persons (like Spock from *Star Trek*) visit Earth. Now, this last person loves explosions and so has hooked up all of the nuclear weapons in the world to a single button. The detonation of all these nuclear weapons will certainly kill many individual animals, could drive all existing species of plants and animals into extinction, and will destroy all existing ecosystems. Imagine, further, that it will flatten Mt. Everest, fill the Grand Canyon, etc. But watching such an explosion would bring significant pleasure to the last person. The last person knows his or her life is about to end and so decides to push the button. Is it morally wrong to do this? Take a moment to think about this.

We could reason like this: if anthropocentrism is true, then only human beings are intrinsically valuable and nature has only instrumental value. Using nature to benefit humans—as these explosions will bring pleasure to the last person—is the only value nature has. So using nature in this way does not fail to respect the value of nature—it is valuable only instrumentally, it brings pleasure to the last human person. Nothing of intrinsic value will be harmed. Thus, if anthropocentrism is true, it seems it would *not* be wrong to treat nature in this way.

But many people have a strong intuition that the last person acts wrongly. We have seen how if anthropocentrism is true, then it's difficult to explain why pushing the button is wrong. But if it *were* morally wrong to push the button, then it looks like anthropocentrism must be false because anthropocentrism implies that pushing the button is *not* morally wrong. Again, take a moment to think about the logic of this. If any theory, like anthropocentrism, implies something else that is actually false, then the theory itself must also be false.

How could we defend the idea that it is morally wrong to behave as the last person does? It could be wrong if, in addition to instrumental value, some parts of nature also have an intrinsic value. Then treating the world as if it were only instrumentally valuable would fail to respect the fact that nature is valuable in itself, intrinsically valuable, and thus such treatment would be wrong just as if we treated an intrinsically valuable human person merely as a means only. Here are some more philosophical questions to pose to your students.

- Do you believe that some things are intrinsically valuable? What could make something intrinsically valuable? For example, what makes an individual human being intrinsically valuable?
- Does the same thing that makes a human intrinsically valuable also make some things in nature intrinsically valuable, or is there some *other* property that could make something valuable for its own sake?
- In what ways does nature have instrumental value, if at all? In what ways does nature have intrinsic value, if at all?
- Could something be valuable even if we don't recognize that it is valuable? That is, is it still instrumentally valuable when we don't recognize its usefulness or intrinsically valuable even when we don't value it beyond its usefulness?
- Do we *discover* that things are valuable or do we *confer* value on them by our act of valuing them?
- Could we explain how the last person acts wrongly *without* invoking the idea of intrinsic value in nature? Consider: what kind of person would do such a thing?

These are difficult and perplexing questions. Teachers, I invite you to pose these and similar questions to your students and engage in discussions, to help them think about the nature of value and, perhaps more importantly, about the value of nature.

SECTION IV

Children's Activism

From the Local to the Global

The chapters in Section IV makes a case for place-based *activism* but, also, an activism that involves children taking on slightly more *political* roles that focus on issues outside of children's immediate neighborhoods. Several authors describe two prominent child-activists as role models, Severn Suzuki (when she was 12 years old at the Rio Summit in 1992) and Xiuhtezcatl Martinez, who more recently began speaking out in response to climate change when he was in elementary school.

Hilary Whitehouse (Chapter 15) asserts that how and what we were taught earlier in our careers must reflect changing environmental conditions. She argues that teachers should enact curriculum that more honestly prepares children for the chaotic future that they will inevitably face. Whitehouse recommends that our teaching ought to reflect this 'new realism,' meaning that it is increasingly necessary for educators to contemplate activism as part of their pedagogy of climate change education. She maintains educators have a moral obligation to teach children to be active in shaping their future, and she describes various forms of child activism, including the example of the children of Vanuatu who are fighting for the survival of their island. Following Whitehouse, Julie Andrzejewski briefly asserts children's legitimate role as activists, but she then narrows the focus of her chapter to teachers, challenging them to show more courage and resolve in both educating themselves and stepping up as activists to help defend a livable planet. Underlying her argument is the powerful idea that teachers' most powerful 'lesson' for students is their own model, or performance, as engaged and critical citizens in the community. Finally, in Chapter 17, children's author of environmental literature (e.g., *The Great Kapok Tree*) Lynne Cherry describes a film project that documents the climate activism of youth and how these stories may inform the work of elementary teachers. Cherry calls on teachers to help young people develop 'self-efficacy'—the belief in themselves to effect change—and be agents of change in the larger world.

15

THE NEW REALISM

A Rationale for Supporting Children's Climate Activism

Hilary Whitehouse

> Children are among the greatest victims of a warming world, but they are also the most powerful protagonists for change. (UNICEF Office of Research, 2014, p. 2)

The children we teach are facing lives increasingly circumscribed by accelerating climate disruption. So many communities are now pummeled by droughts, floods, super storms, and greater regimes of heat or cold. Children around the world face an increasing burden of disease, economic stress, forced migration, restricted food supplies, diminishing access to potable water, and increasing social tragedy. The time has arrived for elementary educators to take climate disruption seriously. No matter what politicians are telling us, the time of avoidance and denial has passed. In the words of Pope Francis, "Doomsday predictions can no longer be met with irony or disdain" (*Laudato Si*, 2015, p. 161).

The New Realism

This is the new realism. Climate disruption is real, and it is happening now. And the effects are about to get more severe. We are experiencing "a historically unprecedented spike in temperatures" and its associated effects (Upton, 2015). The two warmest years on record were 2014 and 2015 (GISTEMP, 2015; NOAA, 2015), and this trend isn't reversing. In March 2015, the average global levels of carbon dioxide exceeded 400 parts per million. Human-caused warming will move our climate system "into a regime in terms of multi-decadal rates of change that are unprecedented for at least the past 1,000 years" (Romm, 2015). Regional rates of change in Europe, North America, and the Arctic will be even higher than the global average (Smith et al., 2015). This is not good news.

I call on teachers worldwide to really ponder these questions: What does disruptive change really mean for our young students, their families, and communities? What should we be doing with students given the accelerating dangers? In the words of UNICEF's UK Director: "We are hurtling towards a future where the gains being made for the world's children are threatened and their health, wellbeing, livelihoods and survival are compromised... despite being the least responsible for the causes... We need to listen to them" (David Bull quoted by Harvey, 2013).

The problem is that teachers can no longer educate for a future where the earth's climate is relatively stable. Unless the ultimate human project is to make the world safe only for jellyfish—which sounds like a joke but isn't given how the oceans are heating and acidifying—then it is time for elementary teachers to take the risks very seriously in how they prepare their students for what lies ahead. We know that just *thinking* about climate change can cause anxiety and trepidation. Climate change *is* "a disturbing subject that casts a shadow across ordinary life" (Randall, 2012), and grief, unease, guilt, helplessness, denial, defensiveness, anxiety, and upset are normal human responses. It can be emotionally painful to acknowledge the urgency of the problem. It is understandable to feel a sense of futility. It is normal to give in to feelings of individual powerlessness given the magnitude of the problem. However, this narrative of powerlessness can be seen as an easy way out "because powerlessness lets us off the hook" (Solnit, 2015). Worry, paralysis, and apathy never solve anything. There are challenges to be met.

Teachers become teachers because they care about children and young people. They understand the extrinsic and intrinsic value of education. They know that education can change the world. None of us would be teachers if we didn't believe in a more optimistic future. We know that to teach is to touch that future, and this is where we find meaning and purpose in our profession. The challenge for teachers is how to teach children about the environmental crisis in a way that will lead to their engaging in actions to address our precarious relationship with the planet. Engaging in positive action is one way of being both realistic and optimistic at the same time. Realistic, because we recognize that climate disruption is a real and serious risk to our livelihoods and well-being. And optimistic, because we have faith in our young students and in ourselves to do what we can where we can to overcome the negative feelings and impacts.

Naomi Klein (2014) sees the climate emergency as a catalyzing force for social and environmental change. Like many, she found that climate science caused her great existential distress, shattering her faith in humanity and in our political and economic structures. However, she was able to construct a new vision for how we all should live in the world: a place where humans collectively use the environmental crises to "leap" to somewhere better than where we are now. So how are we to do this leaping? Do children and young people have to be the passive victims of climate change? Or can we expect children to be able to raise their voices in dissent at the 'business as usual' paradigm that promotes continued carbon pollution and environmental degradation? What is teachers' role in supporting children's climate activism? These are questions asked as part of the new realism.

The Rationale for Activism

Ideas on children's participation "require reformulation as current conceptualizations and their attendant practices are outmoded for the dynamic, complex and challenging times in which we live" (Davis, 2014, p. 26). For the last 150 years, elementary education has concentrated on the development of mandated disciplinary knowledge and skills, largely unconnected to the real problems and issues in community and society. Curricula were designed on the implicit premise that the world's climate was relatively stable, as it has been throughout the Holocene. Now we live in the Anthropocene, and our expectation of relative atmospheric and oceanic stability is outmoded. Established ideas about curriculum and pedagogy are being challenged by the very nature of the climate emergency. In response, teachers have the opportunity to reconsider the place of student action and activism in the traditional curriculum. The moral imperative of *doing* something in response to the existential crisis of climate change, rather than only *learning* about something, changes the nature of teacher's work. Indeed, young children *are* capable social actors who have perspectives and ideas and are capable of participating in public discussions about matters that affect them (McNaughton, Hughes & Smith, 2008).

The case for an activist pedagogy reflects recent political agreements that have expanded moral and international rights of children (Davis, 2014; Guillemot & Burgess, 2014), and that children can and should assert their rights in the face of their experiences of global climate change (Burton et al., 2011; United Nations Alliance on Climate Change, 2014). Lewis (2009, p. 69) makes a strong case for using human rights as a "normative framework on which to build our responses to climate change." She argues that the human rights perspective has strong resonance especially when focused on those who will be severely affected, such as children, particularly those in poorer communities. The real problem of climate change is that "it represents a serious injustice" (p. 70) by most impacting those who have the least to do with its causes.

Teachers have an ethical responsibility to act in the interests of children. The potential losses of livelihoods, homes, and communities are of such magnitude that it becomes ethically necessary for teachers to teach children and young people to act in defense of their rights and their lives. Children, however, are generally denied legal standing. Children do not have voting rights, and they do not have the resources to pay off legislators who are unwilling to pass climate protection laws. Still, children can and do advocate for their own interests. Many children and youth are already forced into "raising their voices and contributing to the conversation through their resourcefulness, imagination, and ethical and well as practical concerns" (UNICEF Office of Research, 2014, p. vi). When children come from communities whose survival is precarious due to climate change, they have no choice but to act, as is discussed later on in this chapter.

The new realism is that climate change affects us all and young age is no protection against this truth. In fact, the effects of climate change are borne unequally by children, who make up 30 percent of the world's population. One sobering statistic is that 80 percent of deaths currently directly attributable to climate change are child deaths in developing countries (UNICEF Office of Research, 2014). Without radical emissions reduction and concomitant habitat protection and rehabilitation, tens of millions of children are at risk. Therefore, it makes sense to identify and enhance opportunities to advance the rights of children and enable children and youth to participate in global and national policy dialogues as well as devising sustainable solutions. Children's activism on behalf of their own interests is necessary as political and economic progress towards directly tackling the threats of climate change has been slow, even obstructed. The ethical educational response is not to deny this unfortunate reality, nor wring our hands or metaphorically bury our heads in the sand, or cover our ears and sing loudly. The ethical educational response is to directly face this challenge by engaging students in social actions, in defense of the planet, but in ways that are developmentally appropriate.

Action to Activism

In his keynote address to the 2014 Australian Association for Environmental Conference, David Orr recommended, "We tell kids the truth about what's happening, but also create hope through action [and encourage children to] be passionate, be political and be positive about their capacity to create change" (Tudball, 2014). There is no shortage of trustworthy, educational programs to teach about climate change in the elementary school. Examples include Australia's CSIRO *Sustainable Futures* school-based program for elementary and middle school, Education Scotland's *Weather and Climate Change* education site, and NASA's *Climate Kids* interactive resources.

Children are encouraged to take action as part of climate change education. Even very young children can take action, when their personal agency is enabled though relationships, such as those they have with their teachers (Calman & Lundegård, 2014). The educational literature is replete with examples and analyses of what works and how actions can be successfully undertaken in early childhood and elementary education (see Corcoran & Osano, 2009; Davis, 2010; Davis & Elliott, 2014; Gray-Donald & Selby, 2008; Gruenewald & Smith, 2008; Hart, 2003; Smith & Sobel, 2010). Partnerships that extend beyond schools and into communities provide opportunities for creative problem solving and inquiry learning that "enable children to lead the way" (Green & Somerville, 2014).

Action-orientated learning (the Danish call it 'action competence') begins with an idea, rippling through a classroom, that gets students excited about what they can do on a personal level, helps them understand *why* they do what they do, and allows them to picture a healthier and thriving future (Jensen & Schnack, 1997; Mogensen & Schnack, 2010). Action-orientated learning only works if students are willing and able to do something. For example, if students have a great idea about how to reduce greenhouse gas emissions, but can't actually make the necessary changes to make the idea a reality, then that is not an example of 'action competence.' Similarly, beach clean-ups are great activities, and most students can participate, but they won't develop personal 'action competence' just by participating—they have to understand *why* they are doing it, and be able to *understand what a clean beach means for all living creatures*.

Climate change education calls for "flexible ... and emergent curriculum approaches that embed climate change learning and action within community contexts" (Kagawa & Selby, 2010, p. 241). Children and their teachers can undertake gardening projects; look after a local creek, park, or forest reserve; plant trees to encourage birds and butterflies back into schoolyards; care for local amphibians whose populations are crashing; get involved in community litter reduction and recycling programs; and use carbon calculators to find out how to lower carbon footprints and design energy-saving projects. There are many options for local actions that are highly engaging, successful, and doable. Social action demonstrates human capability to work at solutions. Every elementary teacher and every child, together, can learn to establish better conditions in their family, school, and community.

What about the next step, the critical need for *activism*? How can elementary schools support children (and teachers) who wish to refashion themselves as agents for change? The majority of children (particularly in relatively stable democratic societies) are conceived as being removed from political struggle in their daily lives. Children are detached from politics (see Kallio & Häkli, 2011) and the traditionally accepted purpose of schooling is not to engage children in the constant renegotiation of the political. Most forms of activism are not generally accepted as part of school practice. However, the nature of the climate emergency is fast undoing this idea as more and more communities become affected. If the climate crisis is a crisis of political will, then the crisis will not be solved unless individuals, schools, and communities take political action on behalf of their own interests. And no group's interests are as threatened by the climate crisis as are children's interests. The challenge is both political and moral.

When we think about climate change education and children's futures we need to consider both action and activism, which is complex and messy and frightening. Activism, as advocacy, takes many forms at different levels and on different scales. Climate activism, "just as life, is complicated" and "the complexity and pervasiveness of global climate change can be leveraged with people from very different backgrounds and experiences to engage them in committing to climate activism" (Fisher, 2015). There is no single vision for climate activism; however, when children are invited to advocate for their own interests they will do so in their own creative and powerful ways.

Teachers can support their young students who are willing to agitate on their own behalf. Social and cultural barriers to child activism at school tend to exist only where children have no need to agitate on their own behalf due to *fortunate* geographies. Children who are victims of *unfortunate* geographies are compelled to take part in civic action. Their survival and that of their families and communities may depend on it. Denying the imperative for child activism is fast becoming a luxury in many parts of the globe.

Child Activism in Vanuatu: Necessary Actions

Children of the island nation of Vanuatu continue to advocate for their own interests out of sheer, bitter necessity (UNICEF, 2014). The nation was devastated by severe tropical cyclone Pam in February 2015. Only five schools in the whole of the nation were open one month after the storm. Though recovery efforts focused on reopening schools and enabling teachers and teacher aides to staff schools, forced exclusion from education has had long-term consequences. The children of Vanuatu have born the brunt of political and economic decisions taken in far-away places by people they will never meet, and who may never have learned of Vanuatu before this super storm hit the capital of Vila and the outlying islands.

Vanuatu's children are 'front line' victims of climate change. They did not cause the problem, yet their lives have been devastated by climate disruption. They have no choice but to join with adults in collective activism. The people of the Pacific Island nations have been protesting for many years against an international world order that expends more taxpayers' money on subsidies to the fossil fuel industries (5.3 trillion dollars in 2015) than is spent on world health (Cody et al., 2015). The movement to alert the world to the dangers of climate change is called Ta Reo Vanuatu, The Voice of Vanuatu, and the Vanuatuan message is, "We are not drowning. We are fighting." The people explain, "Our message to the world is that we are more than just broken down seawalls, dead breadfruit trees and fewer fish. We are also resilience, sheer courage and shared hope, in the face of climate change." School children have made films to advocate for limits to carbon emissions and developed agro-forestry initiatives for carbon sequestration (PACMAS, 2013). Children helped build the canoes used by (the twelve-nation) Pacific Climate Warriors direct action blockade of the Newcastle (Australia) coal port in 2014 (view video at http://350.org/pcw6monthsvideo/).

Pacific Island children have become activists because the idea of losing and having to depart one's 'vanua,' or land, is tantamount to losing or parting with one's life (Taylor, 2014). In the South Pacific, islands and people are inseparable. Children's sense of identity includes both their community and their land.

When the islands go underwater, what happens to the people? The children of Vanuatu do not have the luxury of not thinking about climate change.

Supporting Child Activism

Child activism on climate change is not new. In 1992, at the United Nations Rio Earth Summit in Brazil, a 12-year-old from Canada named Severn Suzuki gave a short speech on the injustice experienced by children in relation to climate change. She said: "At school, even in kindergarten, you (adults) teach us how to behave in the world. You teach us to not to fight with others, to work things out, to respect others and to clean up our mess, not to hurt other creatures, to share, not be greedy. Then, why do you go out and do the things you tell us not to do?" (Laskow, 2012). Twenty-three years later, in 2015, at a United Nations meeting in New York, a 15-year-old American named Xiuhtezcatl Martinez gave "an extemporaneous speech on climate dithering" (McPherson, 2015). He said: "I stand before you representing my entire generation… Youth are standing up all over the planet to find solutions. We are flooding the streets and now flooding the courts. We need you to take action. We are all indigenous to this earth." Martinez works with a group called Our Children's Trust (http://ourchildrenstrust.org) whose mission is "securing the legal right to a healthy atmosphere and stable climate for all present and future generations." The Trust supports young people's civic and legal advocacy as well as education through a program called YouCAN. Young people are taught how to participate directly in government decision-making on emission reduction and transformation to the low-carbon economy. A series of films that show young activists engaging in environmental action can be viewed at http://ourchildrenstrust.org/trust-films.

Communication is a key form of activism. Teachers can help children formulate their concerns on climate risks. Teachers can show children how to craft logical arguments in defense of their own interests and rights. Teachers can encourage children to engage politically and lobby for better policies for climate mitigation and adaptation at the local, state, and national level. Teachers can physically help children by providing transport and meals, and by arranging meetings and press events. When children take their message to the world using social media and the Internet, teachers can supply technical assistance. Children may wish to advocate for affected animals and plants, showing concern for the lives of vulnerable others, who are in a real sense 'voiceless' within human political systems. Teachers can join in with this humane endeavor.

The principle of human rights as a fundamental rationale for activism can be exercised both by children and their teachers. When children feel obliged to act on matters of intergenerational injustice, it is desirable they can rely on the important adults in their lives. Children in high-risk areas are forced to take action now. Child activism in areas not yet suffering disruptive climate change is warranted as well. Eventually, it will affect everyone. The goal we can have is to mitigate the damage, slow it down, and, hopefully, give communities time to adapt to the change already in the system that cannot be averted because extra carbon dioxide persists in the atmosphere for a very long time.

Conclusion

The first papal environmental Encyclical released in June 2015 offered an invitation to all people to consider our common humanity and act in a "new and universal solidarity" (*Laudato Si*, 2015, p. 14). In the words of one commentator, "The practical need to protect the climate system is real—but so, too, is the moral outrage of billions of human beings denied access to a dignified life" (Warner, 2015). The Encyclical reminds us that everyone has a role to play, and this includes the very young and their teachers. To hundreds of millions of people in the world now, social activism in response to the environmental crisis is no longer a luxury. The preservation of life and their social, cultural, and ecological well-being depends on it. As teachers, we have to remember this. The climate will not settle back into that "happy 10,000 years of climatic stability and clemency known as the Holocene" (Hamilton, 2015). We have to act on mitigation to give ourselves time to adapt. If the children in our schools care enough to advocate on behalf of their own interests and rights to a more secure future and, indeed, on behalf of the interests of every living being on the planet, then it is our moral duty to support them.

References

Burton, D., Mustelin, J., & Urich, P. (2011). *Climate change impacts on children in the Pacific: Kiribati and Vanuatu technical report*. Bangkok, UNICEF.

Calman, C., & Lundegård, I. (2014). Pre-school children's agency in learning for education for sustainable development. *Environmental Education Research*, 20(4), 437–459.

Cody, D., Parry, I., Sears, L., & Shang, B. (2015). *IMF working paper 15/105: How large are global energy subsidies?* New York: International Monetary Fund.

Corcoran, P. B., & Osano, P. M. (2009). *Young people, education and sustainability: Exploring principles, perspectives and praxis*. Amsterdam: Wageningen Academic Publishers.

CSIRO (2015). *Sustainable Futures*. Retrieved June 2, 2015, from www.csiro.au/en/Education/Programs/Sustainable-Futures.

Davis, J. (Ed.). (2010). *Young children and the environment: Early education for sustainability*. Melbourne: Cambridge University Press.

Davis, J. (2014). Examining early childhood education through the lens of education for sustainability: Revisioning rights. In J. Davis & S. Elliott (Eds.), *Research in early childhood education for sustainability: International perspectives and provocations* (pp. 21–37). New York: Routledge.

Davis, J., & Elliott, S. (Eds.). (2014). *Research in early childhood education for sustainability: International perspectives and provocations*. New York: Routledge.

Education Scotland (2014). *Weather and climate change*. Retrieved February 15, 2015, from www.educationscotland.gov.uk/weatherandclimatechange/aboutthisresource/index.asp.

Fisher, S. R. (2015). Life trajectories of youth committing to climate activism. *Environmental Education Research*. DOI: 10.1080/13504622.2015.1007337.

GISTEMP Team (2015). *GISS surface temperature analysis (GISTEMP)*. NASA Goddard Institute for Space Studies. Retrieved June 21, 2015, from http://data.giss.nasa.gov/gistemp/.

Gray-Donald, J., & Selby, D. (Eds.). (2008). *Green frontiers: Environmental educators dancing away from mechanism*. Rotterdam: Sense.

Green, M., & Somerville, M. (2014). Sustainability education: Researching practice in primary schools. *Environmental Education Research*. DOI: 10.1080/13504622.2014.923382.

Gruenewald, D., & Smith, G.A. (Eds.). (2008). *Place-based education in the global age: Local diversity*. New York: Lawrence Erlbaum Associates.

Guillemot, J., & Burgess, J. (2014). Child rights at risk. In *The challenges of climate change: Children on the front line* (pp. 47–51). Florence, Italy: Innocenti Insight (UNESCO).

Hamilton, C. (2015). The banality of ethics in the Anthropocene. *The Conversation*. Retrieved August 23, 2015, from http://theconversation.com/the-banality-of-ethics-in-the-anthropocene-part-1-44568.

Hart, P. (2003). *Teachers' thinking in environmental education: Consciousness and responsibility*. New York: Peter Lang.

Harvey, F. (September 23, 2013). Children will bear brunt of climate change, new study says. *The Guardian*. Retrieved February 12, 2015, from www.theguardian.com/environment/2013/sep/23/children-bear-brunt-climate-change-new-study.

Jensen, B. B., & Schnack, K. (1997). The action competence approach in environmental education. *Environmental Education Research, 3*(2), 163–178.

Kagawa, F., & Selby, D. (2010). Climate change education: A critical agenda for interesting times. In F. Kagawa & D. Selby (Eds.), *Education and climate change: Living and learning in interesting times* (pp. 241–243). New York: Routledge.

Kallio, K. P., & Häkli, J. (2011). Are there politics in childhood? *Space and Polity, 15*(1), 21–34.

Klein, N. (2014). *This changes everything: Capitalism vs. the climate*. New York: Simon & Schuster.

Laskow, S. (June 13, 2012). 12-year-old whose awesome speech floored 1992 Rio Summit returns to Rio+20 as a mom. *Grist*. Retrieved March 1, 2015, from http://grist.org/list/twelve-year-old-whose-awesome-speech-floored-1992-rio-summit-returns-to-rio20-as-a-mom/.

Laudato Si' (May 24, 2015). *Encyclical letter of the Holy Father Francis on care for our common home*. Vatican City: Vatican.

Lewis, B. (2009). Environmental rights, justice and climate change. In E. L. Weber, (Ed.), *Environmental ethics, sustainability and education* (pp. 63–79). Oxford, UK: Inter-Disciplinary Press.

MacNaughton, G., Hughes, P., & Smith K. (Eds.) (2008). *Young children as active citizens: Principles, polices and pedagogies*. Newcastle-Upon-Tyne: Cambridge Scholars Publishing.

McPherson, C. (July 13, 2015). Meet the teenage Indigenous hip-hop artist taking on climate change. *Rolling Stone*. Retrieved July 20, 2015, from www.rollingstone.com/politics/news/meet-the-teenage-indigenous-hip-hop-artist-taking-on-climate-change-20150713.

Mogensen, F., & Schnack, K. (2010). The action competence approach and the 'new' discourses of education for sustainable development, competence and quality criteria. *Environmental Education Research, 16*(1), 59–74.

National Aeronautics and Space Administration (NASA) (2015). *Climate Kids*. Pasadena, CA: NASA Jet Propulsion Laboratory & California Institute of Technology.

National Oceanic and Atmospheric Administration (March, 2015). *State of the Climate Report: Global Summary Information*. Retrieved June 4, 2015, from www.ncdc.noaa.gov/sotc/.

PACMAS (Pacific Media Assistance Scheme) Blog (2013). Action against climate change Vanuatu: Growing trees to stem climate change. Retrieved November 15, 2013, from www.pacmas.org/blog-post/action-against-climate-change-vanuatu-growing-trees-to-stem-climate-change/.

Randall, R. (December 5, 2012). The id and the eco. *Aeon Magazine*. Retrieved May 23, 2015, from http://aeon.co/magazine/psychology/rosemary-randall-climate-change-psychoanalysis/.

Romm, J. (March 10, 2015). Rate of climate change to soar by 2020s with Arctic warming 1° F per decade. *Climate Progress*. Retrieved January 12, 2015, from http://thinkprogress.org/climate/2015/03/10/3631632/climate-change-rate/.

Smith, G., & Sobel, D. (2010). *Place- and community-based education in schools*. New York: Routledge.

Smith, S. J., Edmonds, J., Hartin, C. A., Mundra, A., & Calvin, K. (2015). Near term acceleration in the rate of temperature change. *Nature Climate Change, 5*, 333–336.

Solnit, R. (May 15, 2015). One magical politician won't stop climate change: It's up to all of us. *The Guardian*. Retrieved May 17, 2015, from www.theguardian.com/commentisfree/2015/may/15/one-magical-politician-wont-stop-climate-change-its-up-us.

Taylor, R. (June, 2014). Ecocide: The psychology of environmental destruction. *Psychology Today*. Retrieved July 1, 2015, from www.psychologytoday.com/blog/out-the-darkness/201406/ecocide-the-psychology-environmental-destruction.

Tudball, L. (November 7, 2014). Our kids need to learn about climate change. *The Conversation*. Retrieved January 19, 2015, from http://theconversation.com/our-kids-need-to-learn-about-climate-change-33833.

UNICEF Office of Research (2014). *The challenges of climate change: Children on the front line*. Florence: Innocenti Insight.

United Nations Alliance on Climate Change: Education, Training and Public Awareness (2014). *United Nations Framework Convention on Climate Change*. New York: UNACC.

Upton, J. (February 27, 2015). Looming warming spurt could reshape climate debate. *Climate Central*. Retrieved March 23, 2015, from www.climatecentral.org/news/warming-spurt-looms-will-it-change-minds-on-climate-change-18716.

Warner, K. D. (July 18, 2015). Why Pope Francis, spiritual leader of a billion souls, cares about saving the material world. *Reuters US*. Retrieved July 22, 2015, from http://blogs.reuters.com/great-debate/2015/06/17/why-the-leader-of-a-billion-souls-cares-about-the-earthly-realm/.

16

URGENT GLOBAL PROBLEMS REQUIRE TEACHER AGENCY

Julie Andrzejewski

In 1992, 12-year-old Severn Cullis-Suzuki, founder of the Environmental Children's Organization, gave a riveting speech to the delegates at the UN Earth Summit in Rio de Janeiro, Brazil. Some excerpts are especially relevant to educators (1992):

> I am here to speak on behalf of the starving children around the world whose cries go unheard. I am here to speak for the countless animals dying across this planet because they have nowhere left to go. I am afraid to go out in the sun now because of the holes in the ozone. I am afraid to breathe the air because I don't know what chemicals are in it... And now we hear about animals and plants going extinct every day—vanishing forever. Did you have to worry about these little things when you were my age?
>
> All this is happening before our eyes and yet we act as if we have all the time we want and all the solutions. I'm only a child and I don't have all the solutions, but I want you to realize, neither do you!
>
> - You don't know how to fix the holes in our ozone layer.
> - You don't know how to bring salmon back up a dead stream.
> - You don't know how to bring back an animal now extinct.
> - And you can't bring back forests that once grew where there is now desert.
>
> If you don't know how to fix it, please stop breaking it!

I'm only a child yet I know if all the money spent on war was spent on ending poverty and finding environmental answers, what a wonderful place this earth would be!

At school, even in kindergarten, you teach us to behave in the world. You teach us:

- not to fight with others,
- to work things out,
- to respect others,
- to clean up our mess,
- not to hurt other creatures,
- to share—not be greedy.

Then why do you go out and do the things you tell us not to do?

Recognizing Child Agency

As adults, we may believe that we are protecting children by sheltering them from harsh realities about the world. We may argue: why should childhood be disturbed by concerns about global problems such as war, animal extinctions, climate disruption, food/water/air contamination, or environmental destruction? However, Severn's speech raises important challenges to this common thinking. First, children and young people have access to information, true or false, about global problems from many sources that cannot be controlled or censored by adults. Second, children may realize that teachers or other adults are avoiding these topics. Third, without training to evaluate the accuracy of information, children, like adults, can be manipulated by advertisers, entertainment media, political or religious groups, peer pressure, military recruiters, or corporate-influenced "news." Fourth, childhood censorship may prevent children from developing their own consciousness and agency at a time when it is most crucial for them to take action on their own behalf or on behalf of others and the earth. And finally, in the absence of complete information and role models, children may adopt life habits that are harmful to themselves, others, or the earth. Such habits can become difficult to change when accurate information is finally accessible: behavior patterns such as smoking, tanning, bullying, eating harmful foods, exhibiting bigotry, being cruel to animals, using pornography, over-consuming, using drugs, watching television excessively, or playing violent video games.

Severn, now a mother herself, was one of many thousands of children around the world throughout history who have felt compelled to take action in the face of serious social and ecological injustice. Unlike Severn, most children activists remain nameless and unrecorded in history books. In spite of cultural norms that usually marginalize children's activity in civic life, elementary aged youth *can* speak out, organize, and provide leadership for significant social change.

Across the world, with or without the support of adults, children are challenging gender discrimination, female genital mutilation, early marriage, labor exploitation, homelessness, poverty, slavery, war, environmental problems, racism, heterosexism, animal cruelty, and countless community problems. Two more well-known examples are Malala Yuosafzai and Xiuhtezchatl Martinez.

- At age 11, Malala Yousafzai became an advocate for education as a human right, especially for girls. Three years later she was shot in the head, but she survived and recovered to continue and expand her activism. In 2014, she became the youngest person to receive the Nobel Peace Prize.
- Xiuhtezchatl Martinez is an indigenous environmental activist who gave his first speech at age 6, after watching Leonardo DiCaprio's film, *The 11th Hour* (Peterson and Connors, 2007). His Aztec father taught him "that all life is sacred and connected to each of us," and his environmental activist mother encouraged him to speak out. At 12 years of age, he spoke at the Rio+20 UN Summit and at 14 he organizes youth for the non-profit organization Earth Guardians (McCurdy, 2014).

Other recent examples of environmental activism by schoolchildren include the fight against child labor (Lyman, 2002/2003), the redesign of a community park (Comber, Thomson & Wells, 2001) and a child-friendly neighborhood (Malone, 2013), setting up energy efficient 'green' roofs in an urban community (Barton & Tan, 2010), responding to the violence of a puppet play, protecting turtles, acting against vandalism to trees (Pelo & Davidson, 2000), questioning school district budget cuts (Weiss, 2011), and leading voter registration drives (Cowhey, 2006). Adults may be surprised when young people initiate successful actions because of preconceived notions of children and childhood. Since they often suffer in greater proportion than adults from wars, pollution, poverty, and environmental destruction, why should children *not* be allowed to explore and take action on serious social and environmental issues?

Creating Global Problems: Doing What Our Teachers Said Not to Do

Sixty-three percent of all human-generated emissions have been produced in the last 25 years, but science shows us that there is a 40-year time lag between global emissions (our actions) and climate impacts (the consequences).... In December 2010, the UN Environment Program predicted up to a 5 degrees Celsius increase by 2050. This is a shocking piece of information, because a 3.5 degrees Celsius increase would render the planet uninhabitable for humans due to collapsing the food chain at the level of oceanic plankton and triggering temperature extremes that would severely limit terrestrial vegetation, and hence, our ability to feed ourselves.

Dahr Jamail, Climate Disruption Dispatches, *Truthout,* May 1, 2015

There is ample evidence that life on earth today is facing problems unlike any other era, problems that have been known, ignored, and exacerbated by governments, businesses, and other institutional leaders for decades. These problems are not isolated events. Rather, they impact one another in a myriad of ways, increasing the rapidity with which they occur and the intensity of the resulting consequences.

When people can locate accurate information about global problems, the evidence is enormously disturbing. People tend to avoid or deny these realities because they are unpleasant and worrisome, and because they challenge some of our beliefs and favorite daily habits. Yet, if we as teachers of young people *and* as citizens want a chance to influence the outcome of the planet, we must commit ourselves to fully learning the scope of environmental and social injustice in the world today (Jamail, April & May 2015; Klein, 2014). In this chapter, I first provide a brief overview for teachers of the urgency of several key global problems. I conclude with a description of some core actions teachers can take to enhance their readiness to get involved in justice movements, locally and beyond.

Being Greedy: The False Choice of Economy over Natural Law

Indigenous intellectual thinking explains that no matter what laws or priorities humans establish, the laws of nature (natural law) are pre-eminent, which means that the physical processes of nature continue regardless of what beliefs or laws humans create. For example, humans can deny or pretend that climate change is not occurring and continue to extract and use fossil fuels; however, if carbon and methane are emitted into the atmosphere, climate disruption will occur no matter what humans claim or believe, or what laws have been made to protect the polluting companies (Jamail, April 2015; LaDuke, 1996). When human leaders and business enterprises put money, economics, and profits ahead of the natural environment, consequences will inevitably occur in the earth's systemic processes. Business and government leaders' decisions to promote or acquiesce to environmental destruction for the purposes of making the most money have pushed nine thresholds of world sustainability[1] near or over the tipping point. Pitting economic issues (including "jobs") against the environment is a false choice since economies require a healthy environment in order to be sustained into the future.

Hurting Ourselves and Other Creatures: The Ecological Crisis Created by Humans

It has only recently been discovered that there have been five previous extinction events on earth over the course of millions of years during which time a substantial percentage of life was extinguished (Kolbert, 2014). In antiquity, there were human civilizations that became extinct because of their overuse of the natural environment, but these events were localized and did not create global extinctions. However, at this moment in history, humans have used and abused living plants and animals and extracted enough of nature in ways that threaten all forms of life on the planet. Human technologies have plundered massive expanses of the earth's ecosystems and destroyed the habitats of its occupants. The delicate web of life that has emerged over millions of years, whereby plants and animals adapted to remarkable interdependence with one another, has become fragmented in just a couple hundred years. Julie Marton-Lefevre, Director General of the International Union for Conservation of Nature (IUCN), declared, "A sustainable future cannot be achieved without conserving biological diversity—animal and plant species, their habitats and their genes— not only for nature itself, but also for all seven billion people who depend on it. The IUCN Red List is a clarion call to world leaders to secure the web of life on this planet" (2012, p. 2).

Notwithstanding verbal commitments from world leaders, they have not heeded this "clarion call" from the IUCN, bending instead to the influence of those who have enriched themselves at the earth's expense. Human projects have changed the global climate, precipitated the sixth mass extinction of species now occurring, filled the oceans with plastic garbage, contaminated soil, plants, animals, and food with poisons and genetic modifications, cut down the forests, drilled deep into the earth's crust, extracted over 90 percent of the oceans' fish, expanded unsustainable meat production where rain forests and prairies used to thrive, and flagrantly wasted and contaminated our meager potable water supplies. There is no shortage of scientific documentation of these problems (e.g., IPCC, 2014; IUCN, 2012; Jamail, 2015; Urban, 2015; World Wildlife Foundation, 2014).

Fighting with Others: The Profitability of Militarism and Wars

Contrary to the belief that no one benefits from war, the largest profits of any industry are generated by wars. Companies that make weapons and supply soldiers with uniforms, equipment, food, and other expendable products obtain government contracts worth millions or billions of dollars. Indeed, the arms industry spends millions to lobby Congress to help reinforce the continuation of our war economy. Yet, in spite of whistleblowers, investigative reports, documentaries (e.g., *Iraq for Sale*, 2006), and convictions for fraudulent and illegal activities, companies who have violated the law continue to qualify for new government contracts. Cost-plus military contracts encourage waste and overspending since the more money that is spent, the more profits will be gained.

The United States military is the largest polluter in the world. However, military waste and chemical pollution are not included in any of the reports analyzing the ecological footprint of the United States (Nazaryan, 2014; Huff et al., 2010; Sanders, 2009). Without accurate information on this enormous source of greenhouse gases and toxic waste, and the profits made by the military–industrial complex, public opinion about wars is manipulated by fears of terrorism rather than the comparatively more devastating consequences of the war on the natural world (Davenport, 2014). Still, military responses to national, regional, and global problems are repeatedly discussed by media and leaders as the only "realistic solutions." Experts who support diplomacy, negotiation, and peaceful approaches to conflict are either absent or marginalized. The corporate-controlled media environment uses violent entertainment (e.g., films, video games, certain sports) to help normalize military and police violence toward peoples of color and protesters. It is not surprising that the public, including children, becomes habituated to violence as the answer to many social problems.

Not Cleaning Up Our Mess: Extraction, Overconsumption, and Waste

Annie Leonard's film, *The Story of Stuff*, describes the many complicated factors involved in overconsumption so simply and powerfully that it is easy for adults, youth, and children to understand. She explains six core manifestations of our global overconsumption (Leonard, 2007, 2011):

- We humans are extracting (e.g., by mining and deforestation) more natural resources than can be regenerated by the earth, causing extreme damage to the environment, to people, plants, and animals.
- Toxic products result from a production process that uses toxic substances. These products affect the health of the workers making them and the consumers buying them, and leave the environment contaminated.
- These products are manufactured with parts and products transported all around the world at a huge environmental cost.
- Media and advertising convince us that consumption will make us happy, so we spend much of our time watching television, shopping, and working for money so we can buy things we do not need that do not make us happy.
- As a consequence of *planned obsolescence*, products break easily and cannot be repaired while *perceived obsolescence* creates a mindset where usable products are quickly disposed of into landfills or incinerators, both of which result in further contamination of our air, water, and land.

Meanwhile, the human population of the earth has exploded from the first one billion people in 1800 to seven billion in 2011 (Worldometers, 2015) while many other species are in a state of rapid decline and extinction (Kolbert, 2014). Scientists agree that humans are using more than the "biological capacity" of one earth, a fundamentally unsustainable condition, especially when taking the needs of other species into consideration (Tulloch, 2014).

Not Sharing and Respecting Others: Global Inequalities

Every year, new studies report global inequalities based on almost every iden-
tifiable characteristic that humans have observed or, in some cases, invented to
justify discrimination: gender, race, class, ethnicity, disability, age, religion, sexual
orientation, caste, and species. Regardless of repeated teachings of our parents
and teachers to share, respect everyone, and treat others as we would like to be
treated, children observe that many adults do not follow these teachings themselves. For example:

- *Wealth and Income Gaps:* Oxfam research predicts that "on current trends
  the richest 1% would own more than 50% of the world's wealth by 2016,"
  and that "just 80 people (own) the same amount of wealth as more than
  3.5 billion people," the poorest 50 percent (Elliot and Pilkington, 2015).
  Income inequality is noted as the most significant trend by the World
  Economic Forum (Mohammed, 2014).
- *Gender Inequalities:* While some progress has been made in education and
  economic opportunities, women still remain extremely underrepresented in
  political leadership (Hausmann et al., 2015). Violence against women continues unabated. The UN Office on Drugs and Crime reports that "women
  and girls continue to be killed in large numbers worldwide" with millions of
  women experiencing violence on a daily basis (UNODC, 2015).
- *Racial Inequalities:* Historically, racism has been a tool of imperialism, used
  to justify the exploitation of peoples of color and the lands that belonged
  to them. The legacy of this theft continues as racial inequalities have been
  institutionalized in laws and policies that disadvantage people of color in
  their own countries as well as in other countries whether by forced or chosen migration. Racial inequalities are reflected in greater infant mortality,
  educational and health disparities, economic discrimination, imprisonment,
  harassment and violence, enslavement, and lower life expectancy (Irwin
  et al., 2014).
- *LGBT Inequalities:* Even though marked progress has been made globally for
  LGBT people, Human Rights Watch reports that "almost 2.8 billion people
  still live in countries where identifying as gay could lead to imprisonment,
  corporal punishment or even death" (Roth, 2015).
- *Disability Inequalities:* Poverty causes 80 percent of disabilities through
  malnutrition, diseases, pollution, wars, and other poverty-related causes.
  "People with disabilities represent approximately 15% of world's population
  or 1 billion people…80% of people with disabilities live in developing countries" but those living in more affluent countries often still live in poverty
  (Callender, 2013).
- *Species Inequalities:* Speciesism is the "unwarranted belief that human beings
  are superior to all other living beings and that the earth and other forms of

life are here specifically for our use… People have been taught to think of animals as 'other,' peripheral to the lives of humans unless they are companions, can be eaten, sold, used for work, or products can be made from their body parts" (Andrzejewski & Alessio, 2014).

Exercising Democracy: Becoming Active Citizen Teachers

The reality of the global problems we face can be immensely discouraging. In the face of such enormous problems and obstacles, what can we, as teachers, really do? If we want to encourage the agency of our students, I argue that we as educators have the responsibility to first begin the process of becoming active global citizens ourselves. How can we, as teachers, get involved in addressing the type of global problems that Severn identifies?

Investigate Environmental Crises and Learn How to "Clean Up Our Mess"

It takes courage to truly inform ourselves about the serious global problems and not turn away, give up, succumb to fear, get defensive, or let others talk us out of it. To find the uncomfortable truth, we must go beyond the corporate mainstream media to locate accurate resources for ourselves. Independent socially responsible non-profit news and Internet sites, such as *Commondreams, Truthout, Yes Magazine, In These Times,* and *Mother Jones*, routinely publish short articles and videos on environmental and global justice issues. A few corporate newspapers such as *The Guardian (UK)* also have a strong history of independent reporting and management. A progressive alternative to the commercial media news is *Democracy Now,* a daily US-based news hour that can be streamed from the Internet (www.democracynow.org). Comparing independent sources with mass media news can enhance our awareness of media biases (Andrzejewski, 2007).

Documentaries on water, soil, food, oceans, democracy, wars, chemicals/toxins, climate disruption, extinctions, GMOs, animal agriculture, and various social movements working to solve these problems is another powerful avenue to raise our consciousness. They can be found by searching film festivals such as *Films for Action* (www.filmsforaction.org). At the same time, sharpening our skills to critically analyze different claims and evidence is fundamental to participating in community with *critical consciousness*.

Learn How Democracy Is Practiced through Personal and Collective Actions to "Fix It"

Although most schools express commitment to democratic values, what democracy means and how ordinary citizens practice it are often not part of our education. We teachers rarely have had the opportunity to study or experience social movements and the effectiveness of these movements to influence policies and laws. Civics courses, for instance, have been marginalized or entirely eliminated in most middle and high schools across the nation. Only about one-third of elementary teachers integrate civics or citizenship information regularly throughout their curricula (Civic Mission of Schools, 2012). How can we expect children to become engaged in social action if we, as teacher-citizens, have not joined with other concerned citizens in collective actions and social movements? In virtually every community, there are citizen groups advocating for social and environmental justice that would be more effective with our involvement.

The stories of social movements (e.g., labor movement, civil rights movement, women's movement, environmental movement) must be told and learned by both our students and us (e.g., read Zinn, 1999). Movements are made up of many activist organizations working separately and together to achieve important changes. The women's movement made famous the statement, "The personal is political," bringing attention to the importance of our individual actions to social movements.

Attending civic meetings or events in our own communities can give a sense of movement organizing today. The accomplishments and strategies of activist organizations can help us become movement-literate, and serve as a foundation for our own decisions and actions. Research, reports, laws, and international agreements can serve as effective organizing tools to educate ourselves and others. One of the most important international agreements is the Earth Charter (www.earthcharterinaction.org/content/). This document is one of the first of its kind that integrated social and ecological justice. Take a look at this document and imagine how life on earth would be different if humankind lived by these standards.

"Respect Others and Work Things Out": Value Cultural, Philosophical, and Political Differences

Rather than seeking homogeneity or enforcing conformity, learning how to value differences in our everyday activities is a daunting project that presents challenges and opportunities necessary for growth as civic-minded individuals, vital social movements, and democratic schools. Overcoming bigotry, social stratification, education gaps, and bullying require changes in fundamental policies and practices. Becoming more literate and appreciative of the diversity of languages, cultures, and worldviews—even as we may disagree with one another—is essential if we want to work together for justice and our precious life-sustaining planet.

There are several ways we can bridge these barriers. We can learn how environmental issues are integrally related to other social movements (e.g., challenging inequalities, stopping wars, advocating for animals). This understanding will help us strengthen alliances by supporting movements that at first glance might not appear to be "our issues." We can challenge ourselves to make connections to people with whom we disagree and listen to them without judgment. It may be especially difficult to reduce our attachment to having our own way, and to appreciate the leadership of others. These actions all take strenuous effort but, if we take these actions seriously, they can lead to great personal development and, importantly, more democratic and egalitarian communities.

Be a Real Life Role Model for Sharing, Caring, and Acting

There are many ways to make a difference in the world. Unfortunately, our media, and sometimes our schools, influence us to become pleasure-seekers, only inter-ested in entertainment and self-gratification through television, social media, sports, and shopping. But we can provide a different model—by making our per-sonal habits congruent with our values (what we eat, what we buy, how we share and treat others, how we act as citizens, etc.). In this process, it helps to remember that changing ourselves is a journey where guilt and/or self-righteousness are counterproductive.

We teachers can become role models for our students and reluctant colleagues by joining other ordinary citizens to demand changes in policies to protect our food, air, water, and health, to stop wars, to increase equality, and to save species from extinction. Instead of striving to solve all the world's problems, be focused and select just a few issues to work on, if not just one. We can support and join local, national, and global organizations working on whatever issues we feel most passionate about. We can demonstrate that being an active global citizen is a nor-mal part of everyday life and share experiences of our own actions with students when appropriate.

Conclusion

Because Severn Cullis-Suzuki learned early in life that her actions made a difference, environmental activism became her life's work, and she continues to speak around the world urging people to become activists for the planet and all life. As teachers, we must not underestimate the interest and ability of children to make serious contributions to social movements. Let us join the millions of adults and children, who, like Severn, have taken meaningful action to change the direction of our future and, in the process, have provided role models for many others to do the same.

References

Andrzejewski, J. (2007). Alternative press. In G. Anderson & K. Herr (Eds.), *The encyclopedia of activism and social justice* (pp. 78–84). New York: SAGE Publications.

Andrzejewski, J., & Alessio, J. C. (2013). The sixth mass extinction. In M. Huff & A. L. Roth (Eds.), *Censored 2014*. New York: Seven Stories Press.

Barton, A. C., & Tan. E. (2010). "It changed our lives": Activism, science, and greening the community. *Canadian Journal of Science, Mathematics & Technology Education, 10*(3), 207–222.

Callender, T. (August 2, 2013). Addressing inequalities for people with disabilities is central to an effective post-2015 agenda. *World We Want*. Retrieved June 2, 2015, from www .worldwewant2015.org/node/364645.

Campaign for the Civic Mission of Schools (2012). *America's civic learning crisis: Preparation for informed and engaged citizenship is the co-equal goal of education: A fact sheet*. Retrieved May 31, 2015, from www.civicmissionofschools.org/the-campaign/ civic-learning-fact-sheet.

Comber, B., Thomson, P., & Wells, M. (2001). Critical literacy finds a 'place': Writing and social action in a low-income Australian grade 2/3 classroom. *The Elementary School Journal, 101*, 451–464. Retrieved July 16, 2015, from http://newlearningonline.com/ literacies/chapter-6/comber-thomson-and-wells-on-critical-literacy.

Cowhey, M. (2006). *Black ants and Buddhists: Thinking critically and teaching differently in the primary grades*. Portland, MI: Stenhouse Publishers.

Cullis-Suzuki, S. (1992). Full text of Suvern Suzuki's speech to UN Earth Summit. Retrieved April 10, 2015, from http://ssjothiratnam.com/?p=747.

Davenport, C. (October 13, 2014). Pentagon signals security risks of climate change. *The New York Times*. Retrieved May 23, 2015, from www.nytimes.com/2014/10/14/us/ pentagon-says-global-warming-presents-immediate-security-threat.html?_r=0.

Earth Charter International (1997). *The Earth Charter*. Retrieved July 17, 2015, from www .earthcharterinaction.org/content/pages/Read-the-Charter.html.

Elliott, L., & Pilkington, E. (January 19, 2015). New Oxfam report says half of global wealth held by the 1%. *The Guardian*. Retrieved June 2, 2015, from www.theguardian .com/business/2015/jan/19/global-wealth-oxfam-inequality-davos-economic-summit-switzerland.

Hausmann, R., Tyson, L. D., Behhouche, Y., & Zahidi, S. (2014). *The global gender gap report: 2014*. Geneva: World Economic Forum.

Huff, M., Phillips, P., Project Censored, Borjesson, K., & Bendib, K. (2010). US Department of Defense is the worst polluter on the planet. *Censored 2011: The top 25 news stories of 2009–10*. New York: Seven Stories Press.

IPCC (2014). *Climate change 2014 synthesis report: Summary for policymakers*. Retrieved November 14, 2014, from www.ipcc.ch/pdf/assessment-report/ar5/syr/AR5_SYR_ FINAL_SPM.pdf.

Irwin, N., Miller, C. C., & Sanger-Katz, M. (August 19, 2014). America's racial divide, charted. *New York Times*. Retrieved January 23, 2015, from www.nytimes.com/2014/08/20/ upshot/americas-racial-divide-charted.html?_r=0.

IUCN (International Union for Conservation of Nature and Natural Resources) (2015). *The IUCN Red List of Threatened Species*. Retrieved August 3, 2015, from www.iucn. org/about/work/programmes/species/our_work/the_iucn_red_list/.

Jamail, D. (April 27, 2015). Experts warn of "cataclysmic" changes as planetary temperatures rise. *Truthout*. Retrieved May 1, 2015, from www.truth-out.org/news/ item/30449-experts-warn-of-cataclysmic-changes-as-planetary-temperatures-rise.

Jamail, D. (May 1, 2015). Climate disruption dispatches, with Dahr Jamail. *Truthout*. Retrieved June 23, 2015, from www.truth-out.org/news/item/22521-climate-disruption-dispatches-with-dahr-jamail.

Klein, N. (2014). *This changes everything: Capitalism vs. the climate*. New York: Simon and Schuster.

Kolbert, E. (2014). *The sixth extinction: An unnatural history*. New York: Picador, Henry Holt and Company.

LaDuke, W. (1996). A society based on conquest cannot be sustained. In J. Andrzejewski (Ed.), *Oppression and social justice: Critical frameworks* (pp. 199–206). Needham Heights, MA: Simon & Schuster.

Leonard, A. (December 4, 2007). *The story of stuff*. Retrieved May 10, 2015, from www.storyofstuff.com.

Leonard, A. (2011). *The story of stuff: The impact of overconsumption on the planet, our communities, and our health and how we can make it better*. New York: Free Press.

Lyman, K. (2002/2003). Exploring child labor with young students. *Rethinking Schools*, *17*(*2*). Retrieved October 2, 2014, from www.rethinkingschools.com.

Magdoff, F., & Foster, J. B. (2011). *What every environmentalist needs to know about capitalism*. New York: Monthly Review Press.

Malone, K. (2013). "The future lies in our hands": Children as researchers and environmental change agents in designing a child-friendly neighborhood. *Local Environment*, *18*(*3*), 372–395.

McCurdy, J. (December 4, 2014). The 14-year old voice of the climate change generation. *In These Times*. Retrieved February 12, 2015, from http://inthesetimes.com/article/17345/xiuhtezcatl_martinez_voice_of_the_climate_change_generation.

Mohammed, A. (2014). *Deepening income inequality*. Geneva: World Economic Forum. Retrieved January 13, 2015, from http://reports.weforum.org/outlook-global-agenda-2015/top-10-trends-of-2015/1-deepening-income-inequality/.

Nazaryan, A. (July 17, 2014). The US department of defense is one of the world's biggest polluters. *Newsweek*. Retrieved May 23, 2015, at www.newsweek.com/2014/07/25/us-department-defence-one-worlds-biggest-polluters-259456.html.

Pelo, A., & Davidson, F. (2000). *That's not fair: A teacher's guide to activism with young children*. St. Paul, MN: Redleaf Press.

Peterson, L. C., & Connors, N. (2007). *The 11th hour*. Warner Independent Pictures.

Roth, K. (2015). *LGBT: Moving towards equality*. Geneva: World Economic Forum. Retrieved January 12, 2015, from http://reports.weforum.org/outlook-global-agenda-2015/wp-content/blogs.dir/59/mp/files/pages/files/lgbt.pdf.

Sanders, B. (2009). *The green zone: The environmental costs of militarism*. Oakland: AK Press.

Tulloch, J. (July 11, 2014). *World population growth: Are we too many?* Knowledge.allianz .com. Retrieved May 23, 2015, at http://knowledge.allianz.com/demography/population/?354/world-population-growth-are-we-too-many.

UNODC (United Nations Office of Drugs and Crime). (May 19, 2015). Violence against women and girls 'shames every society,' UN anti-crime chief warns. *UN News Centre*. Retrieved June 2, 2015, from www.un.org/apps/news/story.asp?NewsID=50907#.VW36HEtgxDQ.

Urban, M. C. (May 1, 2015). Accelerating extinction risk from climate change. *Science*, *348*(6234), 571–573.

World Wildlife Fund (2014). *Living planet report 2014: Species and spaces, people and places*. Retrieved May 6, 2015, from http://assets.worldwildlife.org/publications/723/files/original/WWF-LPR2014-low_res.pdf?1413912230&_ga=1.4207539.1872814817.1360759912.

Worldometers.info. (2015). Current world population. Retrieved May 23, 2015, from http://worldometers.info/world-population/.

Zinn, H. (1999). *A people's history of the United States*. New York: HarperCollins.

Note

1 Scientists have identified key thresholds relating to various aspects of the physical world that are necessary for sustaining a planetary environment suitable for life (Magdoff & Foster, 2011). These sustainability thresholds include (a) climate disruption; (b) extinction of species; (c) ocean acidification; (d) stratospheric ozone depletion; (e) biogeochemical flow boundary (too much nitrogen and phosphorus); (f) global freshwater use; (g) change in land use (destruction of forests and natural habitats); (h) atmospheric aerosol loading; and (i) chemical pollution (Magdoff and Foster, 2011, pp. 12–13). Some of these thresholds (climate change, biodiversity [extinctions], and biogeochemical flow) have already been crossed, threatening the future of life on the planet.

17

TEACHING CLIMATE CHANGE WITH HOPE AND SOLUTIONS

Lessons from a Film Project

Lynne Cherry

As an author and illustrator of over 30 environmental children's books over the years, I have been invited to visit many schools. I have noticed that children take sad environmental stories to heart and become upset. Messages of gloom and doom elicit reactions of fear, demoralization, and hopelessness. But during those school visits, children have also told me inspiring stories about actions they had taken to preserve land, plant trees, or clean up rivers. I found that sharing these success stories has a motivating influence on other students to try to make a difference themselves.

In this chapter, I describe the *Young Voices for the Planet* (YVCC) documentary film project, a series of films that champions young people's actions in response to serious environmental problems. I also highlight social science research and pedagogy that reflects the importance of teaching about troubling issues with hope and inspiration rather than doom and gloom. The success stories of these young activists offer insights and guidelines for elementary teachers who wish to support children to be agents of change and help promote a sustainable earth.

The Film Project

Nine years ago, photojournalist Gary Braasch published *Earth under Fire: How Global Warming Is Changing the World* (2007), one of the first books for the general public documenting climate disruption. Braasch photographed scientists studying climate change and persuasively made the case for taking immediate action to counter global warming. His book spawned our children's book, *How We Know What We Know about Our Changing Climate* (Cherry & Braasch, 2008). We found that teachers and other educators most valued the climate *solutions* part of the book. They reported to us that the stories in the book showing the actions and positive initiatives of youth addressing climate change tended to dispel feelings of helplessness that their own students had about this global challenge.

Recognizing that young people could play a vital role in initiating change, Gary Braasch and I founded the non-profit organization, *Young Voices on Climate Change*. YVCC has carved a niche in the field of climate education: we champion and publicize inspirational, authentic, and positive youth-led models of social action through a multimedia platform. Our centerpiece project is the film series, *Young Voices for the Planet (YVFP)*, which showcases intrepid youth working on a range of environmental issues. These youth engage local governments, businesses, and school administrators while helping their peers develop confidence in themselves as agents of change in the world. This belief in one's ability to make change is called "self-efficacy." The *YVFP* films document powerful youth models of self-efficacy, of young people who have stepped up to take control of their environment and destiny.

The *YVFP* films allow youth voices on climate change to be heard. These films may also play an important role in motivating student-viewers of these films to engage in social action on behalf of a sustainable earth. Indeed, we have witnessed how the films' positive messaging inspires young people to take action.

Here are the titles and brief descriptions of our first 11 films:

- *Kids vs. Global Warming*: Twelve-year-old Alec erects Sea Level Awareness posts in coastal California, speaks to Congress, and, with Dr. James Hansen, advocates for putting a price on carbon.
- *Girl Scouts*: A group of Girl Scouts distributes CFL light bulbs and educates people about how they can reduce their energy use.
- *Green Ambassadors*: High school students describe how energy is produced and what causes global warming. The "greening" of their school highlights climate solutions.
- *Team Marine*: Students help pass a ban on plastic bags in their city and inspire hundreds of other students to work toward the successful statewide California ban on plastic bags.
- *Anya: Citizen Scientist in Siberia*: Anya is the daughter of the captain of a ship taking American scientists up the Lena River to research Arctic melting. She helps with their research and becomes part of the research team.
- *Plant for the Planet*: Eleven-year-old Felix, inspired by Wangari Maathai, plants millions of trees and describes how they help to mitigate climate change (see Figure 17.1).
- *Dreaming in Green*: Four Miami girls learn that Miami will suffer serious economic loss from sea level rise; they do an energy audit and save their school $53,000 in energy bills.
- *Olivia's Birds and the Oil Spill*: Eleven-year-old Olivia raises $200,000 to clean oiled birds after the BP spill and then speaks to her representative in Congress about supporting renewable energy.

- *Longing for a Local Lunch*: Four high school students create a robust, nutritious, healthy school lunch through a school garden and local community partners.
- *We Sing Out!* The Rivertown kids have a deep environmental ethic. Singing with folk legend Pete Seeger, they "speak out musically" about a renewable-energy-powered future.
- *Save Tomorrow*: After watching *the Young Voices for the Planet* films, nine-year-old Alice is inspired to start a club, "Save Tomorrow," which helps overturn a ban prohibiting solar panels on town buildings in Lexington, Massachusetts.

As a writer and illustrator of environmental books for children, I have come to understand the power of stories to change the way people think. My books such as *The Great Kapok Tree* and *A River Ran Wild* have inspired young people to get involved in saving acres of rainforest and cleaning up rivers. But considering the dire nature of climate change and its rather abstract nature, I thought it more effective to reach students from the upper elementary grades through high school with short films that could be viewed on a handheld electronic device or computer. I now devote most of my working life to documenting youth success stories in the *Young Voices for the Planet* films. No doubt, children and youth of

FIGURE 17.1 Felix leading a tree planting parade in Duisburg, Germany (photograph courtesy of Lynne Cherry).

today will bear the brunt of future climate disruption. It is not surprising that, increasingly, children and youth are emerging as resolute "defenders of the earth."

Theories That Inform My Thinking about Education

My personal experience and convictions about climate change messaging and its ability to empower or disempower have been substantiated by social science research. Here are three theories that have shaped my thinking and behavior as a climate educator and activist.

"Motivated Avoidance" and the Importance of a Positive Approach

The common belief about teaching people about environmental crises has been that if people simply learned the "science," they would be motivated to learn more about climate change and then take actions to address it. But research and our everyday observations show that the opposite is the case.

As guests on Cape and Island National Public Radio, Anthony Leiserowitz, Director of the Yale Project on Climate Change Communication, and I discussed climate change messaging (Goldstone, 2014). We discussed the concept of *motivated avoidance*, which refers to people's tendency to avoid learning about troubling and complicated issues about which they know very little (Shepherd & Kay, 2012). They are *motivated* to *avoid* hearing about what they see as intractable problems that they can't do anything about. The 'motivated avoidance' response was corroborated by the Climate Visuals study done by the UK-based group Climate Outreach (2015). Its research found that emotionally powerful images of climate impacts can be overwhelming emotionally, thus reducing people's inclination to get involved in climate action. However, this study also found that coupling such images with "a concrete behavioural 'action' for people to take can help overcome this [inaction]."

Self-Efficacy and Civic Engagement

In his book *Self Efficacy: The Exercise of Control*, Albert Bandura (1974) examined the concept of *efficacy* and how it influences personal and social behavior. "Efficacy beliefs shape the outcomes people expect their efforts to produce... People of low self-efficacy are easily convinced of the futility of effort in the face of impediments. People with high self-efficacy view impediments as surmountable through perseverance" (p. 4). Those who believe they can manage problems and adversity will tend to view life as less threatening and act in ways to change things. Developing self-efficacy in young people helps to enhance their personal growth as well as their role as global citizens. Bandura describes two ways that self-efficacy is enhanced as it relates to youth/child activism.

When **building mastery**, the individual creates a robust belief in one's ability to take control of one's environment and destiny. The first step in building mastery is to engage youth in projects *guaranteed to succeed*, such as planting trees. Experiencing success nurtures in children and youth a sense of accomplishment and empowerment, motivating them to continue to do things that make them feel good.

Bandura's examination of **social modeling** research shows that messages tend to be effective when delivered by one's peers—people who look like you and with whom you can identify. People learn from one another via observation, imitation, and **modeling**. If people see others like themselves succeed, they come to believe that they, too, have the capacity to do so: "If they can do that, then so can I."

Youth as Change-Makers with Parents and Community

Children and youth can influence their parents and other adults' behavior. For example, Damerell, Howe, and Milner-Gulland (2013) found that children who have participated in environmental education can influence parents to take on more planet-friendly practices, sometimes without the parents even being aware of these effects. The power of young people to influence their parents was also documented in the Project Sunlight study (Unilever, 2013). Eight- to twelve-year-old children and their families in the United States, United Kingdom, India, and Indonesia were found to have a reciprocal effect on each other's pro-social beliefs and behaviors related to the environment. Children and parents learned from each other about green actions, and parents especially were found to be motivated to act on their children's suggestions.

The Unilever study concludes that children can be not only the motivation but also the *trigger* inspiring more adults to change their lifestyles and turn good intentions into positive action.

> When thinking about the planet, we need to take our cue from children's unique perspectives. Children have a natural optimism about the future. They also care about nature, and have an intuitive sense of fairness and justice. Their positive, clear-sighted take on the big issues means that they are less paralyzed by the obstacles than adults. Children provide both a catalyst for action and a prism through which we can view our own responses to social and environmental challenges...Their concerns (about global issues)—coupled with their stake in the future of the planet—give parents some powerful reasons to take action.
>
> (Unilever, 2013, p. 4)

YVFP Films and Lessons for Elementary Teachers

The *Young Voices for the Planet* films provide us with some ideas about the social and curricular *conditions* that might support children's motivation to do civic action. From watching the youth in these films and the conditions surrounding their climate work, I have inferred four instructional (classroom) conditions that might support children and youth, generally, to also step up and take positive action. I invite elementary teachers to consider these instructional conditions and then adapt these to their particular students and teaching situations.

1. Providing models of children and youth doing activism influences others to take similar actions. For example, in the recent movie, *Save Tomorrow*, ten-year-old Alice describes how she was inspired to take action after watching youth taking action in the earlier *Young Voices for the Planet* films. "I didn't know that kids could make a difference," she said. That knowledge gave Alice the courage to start a club, which she named "Save Tomorrow." In the film, another participant, Mari, describes how Alice and she were just kids fighting against powerful forces, although she described her own epiphany about how she wasn't *just* a "helpless little girl." She had become a young person more inclined to take action and "make a difference in the world."

2. It appears that students become motivated if the problem/project comes from their own "backyard," and this can include the classroom, school, or local community. For example, the students documented in "Longing for a Local Lunch" simply want good food for lunch. They were able to get local organic food in their school cafeteria by engaging teachers, school administrators, and local community groups. They even created a barter arrangement with the local food co-op trading the school garden veggies harvested in the summer for vegetables from the co-op during the school year. And they connected with local food producers.

3. Students become engaged if they have some sense that proposed solutions are reasonable and doable, such as the *Save Tomorrow* kids and their work to save a local forest from development. When the youth in *Team Marine* see the effect of plastic debris on their local beaches and the threats that plastic bags pose to sea animals, they work for a ban on plastic bags *in their city*. Successful small projects may lead to greater confidence to then engage in new and possibly more ambitious projects. For example, 12-year-old Alec Loorz, in *Kids vs. Global Warming*, convinced his town to help erect "Sea Level Awareness" posts and that success grew and grew until, at 14 years of age, he presented a "Declaration of Independence from Fossil Fuel" to a Congressional committee.

4. Finally, students tend to become more engaged if the projects are collaborative, including collaborations that are intergenerational and involve both peers and community members. In *Dreaming in Green*, Maddi describes how the youth didn't just do it themselves. They engaged the principal, the community, and local businesses. Maddi and her friends realized that Miami would suffer serious economic loss from sea level rise. They began with a modest project—to do an energy audit. They ended up saving their school $53,000 in energy bills. The effect of the students' efforts cascaded down through the community inspiring other sustainable behavioral changes. When Nicole's father saw how much money the students saved the school through conservation, he traded out the air conditioning units in the office buildings he owned for Energy

Star AC units. He saved so much money that he told other building owners, and they switched to Energy Star units in *their* buildings. The students even helped the airport reduce its energy usage and costs.

Participatory Action Research and Real-world Learning

While engaged in outreach work with the University of Colorado at Boulder, Dr. Deb Morrison used the YVFP films to teach pre-service and in-service teachers how students can be involved in Participatory Action Research (PAR) projects (Morrison, 2014). Participatory action research (PAR) is an exciting approach that involves community people, working with trained researchers, engaged in both research and action to solve local problems. Ideally, this work is carried out collaboratively with youth and an intergenerational community of mentors (e.g., Gaffney, 2008). Typically, PAR involves the people who are most affected by a community problem—and they often work in collaboration with people who have research skills.

Youth and class PAR projects are exemplified in some of the YVFP film projects, such as *Team Marine, Plant for the Planet*, and *Dream in Green,* which are very good examples of high engagement curriculum. The teacher assignment in *Plant for the Planet* is a good example of how an educator can organize learning to allow students to run with their interests and delve deeper. Dr. Morrison argues that teachers can and should organize students to engage in PAR projects like these: collaborations with community partners around real problems of interest to students' immediate experience. Dr. Morrison believes that the *Young Voices for the Planet* films can be a useful tool in helping teachers show children and youth examples of how other youth have tackled real-world problems through research and action. She also explains how teachers engaging in such work with students can better involve students in the learning of science. "Engaging students with real world issues in authentic and meaningful ways, often in more *localized* contexts, helps them to develop scientific understanding and motivates them to be involved in school science, thus increasing their overall academic success" (Morrison, 2014).

The type of learning exemplified in the *Young Voices for the Planet* films, also referred to as problem-based instruction, embodies the best practices of inquiry-based science promoted by the Next Generation Science Standards (NGSS). Students are involved in identifying and researching a specific issue such as how reducing energy consumption can reduce global warming gases going into the air. Students have to be able to argue their reasoning with evidence and in that process, to sift through various types of evidence and interrogate evidence quality. Through the films and other local activities, the students need to communicate their understandings and their supporting evidence to interested audiences, important learner outcomes in the NGSS and the Common Core. I strongly encourage teachers to integrate PAR into their classrooms and tie as much of their teaching as possible to real-world issues and community projects.

Conclusion

As adults, we have a moral imperative to educate children on how to care for all life as well as prepare them for global disruptions already locked into the system. The importance of integrating place-based and solution-based actions in our work with children and youth cannot be overemphasized. For children and youth, taking action *can* act as an antidote to the fear and trauma of growing up in a world overshadowed by the specter of environmental crises. As a result of CO_2 levels in the atmosphere that have not been this high since dinosaurs roamed the earth, climate disruption is inevitable and young people will bear the brunt. By teaching with inspiring youth role models, we aim to support students' *self-efficacy* by providing them with the tools to cope with a new world that they have so unfairly inherited. It is imperative that self-efficacy becomes an integral part of our goals for children and youth, changing the way they think of themselves for the rest of their lives and giving them the power and conviction that they can truly make a difference in the world.

References

Bandura, A. (1974). *Self-efficacy: The exercise of control*. New York: Macmillan.

Braasch, G. (2008). *How we know what we know about our changing climate: Scientists and kids explore global warming*. Nevada, City, CA: Dawn Publications.

Cherry, L., & Braasch, G. (2007). *How we know what we know about our changing climate*. Nevada City, CA: Dawn Publications.

Climate Outreach (2015). Climate visuals. Retrieved November 19, 2015, from http://climateoutreach.org/resources/visual-climate-change-communication/.

Damerell, P., Howe, C. & Milner-Gulland, E. J. (2013). Child-oriented environmental education influences adult knowledge and household behavior. *Environmental Research Letters, 8*(1). Retrieved February 2, 2016, from http://iopscience.iop.org/article/10.1088/1748-9326/8/1/015016/pdf.

Gaffney, M. (2008). Participatory action research: An overview. *Kairaranga, 8*, 9–14. Retrieved January 1, 2015, from http://files.eric.ed.gov/fulltext/EJ908178.pdf.

Goldstone, H. (2014). *Psychology and social science reveal deep underpinnings of climate change denial*. WGBH Atlantic Public Radio, Cape Cod, MA. Retrieved April 22, 2015, from http://capeandislands.org/post/psychology-and-social-science-reveal-deep-underpinnings-climate-change-denial.

Morrison, D. (2014). Personal communication.

Shepherd, S., & Kay, A. C. (2012). On the perpetuation of ignorance: System dependence, system justification, and the motivated avoidance of sociopolitical information. *Journal of Personality and Social Psychology, 102*(2), 264–280.

Unilever (2013). *How children inspire sustainable living: Research among parents and their children in the US, UK, India and Indonesia*. Retrieved July 3, 2015, from www.unilever.com/Images/Unilever-Project-Sunlight-White-Paper_tcm244-417250.pdf.

SECTION V

Explicit Teaching to Support Children's Emotions and Resilience

I believe that environmental crises fundamentally reflect humans' disconnection from the earth and all life. In response, our work as educators must be to help young people find points of reconnection with everything and everybody. Following the imperative to help learners reconnect, an important assumption of the book is that resilience and self-efficacy are enhanced by the quality of connections that people make, connections that are social (with people) and ecological (with the natural world). When children engage in the civic process in their communities, either by doing place-based or beyond-the-local activism, this 'social work' further engenders resilience and self-efficacy.

In Section V, there is a bit more explicit focus on supporting children's resilience, self-efficacy, and emotional stability than in the earlier sections. Molly Young Brown (Chapter 18) offers guidelines for supporting the emotional life of children in times of climate disruption and a set of practices that can be used in the classroom, based in 'The Work That Reconnects' as developed by Joanna Macy and her colleagues. In Chapter 19, Maria Ojala brings a more academic take on children's emotions. She reviews the existing research on how 10–12 year olds are experiencing climate change. Extending Brown's ideas, she suggests several broad perspectives and teaching strategies to help children manage the stress of climate disruption.

Sharon Witt and Helen Clarke provide descriptions of elementary children using small world figurines and models to role play and learn to cope with possible future climate-related scenarios, as they may actually play out in their own neighborhoods. Witt and Clarke describe how children learn to articulate more mature responses to disasters in the context of these mini-world simulations.

Finally, Mayeda Rashid, Kevin Ronan, and Briony Towers provide an overview of the research literature on 'disaster risk reduction' programs (DRR): school and community-based programs that teach children how to prepare for disasters both natural and human-caused. According to Rashid and colleagues, when children are involved as *co-participants* in the planning of DRR, this involvement helps children develop greater levels of resilience and self-efficacy. While DRR educational programs are more common in poorer countries in the global south, disasters associated with climate change are an inevitability for both the global south and north. Even in areas of the world that have not yet been subjected to the worst effects of climate change, it makes sense that teachers and school districts begin the work of DRR now, especially in ways that wholeheartedly engage the ideas and involvement of children.

18

SUPPORTING CHILDREN EMOTIONALLY IN TIMES OF CLIMATE DISRUPTION

Teaching Practices and Strategies

Molly Young Brown

Author's Note: This chapter is adapted from Coming Back to Life: The Updated Guide to the Work That Reconnects, *by Joanna Macy and Molly Brown. The Work That Reconnects is designed to help people discover and experience their innate connections with one other and with the healing powers of the web of life. Pioneered by Joanna Macy in the late 1970s, this highly experiential and interactive work draws from systems thinking, deep ecology, and many spiritual traditions and can be used with both children and adults. The spiral of the work moves through four phases: Gratitude, Honoring Our Pain for the World, Seeing with New Eyes, and Going Forth.*

Many adults, especially teachers, parents, and grandparents, face an agonizing dilemma: how to talk with our children about the ongoing derangement and collapse of biological, ecological, economic, and social systems around the world. We know children will suffer the effects in their lifetimes; perhaps, they already are. Naturally, many of us adults want to shelter children from harsher realities of today's world until they are older, but we also feel responsible to prepare them for the challenges ahead.

"What can I say to these kids? I want them to be happy, feel safe."

"I feel guilty somehow—guilty about the kind of world we're handing them, and deceptive that this is one area I am not being honest with them about what I know and feel."

"I don't want to spoil their childhood by bringing up fears they can do nothing about. But, I wonder, am I protecting them or myself?"

We want so much to protect our children (and ourselves) that we often remain silent about our pain for the world and the threats to the web of life that evoke that pain. But are children all that ignorant of the mounting dangers we face? Do they really not know?

What Do Children Know and Feel?

Reports from teachers and facilitators who work with children indicate that children may know a lot more about what's happening in the world than adults think. And they often carry strong feelings about it. Children may not know all the details about climate change, but they know that adults are worried about something called that. Children pick up feelings of anger, fear, and sadness from adults around them, without necessarily understanding what's stirring those feelings.

The UNICEF-UK (2013) found that "almost three-quarters of young people aged 11–16 are concerned about how climate change will impact on their lives...[and that] two-thirds of young people were worried about how climate change will affect other children and families in developing countries. Awareness of climate change among the young people was high, with 88% of those surveyed claiming to know at least a little about it and just 1% saying they knew nothing about climate change." Another survey commissioned by Habitat Heroes showed that one out of three pre-teens fears an Earth apocalypse in his or her lifetime (Becker, 2013/2014).

When children feel despair for the future, they have developed fewer defenses than most adults; they are not as numbed and detached. Adults depersonalize the peril, talk in abstract terms about "collateral damage" or "acceptable risks," while children see it in concrete terms of homeless families on the street, dismembered limbs, people drowning or trapped in burning buildings, and homes destroyed by bombs, hurricanes, or floods.

During the 1970s, Eric Chivian (1988), staff psychiatrist at the Massachusetts Institute of Technology, interviewed many schoolchildren in his work with Educators for Social Responsibility regarding the threat of nuclear war. He described how children dealt with the knowledge of nuclear weapons and the possibility of war. At the third-grade level, children showed a marked sense of confusion, hopelessness, and fear of abandonment. Some had frequent nightmares. By fifth grade, children had more information and felt anger at the stupidity and hypocrisy of the adult world. By seventh grade, this anger turned to cynicism and gallows humor. In high school, the emotional reactions became more complicated. These teenagers faced critical choices about college, careers, and families, but the shadow of *The Bomb* robbed these choices of reality and meaning. The young people of the seventies began to erect defenses of indifference and defiance. Today, with escalating and multiplying threats to life and health, combined with amplified media exposure, it's reasonable to believe that children are likely to experience even greater confusion, fear, anger, cynicism, and defiance.

Many children, moreover, struggle with serious personal and social problems. They may witness violence almost daily, through media and first-hand experience:

school shootings and lockdowns, drive-by killings, domestic violence, rape, teen suicide, drug and alcohol addiction, homelessness, and child abuse. In the midst of all this, children can feel isolated and lonely, especially if no one wants to hear about their fears, anger, and grief. Remember there is no purely private suffering—inevitably, pain arises within the web of life we share. Many "private" problems, such as domestic violence and child abuse, are triggered and intensified by the stresses inherent in the unraveling of our "Industrial Growth Society." It's all of a piece.

The Effects of Silence

Adults' silence on these threats to safety and well-being and their desire to carry on business-as-usual may take a high toll on children and adults alike. Silence conveys fatalism, seeming to say that our collective future is out of our hands, and there's nothing we can do to change it. Silence can also convey indifference. If teachers avoid talking about these issues, a child can conclude that they don't care—and maybe that they don't even care what will happen to the children themselves!

Silence reinforces repression, which may breed cynicism. Older children may wonder if many grownups even feel anguish over destruction and injustice. If we adults do have these feelings, then we are hypocrites for pretending everything is all right. If we don't have such feelings, perhaps we deserve their contempt. Our teenagers may try to shock us awake, so we see the horror of what we are doing to the Earth and one another. Some forms of heavy metal, rap, and "electronica" music, with loud volume, heavy beats, and angry lyrics, may be manifestations of their fury. At the same time, some rap and hip-hop musicians provide powerful outlets for truth-telling and feelings, detailing injustice and oppression.

The rising incidence of drug and alcohol abuse, crime, suicide, and "screen addiction" among teenagers and even children is sad evidence of the erosion of meaning. A sense of alienation, both from family and future, is also pervasive, manifesting not only in anti-social and self-destructive behaviors, but less visibly in the loss of the capacity to make meaningful choices and commitments.

Teachers of younger children may not see the more extreme reactions that are manifested in older children and teens. I believe that how teachers respond to both their own pain for the world and their students' feelings and concerns will strengthen *or* undermine students' developing emotional resilience. The remainder of the chapter contains teaching practices to help elementary-aged children enhance their mental well-being in the face of climate disruption.

Guidelines for Overcoming the Fear and the Silence

What can we do to break the silence and meet our children on the level of their own deep responses? Sadly, given the destructive processes already unleashed, we parents and teachers cannot make the world safe from catastrophic climate change.

Even if we stopped all fossil fuel use today, climate disruption will continue to unfold for decades, maybe centuries. In a world so full of death and destruction, how can we nurture the little ones' sense of safety and security as they develop their sense of self? Here are some general guidelines, drawn from our own work and that of colleagues who work with children.

- Take joy in life with them, especially in nature.

  First and foremost, help children ground themselves in nature by taking them into natural settings as much as possible. Take time to watch a snail, admire a flower, or hug a tree. Help children overcome the "nature-phobia" resulting from enslavement to television and electronic devices, and recover their innate connection with the natural world. Share your own sense of the sacredness and beauty of the web of life. In a similar way, creating a school garden together builds practical, empowering skills while witnessing first-hand the miracle of life.

  We can also share our delight in music and art (especially the homegrown variety).

- Recognize and honor your own feelings.

  Identify for yourself your own fear, anger, and sorrow for the world. While we want to be honest and open with our children, we don't want to use our conversations with them to vent our own feelings. Attend a workshop in "The Work That Reconnects" (workthatreconnects.org). In a group or alone, take time to talk with the child within yourself; feel your inner child's fears and learn what he or she needs from your adult self.

- Invite children to share their feelings and knowledge.

  Begin by asking open questions, such as "What troubles you about the world today?" When something disturbing happens in the news—and the children know about it—share your own feelings about it in simple words, and offer them the chance to share theirs in a safe way. If you know about actions that people are taking in response, especially anything you are doing yourself, tell the children about those actions. Invite students' response and much discussion, following children's lead and readiness.

- Give your complete attention.

  Once you have broached the subject, don't rush to another lesson or distract yourself and the children with another activity. Take time, even for silence. But don't force the issue. Children have the right *not* to hear or talk about scary things, and usually they have an innate sense of what they are ready to deal with. Do not assume children are oblivious or unconcerned if at a given moment they are not ready to talk about it.

- Listen deeply without intervention.

  Accept the challenge not to interrupt or tell them everything is okay. When we listen deeply to children, they begin to overcome feelings of powerlessness and isolation. Physical contact is reassuring, if not overdone and appropriate to your teaching situation and age of students. "Come sit next to me; I'd like to hear about that."

- Help children affirm and define their feelings.

What remains *unspoken and unacknowledged* can be more frightening than a danger we can talk about together. Many children and adults do not know what they are feeling before they express it. Help children put their vague apprehensions into words or images, even act them out. At the same time, don't think you must relieve your children of their emotional pain. Often, just sharing helps calm their fears, and your fears as well.

- Acknowledge what you don't know.

Children will ask questions you can't answer. Remember that questions are often veiled statements about concerns and fears. Invite children to express the concern behind the question; that may help them more than any answer you can give. Your job is to help the child explore questions and feelings, not necessarily to provide answers. So whether or not you have an answer, you can simply say, "I've wondered about that, too. What do you imagine might happen? How do you feel about that?" Or, when appropriate, "What do you think we might do about that?"

- Support them in taking action in their own right.

We all feel empowered when we act on behalf of our world. Children are no different. They feel validated when we take their ideas seriously and help them find immediate, practical ways of putting these ideas into action. Encourage them to draw or write their imaginings, and share them with one another. Build future lessons around any projects that emerge.

There are many ways that children can contribute to the larger world, especially "hands-on" in their own community. Many children love environmental clean-ups in nearby parks and natural areas because they can see tangible results in the bags of debris collected and in the litter-free landscape they leave behind.

Other possibilities: Write a group letter to the editor of local papers, or to local, state, and national officials. Make posters. Ask local organizations if the children can help in any way, such as helping with mailings. Organize or join a children's action group, to discuss, learn, and raise money for a cause in a variety of ways from bake sales to car washes.

Any of these actions can provide a strong and meaningful sense of peer support and community, so children no longer feel isolated, fearful, and powerless. Taking part in such actions builds self-respect and confidence.

- Show them you care by your own actions.

Children model themselves on the adults around them, either by imitation or rebellion. Because they regard adults as powerful, children tend to feel safer when they see them working to make things better. As much as they may need a safe cocoon when they are very young, as children grow older they will thrive when engaged in a community of shared values and adventures.

To the extent politically possible, share with your students your activist activities outside the classroom or those of people you know. Vivienne Verdon-Roe remembers the second grade class she attended during the Cold War, in which all but one of the children said they expected a nuclear war to occur. When the one hopeful child was asked why he was confident in the future, he said, "Because my mother and father go to meetings to stop nuclear war."

Using *The Work That Reconnects* in the Elementary Classroom

The growing field of environmental education and nature awareness offers terrific activities. The practices here relate directly to the Spiral of the Work That Reconnects (Macy & Brown, 2014) moving through four stages: Gratitude, Honoring Our Pain for the World, Seeing with New Eyes, and Going Forth.

Talking Circle

The Talking Circle is one of the most ancient and powerful communication tools. The process is very simple. A group sits in a circle, including the teacher. An object is chosen to be the talking stick, which is passed around the circle. Whoever holds the stick or object—and no one else—has the right to speak. No one may interrupt and no one may speak out of turn. Anyone wishing to respond to what another has said must wait until the talking stick arrives. People are also free to pass the stick on without speaking. There is no cross talk. What is said in the circle stays in the circle.

The Talking Circle can be used for any and all of the stages of the Spiral, and focused on any issue or theme. Children need to have established a basic comfort level with each other and with the facilitator for the circle to succeed. A Talking Circle focused on gratitude (without calling it that) can help build a sense of common ground and comfort.

Stage One: Gratitude

> Piglet noticed that even though he had a very small heart, it could hold a rather large amount of gratitude.
>
> ~ A.A. Milne

The Spiral begins with gratitude. Gratitude quiets the mind and brings us back to source, stimulating our empathy and confidence. The originating impulse of all religious and spiritual traditions is gratitude for the gift of life. For example, gratitude is at the core of indigenous culture on Turtle Island (North America). Among the Haudenosaunee peoples, in particular, this is seen as a sacred duty.

In times of turmoil and danger, gratitude helps to steady and ground us. It brings us into presence, and our full presence is perhaps the best offering we can make to our world. That our world is in crisis—to the point where survival of conscious life on Earth is in question—in no way diminishes the wonder of this present moment. For the great open secret is this: gratitude is not dependent on our external circumstances. We can let the hardships of this time enlist all our strength, wisdom, and courage, so that life can continue. Moreover, gratitude helps inoculate us against the consumerism upon which the destructive Industrial Growth Society depends.

Gratitude practices come easily to children, and can include many nature-related activities. Megan Toben (2014) of Pickards Mountain Eco-Institute in North Carolina writes:

> When I use The Work That Reconnects with children, I incorporate lots of sensory awareness exercises, mostly from Joseph Cornell's *Sharing Nature with Children*. Of course, as Thomas Berry said, "Children have a natural bond of intimacy with every living thing." We believe this to be true, but we also see a drastic atrophying of the senses in today's media-saturated, sensory-bombarded childhoods. So Joseph's simple practices like blindfolded walks, expanding circles of awareness, and deep listening are fun and nurturing for kids (and adults, actually!).

Open Sentences of Gratitude

Open Sentences is a structure for spontaneous expression. It helps people listen with rare receptivity as well as speak their thoughts and feelings frankly. People sit in pairs, face to face and close enough to attend to each other fully. They refrain from speaking until the practice begins. One is Partner A, the other is Partner B. When the teacher speaks each unfinished sentence, A repeats it, completes it in her own words, addressing Partner B, and keeps on talking spontaneously for the time allotted. The partners can switch roles after each open sentence or at the end of the series. The listening partner—and this is to be emphasized—keeps silent, saying absolutely nothing and hearkening as attentively and supportively as possible. Demonstrate this for young children at the offset.

You may want to invent your own open sentences, or pick from these favorites of ours (#5 always comes last).

1. Some things I love about being alive right now are…
2. A place that is magical (or wonderful) to me is…
3. A person who helps me feel good about myself is…
4. Some things I enjoy doing and making are…
5. Some things I like about myself are…

The Human Camera

This practice, adapted by Pam Wood from the work of Cornell (1999), can be used with even very young children, in which case each little one should be paired with an adult or older child. One person is the photographer and the other is the camera. The photographers guide their cameras, who keep their eyes closed. The photographers search for beautiful and interesting photos, then point their camera's shutters (eyes) at the object or scene they want to "shoot" and press the shutter button to take the photo.

The photographer "presses the shutter button" by tapping the camera's shoulder once to open the camera's shutters. After three to five seconds, two taps tells the camera to close the shutters. Try creative shots: different angles, close-ups, panorama shots, etc. While taking photos, it's best to talk as little as possible. Give photographers about 10 minutes to take at least three photos.

Then the pairs switch roles. When everyone is finished, have each child draw a favorite "photo" they took as the camera on an index card. Share the photos in a group. Here are some debriefing questions:

> What did you notice?
> Which did you like better, being the human camera, or the photographer?
> What will you remember the most?

Stage Two: Honoring Our Pain for the World

In honoring our pain, and daring to experience it, we learn the true meaning of compassion: to "suffer with." We begin to know the immensity of our heart-mind. What had isolated us in private anguish now opens outward and delivers us into the wider reaches of our collective existence. In this stage of the Spiral, we bring to awareness our inner responses to the suffering of our fellow-beings and the destruction of the natural world—responses that include dread, rage, sorrow, and guilt. These feelings are healthy, normal under the circumstances, and inevitable, and we often usually block or bury these feelings for fear of getting permanently mired in despair. Now they are allowed to surface without shame or apology.

Note the term "allowed to surface." We do *not* try to inspire or instill these feelings in anyone else, because compassion—the capacity to suffer with—already flows in us, like an underground river. All we do here is help that river come to the light of day, where its currents mingle and gain momentum.

This stage of the Spiral brings special challenges when working with children. Here we really have to address the question of how to protect our children's basic security and safety (at the base of Maslow's "hierarchy of needs") while being truthful with them about the state of the world. Megan Toben (2014) asks, "What is developmentally appropriate information regarding the various crises for different age groups?" and answers in this way:

> I've certainly tempered the industrial growth story quite a lot for little ones. Mostly what we say is that humans haven't been taking care of the Earth in the best ways, and now we're realizing it and changing our practices so that we are doing better. The kids usually have a pretty good sense of this, mostly through media themes (*Wall-E, Avatar, Ferngully, Captain Planet*, etc.) and want to be a part of the shift.

When working with children, many of the adult practices for Honoring Our Pain are helpful with minor adaptations, offering children the opportunity to safely express the feelings and concerns they *already* carry within them. Here are a few of these practices.

Open Sentences

Here are two versions of Open Sentences for *Honoring Our Pain*, following the procedures outlined above.

I.   Teachers, you may want to work with sentences like these in preparation of working with children:
   1. *If I withhold from children my concerns for the future, I do so because...*
   2. *If I tell the children my concerns for the future, I do so because...*
   3. *In talking with children about the news, what I want is...*

II. With children, you can use sentences like the following:
   1. *One time I felt really glad to be alive was...*
   2. *Something in the world that makes me feel sad or angry is...*
   3. *One way I help take care of our world is...*

Truth Mandala with Children

This ritual provides a simple, respectful, whole group structure for owning and honoring our pain for the world.

Seat everyone, including the teacher, in a close circle, either in chairs or on the floor. Objects can be placed within the circle to represent various feelings: a hard stone for fear, a sturdy stick for anger, dead leaves for sadness, and an empty bowl for numbness or not knowing what to do. If you use the stick, demonstrate that it should be grasped firmly, not waved around or used to hit anything.

Invite children to move into the circle—one at a time—to share their feelings about what's going on in their world that troubles them. They may pick up the object that represents their feelings as they speak. As each person finishes sharing, the others may say, "We hear you," or "We're with you." After demonstrating the process, the teacher sits with the group, and may enter again as a group member. When everyone who wants to share has had a chance to do so, the teacher can call the Truth Mandala to a close by suggesting the group hum or chant or sing a familiar song.

Here are two stories about using the Truth Mandala with children, demonstrating how objects can help children share feelings about anything on their minds and hearts. The first story from Elizabeth Koelsch-Inderst (2014), a social worker in Germany, involves a very small group of boys.

> I did the Truth Mandala in the woods with three boys whose family is in my care. We gathered sticks, stones, leaves and berries, and I explained how we do it: *We say what makes us sad, express our anger, talk about our fears, and whatever else is on our mind.* We also agreed that after each one spoke we would say, "We'll help you."
>
> After some hesitation and giggling at the beginning, each boy went into the Mandala.
>
> C is sad because he has no friends. He picks up the stick and is about to cry when he says, "Mama hits me. I'm so mad at her."
>
> D says, "I still wet my bed without knowing I'm doing it. I'm so ashamed."
>
> And P, the youngest, says, "Papa promised me a cat I could take care of and talk to. And I never got my cat. I'm so sad."
>
> D goes again into the middle, and he says he gets really scared at night and can't sleep when everything is all dark.
>
> C also returns to the middle and says that he's a bad boy and stupid.
>
> We ended the Truth Mandala together; the children cleaned up the sticks, leaves and stones. We then thought about how we would help each other deal with the various issues that had come up. We spoke about courage and joy and about our hopes. Although we hadn't solved our problems, we emerged from the woods laughing and in wonderful spirits.
>
> Since that afternoon the children have been more open with me and speak about what's on their minds. It's almost as if we four had experienced a mystery together in the woods.

Eva Schilcher (2014), dance and eco-therapist also from Germany, tells a story of a Truth Mandala she conducted with twelve kids, nine and ten years old, along with their teachers in an after-school program.

> The teachers in this after-school program had been changed four times within a year without explanation or a chance to say goodbye. When two new teachers arrived to take charge, the children reacted with resistance, rejection, disrespect and aggression. Everyone was at a loss as to how to handle the situation.

To this new team I suggested a Truth Mandala, to give the children a chance to express and understand their emotions, while at the same time letting the adults acknowledge their distress.

The children were alert and attentive as I explained the ritual. Many strong emotions surfaced, expressing pain in their personal lives, such as moving from another city or country, losing friends and beloved caregivers, along with anger at schools and teachers, with also some anxiety about the new team. Sometimes the anger tipped over into sadness. It all bubbled and boiled like a cook pot on the stove. Some wanted to talk and be heard over and over again. Then came laughter and also some uncertainty. I had to remember the rule that we never know how the Truth Mandala will end. Unfortunately the time was limited (by the scheduled hour for homework), so we ended the ritual with the possibility that the children could speak their feelings later and also write them down. Afterwards they made a poster with their recommendations for the future.

The next day the majority of the group was far more relaxed. Children and teachers could see each other in a fresh way, and they interacted with more ease and respect in the following weeks and months—and have continued to grow together for this last half year.

Stage Three: Seeing with New Eyes

We move into the third stage of the Spiral as we realize from personal experience that it is from our connectivity that our pain for the world arises. The very distress that, when we hide it, appears to separate us from other people, now uncovers our connective tissue. This realization, whether it comes in a flash of insight or a gradual dawning, is a turning point in our perceptions. We shift to a new way of seeing ourselves and a new way of understanding our power.

The approach to many ancient temples is guarded by ferocious figures. In facing them down, in moving through our dreads and griefs, we gain entry to the truth that awaits us. We discover our mutual belonging and the promise that it holds for us. Now we can see in our anguish for the world the good news of a larger consciousness at work; it is the universe knowing itself through us. This shift in perception is an inner revolution which religious traditions call *metanoia*—turning around. At the same time, this turning appears as a new paradigm anchored in holistic science. A teacher may not be able to explain this to small children, but it helps to carry this deeper understanding as you work with them.

The Web of Life

In a silent circle, people toss balls of yarn to one another, looping the yarn loosely around their wrists before tossing it to the next person. They toss the balls randomly, without any particular pattern, to people anywhere in the circle. Once the web is complete, the teacher can make observations like the following:

> All of existence is an interconnected web, and we are part of it. Notice how strong it is when we're all holding our strand. Notice how what happens in one place affects the whole web. Notice what happens to the web if one strand is hurt or weakened.
>
> Some people only care about people who are like them or the places near them. This web shows why we care about people who are like us *and* people who are different from us. It is why we need to care about the places on earth near us *and* far from us. We need all kinds of different people, different kinds of life, for the web to be strong. Our destiny is interconnected with the destiny of all people and all forms of life on our planet.

The Evolutionary Gifts of the Animals (Eco-Milling)

Using their own bodies, children learn about our kinship with other life forms, and the debt of gratitude we owe to those who first invented key features of our anatomy. This process can be conducted as a Milling in which people mill around and then partner with someone new for each section, without speaking. At each encounter, the children are directed to pay attention to a particular biological feature that they all share. They are asked to note it in the person before them, to sense the wonder of this gift, and to honor the animal ancestor that bequeathed it. Here are features we tend to take for granted as "our own." They are really gifts from other and ancient beings.

If children find the Milling too challenging, they can stand in a circle and notice each biological feature in their own bodies. Adapt the language below to make sense to your students.

The blood stream. Can you feel the pulse in your partner's wrist? Blood is circulating. That capacity common to all life forms arose with the first multicelled creatures who devised ways to transfer nutrients to their inside cells. As they developed, some of them invented a muscular pump, a heart. That pulsing you feel is the gift of ancient, great-grandmother worm.

The spinal column. Feel the bones in the neck, the back. Those vertebrae are separate, but ingeniously linked. They cover the central neural cord and, at the same time, allow flexibility of movement. Grandfather fish did the design work, because he couldn't swim if his backbone were one solid piece. We can thank him for this marvel that now permits us to stand and walk.

The ear. Hum in your partner's ear; ah, you can hear each other! That's because tiny bones vibrate in the inner ear, and that is a gift from ancestor fish as well. They were once his jawbones and they migrated into the mammalian ear to carry sound.

The limbic brain. Inside the base of the skull lives the limbic region of the brain, a gift from our reptilian grandmothers and grandfathers. It allows deep pleasure. It also allows us to protect ourselves by fighting, fleeing, or freezing stock still.

Binocular vision. See the eyes are no longer on the sides of the head, as with our fish and reptile cousins, many birds, and some mammals. Our tree-climbing primate ancestors moved their eyes around to the front, to function together for three-dimensional vision, so they could know the exact location and distance of a branch to leap for. We thank them for our binocular vision.

Hand. And see how the thumb and fingertips can touch each other; see the size of the space they enclose. That's just the right size for a branch able to hold your swinging body. Grandmother monkey designed that hand. And the branch was designed by sun and wind and gravity, as well as grandfather tree himself as he grew high to reach the light, and limber to allow the wind. So we, with these hands, are grandchildren of tree and sun and wind as well.

The Robot Game

A slightly slapstick illustration of the mechanistic world view we're leaving behind us, the Robot Game is fun to use toward the end of a day's session, when no more serious work is expected.

Children form groups of three, and two children play the role of robots. The robots can only walk straight ahead, like a machine without a steering wheel. They cannot change direction when they reach an obstacle—a wall, a person, or another solid object; but like a motor that can't turn itself off, they keep on moving their legs and arms in place. Stuck in the "on" position, like a positive feedback loop, they are unable to stop chugging away, with danger of overheating and collapse. The third person, the manager, is charged with keeping these mechanisms from running amok, and the only way to do this is by changing their direction of movement. This is achieved by tapping them on the nose: a tap on the left nostril to turn them to the right, and a tap on the right nostril to go left.

The game starts with the two robots standing back to back. At a signal from the guide, the manager sets the two mechanisms in motion by tapping the tips of their noses simultaneously. Off they go in opposite directions, and their manager has to be alert and quick to keep them from stalling at an obstacle and burning out. The game is over when the teacher blows a whistle or when a lot of the robots are overheated. By this time everyone knows something about the limits of a machine—or is too weak from laughter to care.

Stage Four: Going Forth

Open Sentences for Going Forth

Open Sentences such as the following can be used to open up this stage. Responses can be shared in pairs or small groups of three, with each person completing the sentence in turn.

1. One really interesting thing I learned today about the web of life [or _____] was...
2. One change I'd like to make in my daily life that will help care for the Earth is...
3. Something I can do in my community to help the Earth is...

Starfish Story and Ritual

Pass out starfish-shaped pieces of heavy card stock or cardboard. Then tell the Starfish Story as follows (rather than reading it).

> *The Starfish Story* (adapted from "The Star Thrower" by Loren Eiseley [1979])
>
> *Once upon a time, there was a wise man who used to go to the ocean to do his writing. He had a habit of walking on the beach before he began his work.*
>
> *One day, as he was walking along the shore, he looked down the beach and saw a person moving in an unusual way—bending down and then reaching up in an arc. Was it a dancer? He walked faster to catch up.*
>
> *As he got closer, he saw person was a boy. He was not dancing at all. The boy was reaching down to the shore, picking up small objects, and throwing them into the ocean. The man came closer still and called out "Good morning! May I ask what it is that you are doing?"*
>
> *The boy paused, looked up, and replied "Throwing starfish into the ocean." "Why are you throwing starfish into the ocean?" asked the somewhat startled wise man. To this, boy replied, "The sun is up and the tide is going out. If I don't throw them in, they'll die."*
>
> *Upon hearing this, the wise man commented, "But, do you not realize that there are miles and miles of beach and there are starfish all along every mile? You can't possibly make a difference!"*
>
> *At this, the boy bent down, picked up yet another starfish, and threw it into the ocean. As it met the water, he said, "It made a difference for that one."*

After telling the story, designate an area that is the "beach" and an expanse that is the "ocean." Have each child write or draw a picture on their starfish to represent one thing they already do or will do for the Great Turning. When everyone is ready, each child says a few words about what they wrote on their starfish, and then throws it "back in the ocean." Each time, everyone says together: "We made a difference to that one!"

References

Becker, S. (2013/2014). Helping little people cope with the world's big problems. *The Center Post*, p. 15. Retrieved June 24, 2014, from www.rowecenter.org/upload/docs/ROWE-CPFall&Winter2013.pdf.

Chivian, E., et al. (1988). American and Soviet teenagers' concerns about nuclear war and the future. *The New England Journal of Medicine, 319*(7), 407–413.

Cornell, J. (1999). *Sharing nature with children II.* Nevada City, CA: Dawn Publications.

Eiseley, L. (1979). *The star thrower.* New York: Harcourt Brace & Co. (A Harvest Book).

Koelsch-Inderst, E. (February 2014). Email to authors.

Macy, J., & Brown, M. (2014). Coming back to life. Gabriola Island, British Columbia: New Society Publishers.

Schilcher, E. (2014). Email to authors.

Toben, M. (March 2014). Pickards Mountain Eco-Institute, North Carolina. Email to authors.

UNICEF-UK (2013). Poll: British children concerned by effects of climate change. Retrieved June 26, 2014, from unicef.org.uk/Latest/New/British-Children-deeply-concerned-by-effects-of-climate-change-/.

19

PREPARING CHILDREN FOR THE EMOTIONAL CHALLENGES OF CLIMATE CHANGE

A Review of the Research

Maria Ojala

Polar bears standing on shrinking ice floes. Children from developing countries starving because of prolonged drought. Hurricanes and flooding hitting communities close by. These are just a few images that young people are confronted with when media report about global climate change and its consequences. Besides media reporting, young people hear about climate change in school and to some extent through discussions with friends and family. How do young people cope with the emotions that are evoked by this alarming information? How are coping strategies related to feelings of empowerment, environmental engagement, and well-being? What can teachers and other adults do to promote hope and engagement concerning this problem? These are some questions that I address in this chapter. The focus will be on children in late childhood, young people who are around 10 to 12 years old. In many ways, this is an ideal time to seriously begin educating young people about global problems. Children in this age group have started to acquire the capacity for abstract thinking (Evenshaug & Hallen, 2001). At the same time, many older elementary-aged students are beginning to show greater sustained interest in the larger world and its problems (Holden, 2007).

Studies suggest that many young people are worried about environmental problems and pessimistic about the global future (Connell et al., 1999; Holden, 2007; Kelsey & Armstrong, 2012; Taber & Taylor, 2009; for a review see Ojala, 2016). In this chapter, I argue that it is important for teachers to be mindful of their students' emotions and coping strategies concerning climate change in order to promote a constructive learning environment, student engagement, and hope. First, I describe a portion of the research literature on how children cope with emotions concerning climate change. Thereafter, I propose several strategies for teachers to support children in response to this global concern.

Children's Emotions in Relation to Climate Change

When educating about climate change, it is not enough to focus exclusively on knowledge as facts. It is necessary to acknowledge that climate change is an existential, moral, and political problem (see Wals & Corcoran, 2012). Its existential character has to do with the complexity and seriousness of the problem; it concerns the future survival of our planet and of humankind. In addition, the Western way of life is often said to be a main cause of climate change. At the same time, initially at least, the consequences of climate change will primarily fall on people living in poorer countries, future generations, and nature (Gardiner & Hartzell-Nichols, 2012). Thus, the climate threat is also a moral and ethical problem. In addition, climate change is intertwined with overarching societal structures. It could be stressful, especially for young people, to take personal responsibility for problems that fundamentally need to be handled at a political and societal level.

How then do children deal with this complexity? Research from different countries shows that young people perceive climate change as a major concern, and anxiety is a common emotional response (Connell et al., 1999; Holden, 2007; Kelsey & Armstrong, 2012; Taber & Taylor, 2009; for a review see Ojala, 2016). Children worry about pollution from cars and factories, flooding, and hurricanes, for example. Often, children's worry is other-oriented: i.e., about other people's and animals' well-being (Threadgold, 2012; see also Ojala, 2016). Worry can be a catalyst for taking action if dealt with in a constructive proactive manner (Ojala, 2007; Taber & Taylor, 2009). However, it is more problematic that feelings of pessimism concerning climate change and the global future (and cynicism about the adult world) emerge in late childhood and then seem to increase until the late teenage years (Kelsey & Armstrong, 2012; Ojala, 2012b). Young people are, however, not only passive victims of whatever they learn and hear about climate change. They also actively cope with this knowledge and related feelings. These ways of coping are important when it comes to aspects such as learning processes, a feeling of self-efficacy, environmental engagement, and psychological well-being. Hence, it is vital to understand how young people go about coping with the now pervasive problem of climate change.

Emotion-Focused Coping

A model that could be of use in order to understand how children deal with both self-oriented and other-oriented emotions in relation to climate change is the transactional model of coping. In its original form, this model distinguished between two main ways of coping: emotion-focused coping and problem-focused coping (Lazarus & Folkman, 1984). When people use emotion-focused coping, they concentrate on negative emotions and try to get rid of them with the help of various coping strategies, rather than trying to do something about the problem. For example, to get rid of a negative emotion, one can simply deny the problem, distance oneself from the emotion, or use social support to cope.

Research has shown that some young people *de-emphasize* the seriousness of climate change, doing this in at least two ways (Ojala 2012b): first, by *denying* that climate change is a serious problem, which is not that common among 11- and 12-year-olds; and, second, by engaging in *here-and-now thinking*, which is somewhat more common among children in this age group. In here-and-now thinking, children do not deny that there is a problem, but they distance themselves emotionally by claiming that the problem does not affect them and, therefore, is not worth worrying about (Ojala, 2012b; Pettersson, 2014). These children may assert that their immediate local community is a safe place to live in and that the negative consequences will only be visible in a distant future and/or effect other people living in less affluent countries. Instead of evoking empathy, the distant character of the climate threat seems to inhibit emotional engagement among these children.

Studies performed in Sweden show that young people who use de-emphasizing strategies to cope with climate change tend to feel that they cannot influence environmental problems and they are also less environmentally engaged than those who do not use these strategies (Ojala, 2012a, 2013). In addition, if children observe their parents denying the seriousness of climate change, this also seems to lead to the use of de-emphasizing strategies among young people (Ojala, 2015).

A more common emotion-focused strategy among children is to distance oneself from negative emotions (Ojala, 2012b; Pettersson, 2014). One distancing strategy is *distraction*, in which children, when feeling worried, think of something besides climate change (cognitive distraction), or they try to distract themselves by doing something else (behavioral distraction) such as talking to a friend, eating ice cream, or watching television. *Avoidance* is another strategy where the children either deliberately avoid thinking about the climate threat (cognitive avoidance) or avoid information about climate change by, for instance, walking away from the television when news about the climate problem is broadcasted, or looking the other way when a lot of traffic outside makes them think about climate change (behavioral avoidance).

Among adults, distancing strategies are often viewed as dysfunctional because they lead to disengagement. However, for children, distancing may be a reasonable strategy due to the fact that young people have even less control over this enormous global issue than adults (Taber & Taylor, 2009). Young people's use of distancing to deal with climate worries could also to a certain extent reflect their frustration and cynicism with adults' inability to address this global concern (Connell et al., 1999; Pettersson, 2014).

In addition, some children use *social support* to regulate their emotions about climate change (Ojala, 2012b; Pettersson, 2014). They may talk to other people, such as parents and friends, about their concerns, or they just seek the company of others in order to feel calmer. As one child told me in an interview, "Sometimes, I lay in bed at night and worry, then I go down and see my mom and dad." Still, talking with other people about climate worries is not a particularly common coping strategy among children (see Ojala, 2012b). Studies show that people of all ages do worry about this problem, but they tend to avoid public display of negative emotions perhaps because of social rules about emotional expression. Young people may feel social pressure to remain "cool" around issues of global warming, especially when the larger public discourse reflects a silence about this issue (Norgaard, 2011).

Problem-Focused Coping

Children also use problem-focused coping to deal with negative emotions in relation to climate change. When using problem-focused coping, people focus on the problem and work to directly address or solve it, thereby indirectly alleviating the negative emotions. Although not as common as the emotion-focused coping strategy of distancing, problem-focused strategies are still routinely used by children (Ojala, 2012b; Pettersson, 2014). Some of these coping strategies are of a cognitive character. Children think, search for information, and talk with others about what they can do to fight climate change. When feeling worried, some children also engage in concrete actions of a pro-environmental nature. Examples of these actions include biking or walking to school instead of asking their parents to drive them; asking parents to buy eco-labeled products; and making energy-saving changes in their household.

Children who use cognitive problem-focused strategies to handle climate change are more inclined to feel that they can exert influence on climate change, and they also perform more concrete pro-environmental actions (Ojala, 2012a). However, cognitive problem-focused strategies are sometimes associated with lower psychological well-being among children and teenagers (Ojala, 2012a; Ojala, 2013). The reason may be that these strategies are limited to the behavior of the individual. Young people seldom report collective engagement (i.e., working collaboratively, in groups, to effect social change) (Ojala, 2012b, Pettersson, 2014). Individual problem-focused coping can lead to children's isolation and, given the enormous challenges of climate change, it makes sense that this type of coping could undermine children's overall mental outlook. Psychological research shows that when a problem is more or less impossible for the individual to cope with alone, problem-focused coping could lead to anxiety or depression (Clarke, 2006).

Meaning-Focused Coping

In recent years the transactional model of coping has been complemented with a third main coping strategy, meaning-focused coping (Folkman, 2008; Folkman & Moskowitz, 2000). Meaning-focused coping is especially important when a problem cannot be solved right away but still requires or invites active involvement, such as when people have to deal with chronic diseases. Meaning-focused coping entails activating positive feelings such as hope that can enhance psychological well-being (Folkman, 2008). This way of coping can also help people confront the sources of their negative feelings, thereby promoting active engagement. However, the concept of meaning-focused coping has not been used to explore how people deal with societal or global problems.

Ojala (2012b) asked 11- to 12-year-old children not only how they coped with worry about climate change, but also how they went about finding or experiencing hope. She found that they used meaning-focused strategies of positive reappraisal, trust in different societal actors, and drawing on existential hope. *Having trust*, for example, derives from confidence that scientists or engineers will come up with new inventions and technologies or that governments will take meaningful action to address climate change. Trust in science is an especially common coping strategy among children. *Positive reappraisal* is about admitting that climate change is a serious problem while, at the same time, being able to reframe one's perspective. This reappraisal can activate positive emotions, such as hope. Positive reappraisal includes acknowledging the climate problem while also recognizing positive trends; reflecting on the huge increases in societal knowledge about climate change; and actively searching for positive news in the media. However, 11- to 12-year-olds do not use positive reappraisal as often as older youth. This can be due to the fact that the younger children have not yet developed the cognitive maturity that is needed to consider, simultaneously, both positive and negative trends when it comes to climate change (see Ojala, 2012b). Instead some children in this age group draw on sources of *existential hope* with which they, for example, may argue that one just needs to be hopeful concerning climate change although it is a serious problem; otherwise there is no meaning in doing anything.

Studies have found that meaning-focused coping and feelings of hope are effective in helping children mitigate emotional stress in relation to climate change (Ojala, 2005, 2012a). Furthermore, children who use a lot of problem-focused coping can sustain positive psychological well-being if they combine these strategies with meaning-focused coping strategies of positive reappraisal and trust (Ojala, 2012a). Importantly, meaning-focused coping also is related to more environmental engagement among young people (Ojala, 2012a, 2013).

Helping Children Deal with the Emotional Challenges of Climate Change: Teaching Strategies

Scholars argue that it is important to give children the opportunity to reflect on climate change–related emotions such as worry, fear, and anger (see Hicks, 2014; Kelsey & Armstrong, 2012; Ojala, 2007). Many children do worry about climate change but most tend to remain silent about these concerns. Research suggests that reflection on negative emotions (through writing, drama, or art, for example), especially in socially supportive settings, can lead to increased feelings of control, and thereby can help prevent worry or anxiety from devolving into despair and depression (MacGregor, 1991). Through the many types of reflection typically found in elementary classrooms, children's feelings related to climate change can be brought to the surface and examined, including personal values associated with these feelings (Ojala, 2007). For instance, what is the responsibility of countries that have emitted the most carbon to compensate the countries least responsible? How much should we sacrifice or give up (e.g., material possessions) to help support a livable planet? How important is the health of the natural world when compared to economic interests?

When children express strong emotions about social issues, including climate change, teachers may not know how to respond; they may ignore or dismiss children's expressions. Children may experience teachers' silence as a dismissal or marginalization of the validity of their emotions. One study shows that teenagers who perceived their teachers as not taking their emotions seriously concerning societal problems, and who felt that their teachers might respond humorously or even derisively if they expressed them in the classroom, were more inclined to engage in de-emphasizing strategies than teenagers who felt that their teachers respected and validated their emotions (Ojala, 2015b). Thus, there seems to be a relationship between the emotions rules that teachers enforce and the coping strategies that young people use. In addition, Ojala found that boys believed that their teachers were more dismissive of their negative emotions than they were to the negative emotions of girls, which explained why boys, more than girls, de-emphasized the seriousness of climate change. Hence, it is vital for teachers to reflect on how they react to negative emotions of children and to think about whether they might be treating students differently.

Researchers have also pointed to *the importance of discussing future dimensions* in the classroom in order to promote hope concerning global problems (Hicks, 2014). A recent study showed that when teachers included future dimensions in their lessons, young people were more inclined to feel constructive hope concerning climate change as well as being more engaged in pro-environmental behaviors in their personal lives (Ojala, 2015b). Thus, teachers should devote more time to the discussion of probable, preferable, and possible futures in a creative, critical, honest, and constructive manner (again, using multiple ways of expression: drama, art, poetry, etc.) (see Hicks, 2014). In discussing these different futures, it is important to show connections between global futures, on the one hand, and personal and local community futures, on the other hand. This is due to the fact that young people often view personal and global futures as separate, and this may be one reason that young people are not more actively engaged in global problems (Threadgold, 2012). In order to address the difficulty that some 10- to 12-year-old children have in feeling anything concerning climate change due to its distant character, perspective-taking practices can be useful (see Pahl & Bauer, 2011). By working with art, literature, and drama, children can learn about the situations of people living in other parts of the world and how future generations will be affected by climate change.

Working with visions of preferable futures, teachers might ask: "How does a low-carbon society 25 years from now look like?" It is vital to acknowledge that young people will not necessarily agree upon how a preferable future should look (see Hicks, 2014). In addition, it is important to discuss ethical and value issues about what constitutes a just and fair future society (Wals & Corcoran, 2012).

It is important to help young learners compare the "probable" with the "preferable" and come up with realistic "possible" futures; this includes discussing concrete pathways (both societal and individual) to this possible future and promoting agency so that young people can take active part in these pathways. Late childhood is a critical time since it is in this period that many young people develop understandings that private engagement and technical solutions will perhaps be inadequate to fully address climate change and, therefore, "unrealistic hope" could backfire and lead to cynicism and disengagement (see Pettersson, 2014). Consequently, teachers should combine utopian and critical perspectives and "simultaneously create images of what could be possible while exploring and documenting the actual limits imposed by the current system" (Burton, 1983, p. 67).

In order to be able to look realistically at the future and to be able to acknowledge and face one's concerns, *encouraging the two dimensions of meaning-focused coping—positive reappraisal and trust*—is important. In promoting positive reappraisal, one needs to help children simultaneously reflect on both problems (concerns) and progress (hope) concerning climate change: to acknowledge the problems, but to also identify possibilities for change. In this regard, teachers can take into account research about ways to promote flexible thinking and hope about other more mundane problems (e.g., relationship issues) (Cunningham et al., 2002; Gillham & Reivich, 2004). Teachers can help students evaluate their own self-talk. If their view of the global future is very pessimistic, then teachers might ask students, "Is this really the only way to think about it?" Teachers can challenge their students to generate alternative interpretations of any experience. "Are there any positive aspects to focus on? Throughout history, how has humanity solved severe and seemingly unsolvable problems?" Sharing success stories could be one way to work with this dimension in the classroom (see Hicks, 2014).

It is also important for teachers to help students to reflect on trust concerning different societal actors. Teachers can invite guest speakers to the classroom who have long worked on issues related to the environment and climate change and who can share stories of their own persistence in the face of challenges (Colby et al., 2007). Ideally these people should represent various sectors of society: municipal government, business, science, and non-governmental agencies. It is important that these speakers share in a concrete manner how they work with these issues and also how they deal with frustration and failure.

Teachers could also consider engaging children in place-based curriculum that also involves an action dimension, in which children *engage with the community* (school or city) to try to solve or address some problem or issue. Collective engagement seems to be more related to hope and to well-being than more individual pro-environmental behaviors (for reviews see Kelsey & Armstrong, 2012; Winograd, this volume). We should teach children *how* to engage effectively in the local civic process, and this will be shaped by the kinds of issues children pursue, such as cleaning up a local stream or writing letters to the city council about a safety concern in the neighborhood.

Finally, it is also important to show children that living in a sustainable manner does not only require sacrifice (giving up). Living more sustainably, like reducing consumption, could lead to a more fulfilling life, evoking greater positive emotions and happiness. An important part of sustainable living is to create close and respectful relations to other humans and the natural world, and research has shown that just and caring relationships are the most important sources of happiness (Damon, 2008; Seligman, 2002). To do something that goes beyond oneself by working for society and nature is related to psychological well-being, increased altruism, and hope concerning the future (Damon, 2008). Thus, to connect with nature and to learn to love and respect all living beings should be an explicit part of educating for hope concerning the myriad of environmental challenges facing humanity.

References

Burton, M. (1983). Understanding mental health services: Theory and practice. *Critical Social Policy, 7*, 54–74.

Clarke, A.T. (2006). Coping with interpersonal stress and psychosocial health among children and adolescents: A meta-analysis. *Journal of Youth and Adolescence, 35*(1), 11–24.

Colby, A., Beaumont, E., Ehrlich, T., & Corngold, J. (2007). *Educating for democracy*. San Fransisco, CA: Jossey-Bass.

Connell, S., Fien, J., Lee, J., Sykes, H., & Yencken, D. (1999). 'If it doesn't directly affect you, you don't think about it': A qualitative study of young people's environmental attitudes in two Australian cities. *Environmental Education Research, 5*(1), 95–114.

Cunningham, E. G., Brandon, C. M., Frydenberg, E. (2002). Enhancing coping resources in early adolescence through a school-based program teaching optimistic thinking skills. *Anxiety, Stress, and Coping, 15*(4), 369–381.

Damon, W. (2008). *The path to purpose. How young people find their calling in life*. New York: Free Press.

Evenshaug, O., & Hallen, D. (2001). *Barn- och ungdomspsykologi [Child, and youth psychology]*. Lund: Studentlitteratur.

Folkman, S. (2008). The case for positive emotions in the stress process. *Anxiety, Stress & Coping: An International Journal, 21*(1), 3–14.

Folkman, S., & Moskowitz, J.T. (2000). Positive affect and the other side of coping. *American Psychologist, 55*(6), 647–654.

Gardiner, S. M., & Hartzell-Nichols, L. (2012). Ethics and global climate change. *Nature Education Knowledge, 3*(10), 5.

Gillham, J., & Reivich, K. (2004). Cultivating optimism in childhood and adolescence. *Annals of the American Academy of Political and Social Science, 591*, 146–163.

Hicks, D. (2014). *Educating for hope in troubled times: Climate change and the transition to a post-carbon future*. London: Trentham Books.

Holden, C. (2007). Young people's concerns. In D. Hicks & C. Holden (Eds.), *Teaching the global dimension: Key principles and effective practice* (pp. 31–42). New York: Routledge.

Kelsey, E., & Armstrong, C. (2012). Finding hope in a world of catastrophe. In A. Wals & P. Corcoran (Eds.), *Learning for Sustainability in Times of Accelerating Change* (pp. 187–200). Wageningen, The Netherlands: Wageningen Academic Publisher.

Lazarus, R. S., & Folkman, S. (1984). *Stress, appraisal, and coping.* New York: Springer Publishing Company.

MacGregor, D. (1991). Worry over technological activities and life concerns. *Risk Analysis, 11*(2), 315–324.

Norgaard, K. M. (2011). *Living in denial: Climate change, emotions, and everyday life.* Cambridge: The MIT Press.

Ojala, M. (2005). Adolescents' worries about environmental risks: Subjective well-being, values, and existential dimensions. *Journal of Youth Studies, 8*(3), 331–348.

Ojala, M. (2007). *Hope and worry: Exploring young people's values, emotions, and behavior regarding global environmental problems.* Örebro Studies in Psychology 11. Örebro University.

Ojala, M. (2012a). How do children cope with global climate change? Coping strategies, engagement, and well-being. *Journal of Environmental Psychology, 32,* 225–233.

Ojala, M. (2012b). Regulating worry, promoting hope: How do children, adolescents, and young adults cope with climate change? *International Journal of Environmental and Science Education, 7*(4), 537–561.

Ojala, M. (2013). Coping with climate change among adolescents: Implications for subjective well-being and environmental engagement. *Sustainability, 5*(5), 2191–2209.

Ojala, M. (2015). Climate change skepticism among adolescents. *Journal of Youth Studies, 18*(9), 1135–1153.

Ojala, M. (2015b). Hope in the face of climate change: Associations with environmental engagement and student perceptions of teachers' emotion communication style and future orientation. *Journal of Environmental Education, 46*(3), 133–148.

Ojala, M. (2016). Young people and global climate change: Emotions, coping, and engagement in everyday life. T. Skelton, N. Ansell & N. Klocker (Eds.), *Geographies of children and young people handbook.* Volume 8: Geographies of global issues, change and threat. Springer. *Accepted.*

Pahl, S., & Bauer, J. (2011). Overcoming the distance: Perspective taking with future humans improves environmental engagement. *Environment and Behavior, 45*(2), 155–169.

Pettersson, A. (2014). *"De som inte kan simma kommer nog att dö!" En studie om barns tankar och känslor rörande klimatförändringarna* [*"Those who cannot swim will most probably die!" A study about children's thoughts and emotions concerning climate change*]. Uppsala, Sweden: Uppsala Universitet, Forskarskolan i Geografi.

Seligman, M. E. P. (2002). *Authentic happiness: Using the new positive psychology to realize your potential for lasting fulfillment.* New York: Free Press.

Taber, F., & Taylor, N. (2009). Climate of concern—A search for effective strategies for teaching children about global warming. *International Journal of Environmental & Science Education, 4*(2), 97–116.

Threadgold, S. (2012). "I reckon my life will be easy, but my kids will be buggered": Ambivalence in young people's positive perceptions of individual futures and their visions of environmental collapse. *Journal of Youth Studies, 5,* 17–32.

Wals, A., & Corcoran, P. (2012). Re-orienting, re-connecting, and re-imagining: Learning-based responses to the challenge of unsustainability. In A. Wals & P. Corcoran (Eds.), *Learning for sustainability in times of accelerating change* (pp. 21–32). Wageningen, The Netherlands: Wageningen Academic Publisher.

20

RESCUING THE EARTH THROUGH SMALL WORLD PLAY

Sharon Witt and Helen Clarke

Playful pedagogy is a powerful way to develop children's deep understanding of our complex and dynamic earth. This chapter is forward thinking and future centred, and positions elementary children as powerful problem solvers who can readily take an active role in supporting local communities during times of climatic disruption. It illustrates how children can explore and build capability and suggests implications for educators in their encounters with children. An enabling outlook, enacted through a storied approach to disaster, risk reduction, and emergency education, leads to a proactive response to climate change that builds emotional and practical resilience. This chapter offers practical ideas including a model to support planning, which is illustrated through school-based case studies.

A Focus on Weather Disruption Rather than Climatic Catastrophe

Climate change is complex, challenging, and controversial. Due to our profound dependence on nature, climate change shakes the security of the human sense of being at a basic level and can elicit a doom-laden, catastrophising approach (Weintrobe, 2013). This can be overwhelming for teachers when working with elementary children, so it is essential to work through such anxieties and take a developmentally appropriate approach to this topic for young learners. Sobel (2008) urges educators to consider developmental parameters in deciding how climate change education should be undertaken so that it is a meaningful part of children's educational experience and handled in an age appropriate and sensitive way. In an *eco-playful* pedagogy, this topic can be taught with openness and honesty, which respects local context and equips and empowers children for the future. Our focus is not on global catastrophe but on local, disruptive weather

FIGURE 20.1 In the event of an environmental challenge, 'Remember, don't panic!' (photograph courtesy of Sharon Witt and Helen Clarke).

events such as storms, floods, and snowfall, phenomena that are within the grasp of young children. In this way we are careful to "approach these questions from a perspective that maximises hope" (Sobel, 2008, p. 141) rather than hopelessness, and fosters strength not fear. Children tackle challenges with their own level of complexity and their responses guide teachers, whose decisions on how to teach this topic have significant impacts on learning and on life (e.g., see Figure 20.1).

A Matter of Scale: Teaching from the Local and Familiar

Teachers are experts on their own context, local situations, and children's experiences and interests. A focus on events that may happen within the locality, on an everyday scale, involving ordinary people enables children to explore their fears and fascinations in playful 'emergency' scenarios. These involve real-life situations to which communities can respond. Children need time and space to work through such challenges. To take the 'urgency out of an emergency,' teachers can offer learning experiences where both the scenario and the solution are accessible to children on a manageable scale and where the learners maintain agency.

Teacher-led scenarios can offer familiarity, yet challenge. Scenarios can present a situation that is within the child's experience to explore and on a scale where the children can affect a practical solution. As they achieve success and control in their contribution to events in the community, they develop as active citizens with a confident sense of responsibility. In this way, "We create opportunities to practice ecological behaviours as part of the classroom and school culture" (Sobel, 2008, p. 141). Curriculum design also positions teachers with considerable responsibility "to structure learning around questions and to claim time for students to explore, experiment and interpret. In inquiry-based learning, the teacher is a coach, problem poser and facilitator" (Demarest, 2015, p. 5). Climate change education requires such a sophisticated response.

Playfulness: Learning Not to Panic

Children have a right to inhabit the playful world of childhood. In an eco-playful approach, carefully structured and progressive experiences help children build personal meanings in real-life contexts and empower them to cope emotionally with local climatic challenges. Research and practice suggests that an eco-imaginative approach can foster encounters and relationships with natural and built environments that allow children to see different perspectives (Witt & Clarke, 2014) and suggest solutions often missed by adults. This approach to tackling climate change with elementary children is both cognitive and affective; it involves both the head and the heart. Learning about the environment demands knowledge of an array of 'big ideas' including understandings of place, people, scale, human–nature interactions, natural hazards, built environments, transport systems, materials, forces, and sustainability. Further, learning requires attention to a range of discipline-specific vocabulary and also subject-specific and core skills.

Our focus is on 'middle childhood' (Sobel, 2008), broadly the period from six to twelve years. This phase builds on the early explorations of kindergarten, where play is how very young children begin to make meaning of their world. This phase precedes later complexities, where teenage learners sort facts from opinions, explore ideas about bias and controversy, question motives, and make informed arguments. Middle childhood invites experiences that tap into feelings and offer shape and structure to educational experience. Here scenarios intertwine reality and fantasy. A playful approach by teachers invites participation and encourages sharing of thoughts and feelings.

Constructing Achievable Solutions

When teachers position elementary children as resilient problem solvers, the focus is on solutions rather than problems as they need "to explore examples of positive action for change" (Hicks, 2014, p. 122). Complex environmental events represent 'puzzles' for children to solve. These test learners' ingenuity in unique ways. These puzzles require children to use discovery, enquiry, and decision-making skills that encourage creative and critical thinking. Independent learning helps keep minds open. The ideas in this chapter give children opportunities to practice such skills in a risk-free environment and to rehearse solutions to complex events. Climate change is a dynamic issue and requires a flexible approach. Mental and emotional preparation ameliorates anxiety and builds emotional resilience. Rehearsal fosters a calm, measured response, which builds confidence and maintains well-being.

Small Worlds: Big Players

Small worlds are vehicles for teachers to support children in working through life's events. Small world play provides a "stimulating and meaningful context" which "excites, emboldens and empowers" and "gives children time to experiment, create and reflect" (Bromley, 2004, p. 1). Through using a small worlds approach, abstract ideas of climate change can be made accessible to classroom teachers and to elementary children. This holistic approach starts from "inside the child's world, recognising children's inherent fascinations with nature and with people, and then builds from these starting points to create sturdy community valued knowledge" (Sobel, 2008, p. 3). Although these stories may be of small proportions, "They provide cognitive accessibility because all the disparate elements of a place are brought into one view" (Sobel, 2008, p. 46). A seemingly mundane improvisation provides opportunities to imitate, symbolise, and imagine. Scenarios are brief tasters, glimpses of the future, to prompt discussion, thought and action. These can be "…designed to provide a series of different pictures of the future so we can explore ways in which the future might work out" (Hicks, 2014, p. 134). For many children, "Small world play will be a very significant experience indeed, offering them control over the miniature environment, and the opportunity to become deeply engaged" (Bromley, 2004, p. 1). As curriculum makers, teachers research, plan, and mediate a topic. Teachers know their children and follow their interests in ways that extend and complement the Common Core Standards in the creation of engaging, challenging, and empowering activities that position young children as agents of change.

A Process Planning Model: Responding to Environmental Challenge

The enquiry-based model in Table 20.1 has emerged over four years in our work with student teachers and children in local schools in the South of England, United Kingdom. The model is process-led rather than focused on pre-determined outcomes; it emerges from the children's ideas and is place responsive (see Table 20.1).

TABLE 20.1 A process planning model: Responding to environmental challenge

	Process	Key questions	Skills and attitudes
PARTICIPATION	Setting the scene and eliciting ideas	**Establishing context** Where is this place? What is this place like? What do we know about this place? What happens in this place? How do we feel about this place? How do we fit into this place?	observation questioning communication
	Creating a small world environment	**Place making** What is this landscape like? What sort of place is it? Who uses it? How is this place connected to other places?	modelling use of scale selection of materials decision making communication
	Posing a challenge	**Building awareness** What is the issue? Why is it an issue? Who might this event affect? What views, feelings, and attitudes do we have?	enquiry questioning empathy
	An event	**Participation in the event** How has the environment been affected? How has the landscape changed? What is the effect on the local people and wildlife? What is the effect on the built environment?	cause and effect role play simulation modelling
	Taking action in response to an event	**Proposing solutions** What views, feelings, and attitudes do the children have? What decisions will need to be taken to respond to the event? Who can take control? Whose responsibility is it?	analysis problem solving decision making empathy
	Positive outcomes	**Evaluating actions for a positive future** What happens to the environment now? How can we plan for a future environmental event?	evaluation problem solving resilience

This model aims:

- To invite children to explore complex scenarios in safe situations, which allow rehearsal of environmental change events.
- To create mini-worlds enabling children to articulate sophisticated responses.
- To construct a proactive response to climate change and sustainability practices that build emotional and practical resilience, through a storied approach to disaster, risk reduction, and emergency education.
- To encourage young children to ask deep questions and be involved in values-led education.

These aims may be used by teachers to inform learning intentions in their planning.

Focus of the Enquiry: Extreme Weather Events

Teachers can adapt such a model for a range of purposes. Here we consider extreme weather in the context of climatic disruption. A range of events could be considered including storms, drought, floods, snowfall, erosion, or other local phenomena. Various forms of disruption might ensue, for example, interruption to transport or power, damage to buildings, closure of services such as schools, shortages of water or food supply, and incidents of pollution. In each case, teachers use their professional judgement to help children to articulate their response in terms of feelings, ideas, questions, and attitudes.

Description of Practice: Using the Planning Model

The following school-based case studies illustrate the model in practice as student teachers work with 10- and 11-year-olds in a primary school in the South of England, United Kingdom. Activities included small world play with miniature figures, talk and recording through photography, animation, and cartoons. These creative and imaginative strategies motivated and inspired the children to engage with complex and challenging issues. Children were encouraged to create models and to engage in role play that developed empathy for, and understanding of, possible future scenarios within their own neighbourhood. These activities captured natural interest, created meaningful contexts, imitated and enacted events, developed narrative, elicited vocabulary, motivated collaborative enquiry, and developed skills of critical literacy. Each stage of the planning model is now considered in turn.

Description of Practice: Setting the Scene and Eliciting Ideas

Student teachers gave pupils opportunities to explore their school grounds. These included observations of natural and man-made environments, experiencing the elements, and reconnecting to significant places. Some children took miniature figures with them to seek a different view, to consider scale and perspective and to discuss scenarios (see Figures 20.2a and 20.2b). The practitioners respected the children as experts in their school environment and as learners with local knowledge.

Student teacher reflections:

> "There was a lot of earnest talk and close looking. The children were the guides in their school grounds; they took control, pointed out features, and showed ownership and belonging that they later applied in their small world scenarios."
>
> "Children 'tested' their grounds; they stood in the breeze, stamped on surfaces, collected natural materials …"
>
> "Children worked in small groups with adults; they jumped and stamped in embodied learning. And simultaneously they were involved in sophisticated talk."

Description of Practice: Creating a Small World Environment

Pupils were invited to create an environment in a small plastic play tray. They drew on their familiarity with local landscape and used a range of natural and man-made materials to re-construct features. Their explorations involved place-making, where decisions were taken about the site and the situation of their 'story.' Robertson (2014, p. 75) reminds us that "the act of creating something is central to the thinking process." See Figure 20.3.

FIGURE 20.2A Children notice that recent weather had left the playground wet and littered with debris. Here children simulate a vehicle damaged by a fallen tree (photograph courtesy of Sharon Witt and Helen Clarke).

FIGURE 20.2B A casualty is helped from danger! (Photograph courtesy of Sharon Witt and Helen Clarke.)

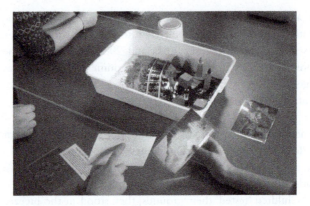

FIGURE 20.3 This group created a railway scene. The teacher used photographs of extreme weather to prompt discussion (photograph courtesy of Sharon Witt and Helen Clarke).

Student teacher reflections:

"The children were immediately intrigued by the situation and were engaged throughout."

"I would definitely use this method again as it gave the children a different perspective to work from. One child noted, 'This must be what happens to an ant when it rains!'"

"Fettes (2005) notes that imagination is central to the process of becoming a teacher."

Description of Practice: Posing a Challenge

A forthcoming weather event was introduced to the children in a variety of ways, including video clips, weather forecasts, and television and radio news reports. These prompted the children to talk about their personal knowledge of weather phenomena and also to discuss the experiences of others. Conversations encouraged children to express their feelings towards previous extreme weather events and future possibilities (see Figure 20.4).

Children's reflections:

"I feel scared and frightened in storms."
"I feel sorry for the people whose house gets wrecked."
"I sometimes worry about trees falling on me when the wind blows."

Description of Practice: Planning a Response

Children were challenged to mitigate the effects of an extreme weather event in their small world. They had a responsibility and a voice. Technology enhanced

FIGURE 20.4 Teachers used video clips, displayed on mobile devices, in group discussion (photograph courtesy of Sharon Witt and Helen Clarke).

FIGURE 20.5A Children issued weather warnings and publicized emergency action plans (photograph courtesy of Sharon Witt and Helen Clarke).

FIGURE 20.5B Children planned and constructed flood barriers for small worlds (photograph courtesy of Sharon Witt and Helen Clarke).

communication and recording; learners accessed video materials, made movie clips, and produced information leaflets (see Figures 20.5a and 20.5b).

Student teacher reflections:

"The children talked their way to a solution."
"We saw conversations not just question and answer."

Description of Practice: An Event

Children simulated the extreme weather event. They deluged small worlds with water to create floods, they added artificial snow for seasonal effect, and they used an electric hairdryer to model storm conditions (see Figures 20.6a and 20.6b).

FIGURE 20.6A Extreme weather events arrived in the small worlds. A town is flooded... (photograph courtesy of Sharon Witt and Helen Clarke).

FIGURE 20.6B ...and a storm causes a traffic incident (photograph courtesy of Sharon Witt and Helen Clarke).

Children's talk during a flood scenario:

"If I put a really tall building near to the river, it might fall down."
"Sometimes you get trees in the middle of the river."
"One side was less affected it could have been higher land."
"There was damage to houses but we live on the top of the hill so we will be fine."
"If it was winter that would be the worst time for a flash flood, you could lose electricity and be freezing."
"It might damage pipes and leak sewage everywhere."
"People might get trapped."
"There might not be drinking water."
"The stream isn't meant to be there."
"He's stuck, that isn't good."
"That car is not in the best of positions."
"You can see the devastation, you can see the difference."

Description of Practice: Taking Action in Response to an Event

Children made adjustments in the small world scenarios. They evaluated their interventions and considered the effect of actions and responsibilities. Children experienced agency and took control of the situation (see Figures 20.7a and 20.7b).

Children's suggestions for action:

"We'd need sandbags."
"We could make a ramp for the water."
"We should shut all windows and doors."
"We must move valuable furniture."

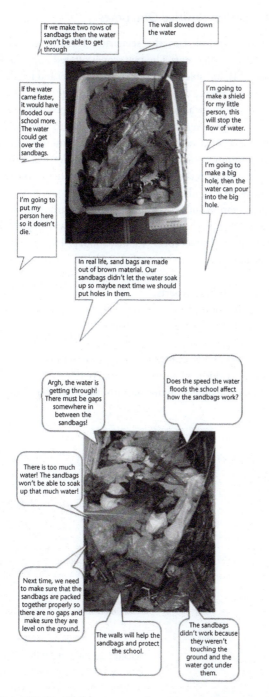

FIGURES 20.7A and 20.7B   Children respond to the event (photograph courtesy of Sharon Witt and Helen Clarke).

Description of Practice: Positive Outcomes

Children confidently responded to the scenarios. These were safe rehearsals of potentially serious real-world events. The tray scenes offered opportunities to model thoughtful responses. "Being able to express your thoughts and feelings, beyond the spoken or written word, offers a different way of communicating" (Robertson, 2014, p. 75). The children communicated in sophisticated and personal ways. They made both individual and collective responses and all had a part to play. Teachers addressed emotional responses as they arose. Miniature figures and animals were rescued from tricky situations, communications were repaired, and order was restored. The children were empowered to help the small world communities to move forward after the event (see Figures 20.8a and 20.8b). Student teachers saw how, "through creating miniature representations of ecosystems, or neighbourhoods, we help children conceptually grasp the big picture. The creation of small worlds provides a concrete vehicle for understanding abstract ideas" (Sobel, 2008, p. 45).

Student teacher reflections:

> "The children were the experts."
> "They had really good ideas."
> "Small worlds allowed place exploration."
> "Children could physically see concepts such as flooding in action."
> "The children created worlds that could be manipulated."
> "They saw the world from another perspective."
> "They could see the bigger picture, not just their lives but impacts on others."

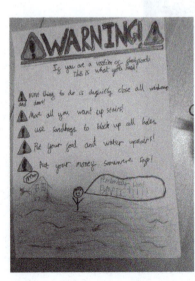

FIGURES 20.8A and 20.8B Children recorded their responses and issued advice for future events (photograph courtesy of Sharon Witt and Helen Clarke).

Over to You

Educators have a significant role in helping children to negotiate the complex issue of climate change. We invite you to take inspiration from this case study, to try this model, to personalise it for your circumstances, and to continue to adapt approaches for your own setting. We recommend the addition of eco-playfulness to practice. When teachers employ imagination we know good things happen. Visioning the future requires imagination and hope, and taps into what it means to be human; it uplifts and empowers (Hicks, 2014). Social psychology suggests people who have self-transcendent values show concern for environmental problems and have higher motivation to act to address issues (Crompton, 2013). This type of work with children is about creating spaces to consider our place in the world and our responses to challenges. There are possibilities in today's classroom to promote opportunities for play, imaginative thinking, and hopeful responses. This approach is one of respect for children as active citizens.

Central to building positive responses to environmental challenge is a re-examination of our relationship with nature. Immersion in nature (Sobel, 2008; Boxley et al., 2014) provides a life foundation and 'sources of strength' (Hicks, 2014) that enables children to face difficult environmental issues as they mature. "By working on small, manageable, cognitively accessible environmental problems at a micro-level" we develop "the sense of agency, the locus of control ... crucial in shaping stewardship behaviour" (Sobel, 2008, pp. 149–150). In our examples, children demonstrate this in their protection of school grounds and local communities.

Summary

- Position yourself as teacher to allow eco-playful responses to climate events.
- Position your children as problem solvers, decision makers, and change agents.
- Build a futures-oriented curriculum for resilience and hope.

Bardwell (1991) stresses the importance of modelling success stories to students if they are to begin to create their own view of what is needed. We offer our model as a "refreshing change from the typical doomsday warnings or edicts for appropriate action" (Bardwell, 1991, p. 9). Although climate change is a new challenge, it also gives opportunities for empowerment. The small worlds described in this chapter provide narrative contexts for children, which deepen understanding of probable and preferable local futures (Hicks, 2014). A respect for childhood, for its playfulness and resilience, reminds educators that in the face of environmental challenges it is possible for young learners to build familiarity not fear, relationships not rifts (Monbiot, 2013). An eco-playful approach promotes hopeful, pro-environmental behaviours, and is likely to bring happy endings to our environmental narratives with children.

References

Bardwell, I. (1991). Success stories: Imagery by example. *Journal of Environmental Education,* *23*, 5–10.

Boxley, S., Clarke, H., Dewey, V., & Witt, S. (2014). Talking with trolls: A creative and critical engagement with students' nature naivety. In K. Winograd (Ed.), *Critical literacies and young learners: Connecting classroom practice to the Common Core* (pp. 70–85). New York: Routledge.

Bromley, H. (2004). *The small world recipe book: 50 exciting ideas for small world play.* Birmingham: Lawrence Educational Publications.

Crompton, T. (2013). On love of nature and the nature of love. In S. Weintrope (Ed.), *Engaging with climate change: Psychoanalytic and interdisciplinary perspectives* (pp. 221–226). London: Routledge.

Demarest, A. B. (2015). *Place-based curriculum design: Exceeding standards through local investigations.* Oxford: Routledge.

Fettes, M. (2005). Imaginative transformation in teacher education. *Teaching Education,* *16*(1), 3–11.

Hicks, D. (2014). *Educating for hope in troubled times: Climate change and the transition to a post-carbon future.* Stoke on Trent: Trentham Books.

Monbiot, G. (2013). *Feral: Searching for enchantment on the frontiers of rewilding.* London: Allen Lane.

Robertson, J. (2014). *Dirty teaching: A beginner's guide to learning outdoors.* Bancyfelin: Independent Thinking.

Sobel, D. (2008). *Childhood and nature: Design principles for educators.* Portland, ME: Stenhouse Publishers.

Weintrobe, S. (2013). *Engaging with climate change: Psychoanalytic and interdisciplinary perspectives.* London: Routledge.

Witt, S., and Clarke, H. (2014). Seeking to unsettle student teachers' notions of curriculum: Making sense of imaginative encounters in the natural world. *Proceedings of Teacher Education for Equity and Sustainability (TEESNet) Seventh Annual Conference,* Liverpool Hope University. Retrieved July 1, 2015, from http://teesnet.ning.com/page/resources.

21

CHILDREN AS CHANGE AGENTS IN REDUCING RISKS OF DISASTERS

Mayeda Rashid, Kevin R. Ronan, and Briony Towers

Vignette One: The Miracle of Kamaishi

On March 11, 2011, the Great East Japan Earthquake set off a tsunami so devastating that more than 15,800 people died and 2,660 people are still missing. But in Kamaishi, Iwate Prefecture, teachers' quick actions reportedly saved more than 3,000 students of Kamaishi elementary and junior high school. The series of events brought hope to the people in time of such a disastrous event and has been dubbed "The Miracle of Kamaishi."

Owing to the tsunami, more than 1,000 Kamaishi residents lost their lives, but only five of them were school children who were absent from school on that day. For several years before the tsunami, Toshitaka Katada, a professor of civil engineering at Gunma University, collaborated with the teachers of Kamaishi Prefecture to deliver school-based disaster preparedness education. The students practiced evacuation drills and were taught different methods for disaster preparedness, mitigation, and prevention. Consistent with data from the World Health Organisation, Katada believed that in times of disaster children are the most vulnerable, so educating children about their safety and helping them prepare for disaster through prevention and preparedness activities was one of his priorities.

When the earthquake struck, the teachers and students of Unosumai Elementary School gathered on the third floor of the school building, where they thought they would be safe. Then some of them noticed that at the nearby Kamaishi Higashi Middle School, students were evacuating the school grounds and running for higher ground.

The Unosumai school children and staff had practiced this response with the middle school in the past and they decided to join them on the hillside. Together they could reach the safe location while behind them the mega-tsunami swallowed their schools and the town. (NHK World TV, 2012)

Research has shown that disaster-related fears are prominent among children (Muris, Merckelbach & Collaris, 1997). Most children do have questions and concerns about hazards and disasters, particularly when these are subject to media coverage during and after an event. Research in both psychology and education suggests that avoiding the topic does not serve the best interests of children: avoidance tends to maintain or increase children's fears whereas approaching the issue directly can help reduce them (Ronan & Johnston, 2005; Towers, 2015). Teachers' efforts to initiate age-appropriate activities and facilitate children's learning about hazards in their local environment are thus worthwhile, particularly when learning activities support children to engage in approach- versus avoidance-coping strategies.

By teaching children knowledge and skills for 'disaster risk reduction' (DRR), teachers can help children manage fears and anxieties stemming from the anticipation of disasters. This includes helping them move from the idea that disasters, and other risks in life, are *insurmountable* threats to the idea that they are *challenges* and problems that have solutions (Ronan & Towers, 2014). The idea here is that children with DRR knowledge and skills – along with attendant "adaptive capacities" like approach (versus avoidance) coping, risk assessment, and problem-solving – are also more confident and capable problem-solvers in relation to hazards and disasters, both human-caused and natural (Ronan & Towers, 2014). The core goal of DRR education is to help reduce risk (e.g., saving lives, reducing psychosocial consequences) while enhancing students' intra- and inter-personal resilience.[1] DRR education also entails learning that helps children begin to think of themselves as global citizens with a sense of agency, compassion, and empathy.

School-based DRR education can translate into life-saving outcomes. As demonstrated in the documentary, "The Kamaishi Miracle" (NHK World TV, 2012), the school disaster education program in Kamaishi Higashi Junior High School was based on three simple "rules of survival": don't make any assumptions; do your best; and go as quickly as you can. The education programme also included conducting joint evacuation drills with neighboring schools. In these drills, older students practiced evacuating and provided instruction to elementary school students on how to do this effectively. As a result, at the time of the earthquake, students put their learning into action and evacuated to higher ground. Reports also indicated that some students who were not at school that day were able to apply their knowledge of earthquake response and convince their families to evacuate (NHK World TV, 2012).

While teachers may like the idea of including DRR in the curriculum, they are confronted by a range of obstacles which involve an overcrowded syllabus, difficulty in locating developmentally/age-appropriate learning activities, a lack of confidence in teaching children DRR, a lack of support from school leadership, and weak partnerships with local emergency management agencies. The fundamental question is how do we help teachers and schools (and larger entities like departments of education) effectively implement DRR education that reduces disaster risk and increases children's resilience.

DRR Education for Children: Background and Expanded Rationale

According to the United Nations International Strategy for Disaster Reduction (UNISDR, 2009), disasters are defined as:

> A serious disruption of the functioning of a community or a society involving widespread human, material, economic or environmental losses and impacts, which exceeds the ability of the affected community or society to cope using its own resources.

The evidence suggests that the frequency and impacts of disasters is increasing. For example, in 2012, a total of 120 countries were hit by a total of 357 disasters (excluding biological disasters, e.g., epidemic, insect infestation, and animal stampede), affecting 122.9 million people, causing more than 9,655 deaths and producing $157.3 billion in damages (Guha-Sapir et al., 2013).

Children are one of the most vulnerable demographic groups in disasters. For example, the World Health Organization (WHO) estimated that children account for 30 to 50 percent of disaster fatalities (WHO, 2008; WHO & partners, 2011). Children are also highly vulnerable to severe psychosocial reactions (Norris et al., 2002; Ronan & Johnston, 2005). Importantly, while children may be more vulnerable to the impacts of disasters and require the protection of adults, they also have a right to participate in disaster risk reduction. This includes having the strategic knowledge for dealing with adverse circumstances and developing resilience. When children are provided with adequate support and guidance, they can develop knowledge, skills, and confidence for dealing with a range of disaster risks (Ronan & Towers, 2014; Towers, 2015). Research also suggests that children are highly motivated to share their knowledge with others which can, in turn, increase their resilience at the household and community level (Plan UK, 2010; Johnson et al., 2014c). Taking this participatory view, children are not seen as the passive victims with no role in DRR but, rather, as active agents who can take action to reduce their own risk as well as contribute to larger household and community mobilization efforts (Haynes et al., 2008; Mitchell et al., 2008; Tanner et al., 2009).

Vignette Two: The Story of Tilly Smith

In 2004, a ten-year-old British girl named Tilly Smith reportedly saved nearly a hundred people from a tsunami by warning them minutes before it reached the Maikhao beach in Thailand. Most of the beachgoers were foreign tourists unconcerned about tsunamis and unaware of early signs. Just two weeks before the incident, when Smith was in Danes Hills School, Oxshott, Surrey, her geography teacher Andrew Kearney taught the class about tsunamis, including early warning signs. When the earthquake in the Indian Ocean hit, Smith remembered this geography lesson. She immediately warned her parents when she noticed receding water from the shoreline and also bubbles on the sea surface. Her parents and she alerted nearby beachgoers and the hotel in which they were staying. Due to their warning, it was possible to evacuate the beach before the tsunami got to the shore and avoid casualties on that beach. (*UNISDR*, 2011, Aug 11)

Based on the dual principles of child protection and participation (United Nations, 1989, UNCRC Article 4 and 12), there is a sound rationale for teaching children DRR and resilience knowledge and skills. Understanding the needs of children and actively including them in household and community DRR has become a part of international frameworks for DRR (Ronan et al., 2014). For example, the recently published Synthesis Report on Consultations on the Post-2015 Framework on Disaster Risk Reduction (UNISDR, 2013) placed children at the very center of DRR efforts: "In particular children and youth have been singled out as having specific needs in terms of school safety, child-centred risk assessments and risk communication. But, more importantly, if appropriately educated and motivated on disaster risk reduction, they will lead and become the drivers of change" (p. 7).

DRR in the Elementary School Curriculum: Research

A recent review of the research shows that children *can* learn how to cope with disasters and become more resilient as a result of DRR programs (Johnson et al., 2014a). This includes increased knowledge, reduced anxieties and fears, and increased preparedness at both the individual and household levels. For example, Ronan and Johnston (2001) found that children in New Zealand who were involved in some hazards education programs were reported to have more realistic perceptions of risk, reduced disaster fears, and increased knowledge of protective behaviors compared to those not involved in such programs. Additionally, their parents also reported more home-based DRR activities (e.g., adding lips to shelves, having a smoke detector, storing emergency equipment, learning first aid, learning how to put out fires, doing home inspections) compared to parents of children not involved in a hazards education program. Children and youth have great potential as a trusted source of information in communicating disaster knowledge to friends and family members (see also Ronan et al., 2008; Webb & Ronan, 2014).

A recent study conducted in a lower socioeconomic area with high bushfire risk in Canberra, Australia, showed that children and youth were very motivated to learn about disasters and risk reduction (Webb & Ronan, 2014). Half the students were identified as typically 'unengaged' in educational/vocational programs, but along with the other (typically 'engaged') students, they attended *every* session.[2] Moreover, benefits to children and youth participants included significantly increased knowledge and preparedness skills, increased confidence, and reduced fears. Parents also reported that their children and they had implemented an average of six more home-based DRR activities by the end of the programme.

Vignette Three: Children Teach What They Are Taught

In Indonesia, DRR awareness material were developed and integrated within the education system to teach children about common disasters and action plans. Schoolchildren were taught DRR skills including how to respond (e.g., safety behaviours, sheltering). Children learned what to do while facing an earthquake and were encouraged to share their knowledge with their parents. In May 2006, the Yogyakarta region of Indonesia suffered an earthquake of 6.3 magnitude. Five thousand deaths were reported, though the death toll could have been even higher. Apparently, the local DRR program is credited for helping save lives. During the earthquake, for example, those families of children trained in DRR used the safety measures, including finding shelter under stable objects (e.g., tables). (GTZ, 2006)

DRR Curriculum

At the elementary school level, DRR curriculum should help students learn the following: (a) disaster risks; and (b) knowledge, skills, and strategies for reducing risks and enhancing resilience. These two content domains should be viewed as interdependent. Without an understanding of how disaster risk is created, strategies for reducing risk might be misdirected or ineffective. Without an understanding of risk reduction, students may assume that disasters are inevitable or unavoidable which would likely increase disaster-related fears and anxieties.

Understanding Risk

In order to understand disaster risk, students need to understand several key concepts including hazard, exposure, vulnerability, and capacity, and how these concepts interact with disasters. It is especially important that DRR curriculum makes a clear distinction between hazards and disasters. Specifically, a hazard is a phenomenon, situation, or human activity in which there is a *potential* threat to life, health, environment, society, and property (UNISDR, 2009, p. 7). A disaster, by contrast, is an event that causes serious disruption to the normal ways of a community or society involving extensive human, infrastructural, economic, or environmental losses that the affected community or society cannot bear on its own (UNISDR, 2009, p. 9). On their own, floods, earthquakes, tsunamis, volcanic eruptions, bushfires, droughts, and landslides are hazards. It is only when the impacts of these hazards cause widespread destruction of human lives and property that disasters occur. Whether or not a hazard event causes widespread disruption is dependent upon the level of exposure, vulnerability, and capacity in a given area.

The way in which hazard, vulnerability, capacity, and exposure[3] interact to create disaster risk can be illustrated with a simple example taken from Gallopın (2006). First, when a flood occurs, homes with more flimsy construction are hit harder than the more solid constructions (vulnerability). Second, the poorest homes in many communities are located in the places most susceptible to flooding (exposure). Third, the families with the greatest resources have a greater availability of means to evacuate to a safer location and repair water damage upon their return (capacity). Finally, the magnitude of the final impact will also depend on the velocity and depth of the floodwaters (attributes of the hazard event). By focusing on not just the hazard but exposure, vulnerability, and capacity, this increases students' opportunities for enhanced problem-solving and risk-reduction skills in their households, schools, and communities.

Reducing Risk

Students should understand the stages of disaster risk reduction. These stages include *prevention, mitigation, preparedness*, and *response* (and *recovery*). The term *prevention* refers to "the complete avoidance of losses of hazards and related disasters through action taken in advance" (UNISDR, 2009, p. 22). An example of prevention is land-use regulations that do not permit any settlement in high-risk areas such as flood plains. However, it is rare that losses can be completely avoided, and mitigation is a more realistic option. The term *mitigation* refers to "the lessening or limitation of the adverse impacts of hazards and related disasters" (UNISDR, 2009, p. 19). Mitigation measures can be 'structural' (e.g., flood levees, fuel reduction burning, hazard-resistant construction) or non-structural (e.g., public awareness, warning systems, evacuation, other key safety-related behaviors). *Preparedness* refers to the "knowledge and capacities developed by governments, professional response and recovery organizations, communities and individuals to effectively anticipate, respond to, and recover from, the impacts of likely, imminent or current hazard events or conditions" (UNISDR, 2009, p. 21). It includes activities such as contingency stockpiling of equipment and supplies, the development of arrangements for evacuation, emergency drills and field exercises. The term *response* is used to refer to "the provision of emergency services and public assistance during or immediately after a disaster in order to save lives, reduce health impacts, ensure public safety and meet the basic subsistence needs of the people affected" (UNISDR, 2009, p. 24). However, emergency services rarely have the capacity to support all of those affected and citizens are often required to be self-reliant. For example, in many cases, citizens need to arrange their own transport for evacuation or implement response strategies such as 'duck, cover, hold' or 'shelter-in-place.'

Ideally, once students have learned about hazards, vulnerability, capacity, and exposure, they will be able, alongside adults, to assess disaster risk in a variety of settings including their schools, households, and communities. They can then set about learning DRR strategies across the spectrum of prevention, mitigation, preparedness, and response. Students can also learn about the DRR strategies that have been implemented in their particular community. They can learn about existing planning regulations and assess whether these are adequate (prevention) (Izadkhah & Hosseini, 2005; Ronan & Johnston, 2003). They can learn about existing warning systems and methods through which warnings are disseminated at the local level (mitigation) (UNESCO/UNICEF, 2013). They can learn about current local emergency management arrangements including plans for evacuation and sheltering-in-place (preparedness) (UNESCO/UNICEF, 2013). Children can also learn basic first aid and other skills that would increase their chances of survival during a disaster, including key safety messages and behaviors and associated emotional regulation strategies (response) (UNESCO/UNICEF, 2013). Research reviewed earlier also demonstrates that children can influence their families to develop household emergency management plans and prepare more effectively. However, it should also be recognized that in some family contexts, children may struggle to engage their parents in such activities. Thus, the curriculum should incorporate some straightforward DRR measures that children can implement independently, such as enacting key safety behaviors and other measures (e.g., packing an emergency kit containing essential items and treasured possessions) (Towers, 2015).

Student-Centred Learning

It appears that DRR that employs student-centred teaching approaches result in better results than traditional teacher-centred and worksheet- and lecture-based approaches. Student-centred learning refers the idea that students should have choice and participate actively in decisions about what to study and how to study (O'Neill & McMahon, 2005). Lea et al. (2003) synthesizes student-centred learning to include the followings tenets: reliance on active rather than passive learning; an emphasis on deep learning and understanding; increased responsibility and accountability on the part of the student; an increased sense of autonomy in the learner; an interdependence and mutual respect between teacher and learner; and a reflexive approach to the teaching and learning process on the part of both teacher and learner.

Selby and Kagawa identified a set of student-centred learning modalities identified in case studies taken in programmes in 30 countries that promote child- and youth-focused DRR curricula (UNESCO/UNICEF, 2012). These include the following:

- *Interactive learning*: brainstorming, group discussion, and interactive multimedia presentations on topics related to disaster risk/climate change
- *Inquiry learning*: individual and team case study research, Internet searching, interviewing, project work
- *Affective learning*: expression of feelings, hopes, and fears regarding hazards and disasters
- *Surrogate experiential learning*: fictional and documentary films, board games, role play, drama, and simulation on disasters and climate change
- *Field experiential learning*: field visits to disaster support services facilities, hazard mapping and vulnerability assessment of home, school, and community, community hazard surveys
- *Action learning*: poster campaigns, street theatre on disasters and climate change, student-led school assembly, risk-reduction campaigns and projects (such as tree planting)
- *Imaginal learning*: using imagination to visualize positive and negative scenarios of past and future hazard and disaster, thinking what to do in crisis situations, sharing stories with one another
- *Somatic and expressive learning*: employing different types of artistic expression, body sculptures and human tableaux

However, Selby and Kagawa (2012) also found an extensive reliance on textbook-based rote learning in most of these countries (see also examples in Ronan, 2015), an approach that is largely ineffective in teaching children disaster preparedness and mitigation knowledge and skills (UNESCO/UNICEF, 2012). For example, a study on a drills-based/rote approach showed that almost 100 percent of children in that DRR education and drills-based program knew the most important protective behaviour (duck, cover, hold under a stable object). However, these students also endorsed a number of other behaviors (e.g., running outside) *that would put them at increased risk* (Johnson et al., 2014a). In addition to knowing what to do (e.g., duck, cover, hold), children (and adults) also need to know why a particular DRR message is important as well as how to enact that set of behaviors under various conditions. In other words, children need to learn not only the "what" in relation to DRR (e.g., key safety and risk reduction behaviours), they also need to know the "why" and the "how" in relation to these activities (Ronan & Towers, 2014; Towers, 2015).

We recommend the following practices for carrying out DRR in schools, particularly in the elementary school setting (Johnson et al., 2014b, 2014c; Johnston et al., 2015; Ronan & Towers, 2014; UNESCO/UNICEF, 2012, 2013).

Graduated Sequence of Learning

Research supports the value of a sequence of courses instead of teaching DRR as a one-off teaching event (e.g., Ronan & Johnston, 2001; see also Ronan, Crellin & Johnston, 2010). Continuous integration of preparedness education into school curricula, geared to the next developmental level, can help children understand preparedness and effective management of risk as a societal value, not some extemporized assignment (Gustafson, 2009). We would also add that it is possible to incorporate this graduated sequence of learning in a manner that doesn't impinge unduly on a crowded curriculum (e.g., through linking this curriculum to school drills).

Integrated Curriculum

Disaster preparedness education can be integrated across different subjects. For example, Bangladesh has introduced disaster and climate change–related themes like hazards, vulnerability, and preparedness across a range of subjects: in the teaching of Bengali and English language, students study poems, read stories, and write essays about disasters and DRR; in social studies, they learn about the influence of poverty on disaster vulnerability; and in science, they learn about the physical characteristics of hazards (UNESCO/UNICEF, 2012).

Encouraging Interaction between Parents and Children

DRR programs can promote child–parent interaction, such as structured home-based discussions (e.g., development of home emergency plans, specified home-based activities including practice and stockpiling emergency supplies) that can start with simple discussions and straightforward activities that progress to more complex other tasks over time. In Australia's *Families Preparing Together* curriculum, students create a family evacuation plan to be displayed around the classroom that, later, is taken home to be shared and discussed with family members (Australian Emergency Management Institute, 2015). Another example is the School Safety Initiative in India which engages children to conduct "hazard hunts" in and around their homes (United Nations, 2007). Importantly, the emotional response of parents has a direct and often powerful impact on children who are coping with hazards and the threat of disasters (Ronan & Johnston, 2005). Therefore, school education programmes should also help parents understand the value of managing their own emotional reactions before, during, and after disasters.

Promoting Self-Confidence by Presenting Realistic Information

Presenting realistic information about risks combined with learning activities that children can practice with families enhances children's self-confidence. For example, as introduced earlier, research shows that preparedness programs can help children reduce their fears of hazards, including in situations where their risk perceptions increase (Ronan & Johnston, 2001; Ronan and Johnston, 2005). However, programs should avoid giving stark or hopeless information that might influence children to emotionally withdraw or, worse, cause distress (Ronan & Johnston, 2005). Representing disasters as challenges and problems to be solved is preferable to framing them as insurmountable threats.

Addressing Children's Particular Needs

Special consideration must be given to children's particular learning needs or cultural background. For example, bilingual children can serve as a communication link between relief efforts and family members and surrounding community who may not fully understand English or the instructional language. During Hurricane Katrina in 2005, many children from non-English-speaking families helped FEMA in the evacuation by translating information to family members regarding shelters, supplies, food, and registration (Mitchell et al., 2008). Additional considerations (e.g., encouraging participation by promoting caring relationships, buddy systems among peers, and welcoming attitudes) are required for children with a range of disabilities to account for their needs in preparedness and response contexts (Boon et al., 2011; Mutch, 2014).

Interactive Learning

Teaching DRR through social interactive activities tends to increase children's learning, including child-led discussions and problem-solving in class (and in other contexts) (Ronan & Johnston, 2003; Webb & Ronan, 2014). Other interactive approaches include peer-to-peer learning and mentoring (e.g., older children helping to teach younger children, as was done in Kamaishi). In terms of instructional materials, board games, interactive multimedia tools, visual teaching aids, and workbooks on disaster education as well as school-wide and inter-school events dedicated to promoting disaster reduction are also reported to be effective (UNISDR, 2009).

Engaging Local Emergency Management Agencies

DRR education programs for children include not only school-based programs but also programs carried out in community settings. This can include initiatives that can then also involve children and youth who do not attend school (e.g., Webb &

Ronan, 2014). For example, in Sri Lanka, one community participation project built a roof water catchment and storage structure near a school to replace one destroyed by the Asian tsunami. This was not an improvement in the everyday school water supply; rather, it provided an emergency water source for future disasters (Wisner, 2006). In addition, preparedness education programs can be integrated with existing community-based initiatives through parent–teacher groups, community and neighborhood groups, and other more specific DRR community initiatives. Various educational programs or preparedness competitions can also be organized through partnerships, starting with a local emergency management agency, a known facilitator for promoting school-based implementation of DRR education programs in classrooms (Johnson et al., 2014a). For example, in Jamaica, collaboration between Jamaica's disaster preparedness agency and schools in Jamaica underpins a Disaster Awareness Day and Disaster Preparedness Day in schools. This includes an innovative disaster-themed culinary competition during the annual Independence Festival where the students prepare recipes and meals with their own creativity using ingredients that would be available after a disaster – those with a long shelf life that do not require refrigeration (Wisner, 2006).

Conclusion

DRR education can empower children not only to protect themselves, but also to become agents of change in promoting safer homes and communities. From the perspective of participatory DRR education programs, children, teachers, and schools are at the center of a culture of safety and risk reduction. Learning about risk reduction and resilience can help solve problems linked specifically to disasters but also can be generalized to other risk-related problems (Ronan & Towers, 2014). Teacher training and capacity building for school-based DRR education should be a focus in both teacher education and community–school collaborations. Despite the challenges of yet another program, a motivated teacher, school, or school district can begin to initiate DRR programming that is developmentally appropriate, reflects community needs, and is integrated into the curriculum. In doing so, we are confident that children can, indeed, be more prepared for the inevitable disasters associated with environmental crises in the years ahead.

References

Australian Emergency Management Institute (2015). People, get ready: Families preparing together. Retrieved August 25, 2015, from https://schools.aemi.edu.au/sites/default/files/Files/AEMI005_PGR%20FPT_230914.pdf.

Boon, H. J., Brown, L. H., Tsey, K., Speare, R., Pagliano, P., Usher, K., & Clark, B. (2011). School disaster planning for children with disabilities: A critical review of the literature. *International Journal of Special Education, 26*(3), 223–237.

Gallopín, G. C. (2006). Linkages between vulnerability, resilience, and adaptive capacity. *Global Environmental Change, 16*(3), 293–303.

GTZ (2006). Disaster reduction: Knowledge, transfer, practice. *Proceedings of the 7th Forum and Disaster Reduction Day.*

Guha-Sapir, D., Hoyois, P. & Below, R. (2013). *Annual disaster statistical review 2012: The numbers and trends.* Brussels, Belgium: Centre for Research on the Epidemiology of Disasters.

Gustafson, T. S. (2009). Empowering children to lead change: incorporating preparedness curricula in the K–12 educational system (unpublished master's thesis). Naval Postgraduate School, Monterey, California.

Haynes, K., Barclay, J., & Pidgeon, N. F. (2008). The issue of trust and its influence on risk communication during a volcanic crisis. *Bulletin of Volcanology, 70*(5), 605–621.

Izadkhah, Y. O., & Hosseini, M. (2005). Towards resilient communities in developing countries through education of children for disaster preparedness. *International Journal of Emergency Management, 2*(3), 138–148.

Johnson, V. A., Johnston, D. M., Ronan, K. R., & Peace, R. (2014a). Evaluating children's learning of adaptive response capacities from ShakeOut, an earthquake and tsunami drill in two Washington State school districts. *Journal of Homeland Security & Emergency Management, 11*(3), 347–373.

Johnson, V. A., Peace, R., Ronan, K. R. & Johnston, D. M. (2015). Improving the impact and implementation of disaster education programs for children through theory-based evaluation. Manuscript under review.

Johnson, V. A., Ronan, K. R., Johnston, D. M., & Peace, R. (2014b). Implementing disaster preparedness education in New Zealand primary schools. *Disaster Prevention and Management, 23*(4), 370–380.

Johnson, V. A., Ronan, K. R., Johnston, D. M., & Peace, R. (2014c). Evaluations of disaster education programs for children: A methodological review. *International Journal of Disaster Risk Reduction, 9*, 107–123.

Lea, S. J., Stephenson, D., & Troy, J. (2003). Higher education students' attitudes to student-centred learning: Beyond 'educational bulimia'? *Studies in Higher Education, 28*(3), 321–334.

Mitchell, T., Haynes, K., Choong, W., Hall, N., & Oven, K. (2008). The role of children and youth in communicating disaster risk. *Children, Youth and Environments, 18*(1), 254–279.

Muris, P., Merckelbach, H., & Collaris, R. (1997). Common childhood fears and their origins. *Behaviour Research and Therapy, 35*(10), 929–937.

Mutch, C. (2014). The role of schools in disaster preparedness, response and recovery: What can we learn from the literature? *Pastoral Care in Education, 32*(1), 5–22.

NHK World TV (2012). *The Kamaishi Miracle* [Video documentary]. Japan: NHK World TV. Retrieved June 13, 2015, from www.youtube.com/watch?v=5KiyKFEVJKM.

Norris, F.H., Friedman, M.J., Watson, P.J., Byrne, C.M., Diaz, E., & Kaniasty, K. (2002). 60,000 disaster victims speak: Part I. An empirical review of the empirical literature, 1981–2001. *Psychiatry, 65*, 207–239

O'Neill, G., & McMahon, T. (2005). Student-centred learning: What does it mean for students and lecturers? Emerging issues in the practice of university learning and teaching, *1*, 27–36. Retrieved September 3, 2015, from www.aishe.org/readings/2005-1/oneill-mcmahon-Tues_19th_Oct_SCL.html.

Plan UK (2010). *Child-centred disaster risk reduction: Building resilience through participation.* London: Plan UK.

Ronan, K.R. (2015). Advances and continuing challenges towards HFA2 and post-2015: *2015 Global Assessment Report on Disaster Risk Reduction.* UNESCO/UNICEF. Retrieved June 13, 2015, from www.preventionweb.net/english/hyogo/gar/2015/en/bgdocs/UNICEF%20and%20UNESCO,%202014.pdf.

Ronan, K.R., & Johnston, D.M. (2001). Correlates of hazard education programs for youth. *Risk Analysis, 21*(6), 1055–1063.

Ronan, K.R., & Johnston, D.M. (2003). Hazards education for youth: A quasi-experimental investigation. *Risk Analysis, 23*(5), 1009–1020.

Ronan, K.R., & Johnston, D. M. (2005). *Promoting community resilience in disasters: The role for schools, youth, and families.* New York: Springer.

Ronan, K.R., & Towers, B. (2014). Systems education for a sustainable planet: preparing children for natural disasters. *Systems, 2,* 1–23. doi: 10.3390/systems2010001.

Ronan, K.R., Crellin, K., Johnston, D.M., Finnis, K., Paton, D., & Becker, J. (2008). Promoting child and family resilience to disasters: Effects, interventions, and prevention effectiveness. *Children, Youth and Environments, 18*(1), 332–353.

Ronan, K.R, Crellin, K., & Johnston, D. M. (2010). Correlates of hazards education for youth: A replication study. *Natural Hazards, 53*(3), 503–526.

Ronan, K.R., Petal, M., Johnson, V., Alisic, E., Haynes, K., Johnston, D. M., & Davie, S. (2014). School curricula, education material and relevant training include disaster risk reduction and recovery. *HFA Progress Report – Indicator 3.2.* Geneva: United Nations International Strategy for Disaster Reduction.

Tanner, T. M., Garcia, J., Lazcano, F., Molina, F., Molina, G., Rodríguez, G., Tribunalo, B., & Seballos, F. (2009). Children's participation in community-based disaster risk reduction and adaptation to climate change. *Participatory Learning and Action,* 54–64. London, UK: Institute of Environment and Development.

Towers B. (2015). Children's knowledge of bushfire emergency response. *International Journal of Wildland Fire, 24*(2), 179–189.

UN/UNISDR (2009). UNISDR terminology on disaster risk reduction. Geneva, Switzerland. Retrieved October 1, 2015, from www.unisdr.org/we/inform/terminology.

UNISDR (2009). Regional analysis on DRR education in the Asia Pacific region: In the context of priority of action 3 of the Hyogo Framework for Action. Bangkok, Thailand. Retrieved October 2, 2015, from www.unisdr.org/files/12081_RegionalAnalysisonDRREducationinthe.pdf.

UNISDR (2011, Aug. 11). *Lessons save lives: The story of Tilly Smith.* [Video file]. Retrieved June 13, 2015, from http://youtu.be/V0s2i7Cc7wA.

United Nations (1989). *United Nations Convention on the Rights of the Child (UNCRC)* Geneva, Switzerland: United Nations.

United Nations (2007). *Towards a culture of prevention: disaster risk reduction begins at school-good practices and lessons learned.* Geneva, Switzerland: International Strategy for Disaster Reduction. Retrieved September 15, 2015, from www.unisdr.org/files/761_education-good-practices.pdf.

United Nations Educational, Scientific and Cultural Organization/United Nations Children's Fund (2012). *Disaster risk reduction in school curricula: Case studies from 30 countries.* Paris/Geneva: UNESCO/UNICEF.

United Nations Educational, Scientific and Cultural Organization/United Nations Children's Fund (2013). *Towards a learning culture of safety and resilience: Technical guidance for integrating disaster risk reduction in the school curriculum.* Paris/Geneva: UNESCO/UNICEF.

United Nations International Strategy for Disaster Reduction (2013). *Synthesis report on consultations on the post-2015 framework on disaster risk reduction (HFA2).* Geneva, Switzerland. Retrieved October 3, 2015, from www.preventionweb.net/english/professional/publications/v.php?id=32535.

Webb, M., M., & Ronan, K. R. (2014). Interactive hazards education program for youth in a low SES community: A quasi-experimental pilot study. *Risk Analysis, 34*(10), 1882–1893.

Wisner, B. (2006). Let our children teach us! A review of the role of education and knowledge in disaster risk reduction. *A report by the ISDR System Thematic Cluster/Platform on Knowledge and Education.* Bangalore, India: Books for Change.

World Health Organization (2008). *Manual for the health care of children in humanitarian emergencies.* Geneva: World Health Organization. Retrieved June 14, 2015, from http://apps.who.int/iris/bitstream/10665/43926/1/9789241596879_eng.pdf.

World Health Organization, United Kingdom Health Protection Agency, Save the Children and partners (2011). Disaster risk management for health: Child health. *Disaster Risk Management for Health Fact Sheets.* Global Platform for Disaster Risk Reduction. Retrieved September 19, 2015, from www.who.int/hac/events/drm_fact_sheet_child_health.pdf.

Acknowledgements

The funding support of Australia's Bushfire and Natural Hazards Cooperative Research Centre (BNHCRC) is gratefully acknowledged. This chapter was part of a larger scoping and review exercise for a 3-year BNHCRC-funded project on "building best practice in child-centred disaster risk reduction."

Notes

1 The United Nations International Strategy for Disaster Resilience (UNISDR, 2009) defines resilience as "the ability of a system, community or society exposed to hazards to resist, absorb, accommodate to and recover from the effects of a hazard in a timely and efficient manner."

2 The program was carried out at a local youth centre.

3 According to UNISDR (2009) definitions of exposure, capacity, and vulnerability are: *exposure*: "people, property, systems, or other elements present in hazard zones that are thereby subject to potential losses"; *capacity*: "the combination of all the strengths, attributes and resources available within a community, society or organization that can be used to achieve agreed goals"; *vulnerability*: "the characteristics and circumstances of a community, system or asset that make it susceptible to the damaging effects of a hazard."

SECTION VI

Opportunities for Professional Development
Teachers Moving Ahead, with Urgency

The final section in this volume, Section VI provides a bit of review and also forges new ground, especially as it relates to professional development. The chapters in this section reinforce the quintessential idea of the book, that it is time for teachers to bring a greater intentionality to the explicit study of environmental challenges and then engage students in related civic actions, in community. Kathleen Kesson maps out a professional development structure for teachers ready to rethink how they approach environmental issues with young people. Kesson uses ideas from Greek philosophy to provide some conceptual grounding for professional development and, then, she suggests prompts to guide teachers' discussions. Kesson's framework for teachers' professional development is best implemented collaboratively, with like-minded colleagues who are ready and willing to begin incorporating the key ideas and strategies from this book. The second reading is by a youth activist, Amy Krol, who tells her story growing up in rural Oregon, immersed in the natural wonders of her area, and then a brief account of her early political activism. Amy's advice to elementary teachers is both simple and powerful, such as her suggestion to study Indigenous people's relationship with nature and to use these ideas to reshape curriculum.

Finally, the final chapter brings together some of the core ideas in the book. One big idea, which I allude to several times in the chapter, is the relationship between civic activism and resilience. The student as 'agent of change,' part of the book's title and oft repeated throughout the volume, is a euphemism for students' experience as participants in the decision-making process around real issues and problems that are in their zone of interest. Even pre-school children are ready for place-based curricula, following Jerome Bruner's idea "that any subject can be taught effectively in some intellectually honest form to any child at any stage of development" (1960, p. 33). The challenge is for teachers to be alert to the problems in the classroom, school, and community that might be interesting to students, and then teach them all those skills in the Common Core and other mandated government standards *but in the context of their participation in authentic community life.*

Reference

Bruner, J. (1960). *The process of education.* Cambridge, MA: Harvard University Press.

22

CULTIVATING CURRICULUM WISDOM

Meeting the Professional Development Challenges of the Environmental Crisis

Kathleen Kesson

Australian philosopher Glenn Albrecht has coined the term "solastalgia" to define the *psychological reaction to the destruction of one's homeland*, whether through floods, hurricanes, tornadoes, or strip mining. Once just a syndrome of people who experience disasters or live in "sacrifice zones" (areas of the planet that have been economically exploited and/or environmentally destroyed in the name of profit), climate change now presents us with a universal human experience of solastalgia. Albrecht writes: "As bad as local and regional negative transformation is, it is the big picture, the Whole Earth, which is now a home under assault. A feeling of global dread asserts itself as the planet heats and our climate gets more hostile and unpredictable" (in Klein, 2014, p. 165).

We must start from the premise that children are already being educated about climate change simply from living in a society immersed in televised images and the Internet and that to varying degrees, they (and we!) are experiencing some level of solastalgia. The preceding chapters in this text have presented an impressive array of activities and perspectives to draw from to help children make sense of what they are hearing and seeing and come to terms with the fears that they likely are feeling. We have read many excellent ideas about how to provide them with the knowledge and skills they will need to live in a world characterized by uncertainty and the possibilities of mass extinctions, disruptions, and dislocations. I want to turn our attention now to the knowledge and dispositions required of teachers who wish to move forward with this work.

Maxine Greene highlights a professional dilemma of teachers when she says, "…the practicing teacher within the classroom today has to make existential choices at particular moments of classroom life. This means choices made on the teacher's own responsibility, with all the anxiety that comes from there being no 'right answer'" (2004, p. 230). When teaching the environmental crisis and climate change, the sensitivity of the subject matter coupled with the complexity of emotions and perceptions in the minds of children present educators with a daunting task. It is no wonder that teachers might experience anxiety when they seek to make the study of climate change a part of their classroom. It is akin to the teaching of evolution; one knows they may be headed into a minefield of conflict and confrontation. In taking on this challenge, we teachers need more than information; we need to become wise in our judgments of means and ends, capable, as David Jardine puts it, of offering children the knowledge they need "to live… to be on an earth that will sustain their lives" (1997, p. 217). Taking responsibility for "existential choices" requires a sophisticated intelligence that signifies more than mere technical/pedagogical knowledge. Given the gravity of the prospect of climate change, given the human disruptions it is already causing and the unpredictable and uneven suffering projected, given current rates of extinctions (over 1,000 times higher than natural background rates according to recent studies) (De Vos et al., 2014), and given the universal moral quandaries this all puts us in, I want to suggest that educators must cultivate *wisdom* in order to guide the young generation into new ways of thinking and being that are consistent with the continuance of life on this planet for all of its inhabitants.

Cultivating Curriculum Wisdom

Curriculum work is multi-faceted. Good curriculum thinking, as John Dewey (1902) long ago noted, must begin with a deep understanding of the learner, the teacher's role being that of a thoughtful bridge builder between academic subject matter and the psychology of the child. In terms of subject matter, practitioners must possess information from a variety of disciplines to develop their climate change curriculum: meteorology (about weather and climate), geology (magma processes and glacier fluctuations), chemistry (the role of CO_2 in the atmosphere), and botany (for plant growth data). Teachers must also understand the nature of scientific inquiry and develop the capacity to assess competing scientific analyses and claims. But climate change is not just a scientific problem. In order to really come to terms with the issue, teachers need to understand the economics of a global system that prioritizes profit over human health and security, the politics of the relationships between developed/developing worlds, and the use and misuse of technology. Teachers need to connect global issues with their personal lives if they are to become invested in taking responsibility for the state of the world. And this is no easy task. Taking this level of responsibility requires that we examine our own consumption patterns and ways of living, reduce our impact in any way we can and, at the same time, recognize the cultural and structural changes that need to be made if we are to survive. Through this reflection on the contradictions of our modern lives we can present models of appropriate living for our students and, hopefully demonstrate a caring struggle to bring our lives into balance with the larger needs of the planet.

In our book *Curriculum Wisdom: Educational Decisions in Democratic Societies* (2004), James Henderson and I developed a matrix of inquiry modes that together form a "map" of the terrain of wise educational decision-making in societies that subscribe to democratic ideals. We used ancient Greek terms for these inquiry modes, in part to remind educators that the act of teaching is a profoundly philosophical journey, concerned as it must be with questions of significance: What is worth knowing? What kind of world do we wish to create? How do children grow to be caring, compassionate, knowledgeable human beings? What is the appropriate role of the teacher? *Wisdom* is not a word one often hears in the public discourse around education. In the current "audit culture" we inhabit (see Taubman, 2009), the activities of teaching and learning are spoken of in instrumental terms with words and phrases like value-added assessment, data-driven instruction, accountability, rubrics, and benchmarks. This kind of technical language can cause us to forget that education is a profoundly human endeavor, one concerned with questions of existence, meaning, purpose, connection, significance, and values.

Our inquiry modes are distinct, yet overlapping in the kinds of questions they pose and habits of mind they foster. None of them are sufficient in and of themselves; I believe all are essential to the cultivation of the democratic spirit, or *ethos*. I want to suggest that such sophisticated, multi-layered habits of mind and approaches to problem solving are essential for life in a postmodern, complex democracy, even more as we seek to develop the knowledge and dispositions necessary to shepherd young people through these epic times. What follows is an introduction to the modes of inquiry and some critical questions for you to ask yourself in relation to these when planning your teaching about the environment in these times of crisis.

Modes of Inquiry

Theoria is the word from which we derive the English word "theory," and in both Greek and Latin it signifies "contemplation" – looking attentively at things, either with the physical eyes or the eyes of the mind. Contemplation is surely the ground of wisdom. *Theoria* represents intelligence, but a special kind of visionary intelligence, one that is characterized by the presence of both reason and intuition. Mindful of the various aspects of a situation, but unconstrained by conventional ideas or habitual thinking, *theoria* allows us to speculate, to imagine, and to envision possibilities. The capacity to recognize both what is and *what might be* is an essential habit of mind for an educator hoping to inspire young people with the possibilities of a better world in the face of climate change. The following discussion prompts are an invitation to reflect with your colleagues about these important matters:

- When you imagine a better world, what does it look like?
- In your busy life, where and when do you allow yourself the opportunity for this kind of visionary thinking?
- What sustains your hope and optimism that we will find solutions for our present problems and develop the collective will to solve them?

Poesis, the Greek root of the word "poetry," is derived from an ancient term which means "to make." An engagement with *poesis* is an engagement with the tacit, aesthetic dimensions of experience – the emotional, the perceptive, the intuitive, and the creative. John Dewey (1934) brilliantly explores the potential of ordinary experience to be a profoundly aesthetic event, and perception, creation, activity, discrimination, reflection, and culmination as interrelated and interactive components of holistic, gestalt-like experiences. In contrast to the continual stream of everyday experience, an *aesthetic* experience brings the world into sharper focus, creates a sense of wonder or awe, evokes connections in our minds, and brings a sense of fulfillment. I believe that such an aesthetic encounter with the living world is essential, if we are to care enough about nature (which includes human nature) to heal the wounds of our planet.

Edmund Wilson gave us the concept of *biophilia*, defined as the "innate need to relate deeply and intimately with the vast spectrum of life around us" (Kellert & Wilson, 1993, p. 42). How are we to facilitate *deep and intimate experiences of the life around us* for our students if we have not had them ourselves? In addition to actually spending time in nature, which is of primary importance, the arts – music making, poetry, singing, movement, craft work, painting – offer opportunities to engage with questions of meaning and connect with our deepest feelings, such as those of solastalgia, and move us to new heights of awareness about the profound implications of our current environmental situation. Educational decisions informed by *poesis* pay attention not just to the instrumental knowing of facts, but to the many tacit dimensions of experience. *Poesis* transforms teaching from a role or a function into a calling. Again, with your colleagues, take the time to reflect upon some questions, with the aim of increasing your "aesthetic intelligence":

- Can you recall and describe a time when an experience in nature moved you to emotional heights?
- What art forms do you resonate with on a feeling level? Can you talk about a painting or a piece of music that transports you, or which intensifies your experience of life?
- Explore your deepest feelings about climate change through painting or drawing or poetry. What do you learn from this?

Dialogos, the ancient Greek root of our word "dialogue," means to speak, to converse. Dialogue, however, is more than simply talking – it is talking with the intent of coming to shared understandings. The spirit of *dialogos* embodies a commitment to *multiperspectival inquiry*, the awareness that perception and subjectivity are shaped by a number of cultural factors, including racial, class, ethnic, sexual, gendered, age and ability-related identities. Understanding such socially constructed difference can lead to the "disposition to honor diversity" and the recognition that in a pluralistic society, no one cultural element is the norm, and that all perspectives must be treated with respect. With the ability to entertain contradictory perspectives, intelligence is sharpened and made subtler. *Dialogos* requires that we keep our personal and professional beliefs "bracketed" through multi-perspectival dialogue and critical self-examination. Some discussion questions to consider:

- How is your understanding of climate change shaped by your own social and cultural "location" (personal geography, age, income level, education, etc.)?
- How do you extend yourself into the perspective of others who are perhaps more immediately threatened by the effects of climate change than you?
- Can you describe a time when you were involved in an effort to "dialogue across differences" in order to solve a problem or come to a deeper understanding? What was that like for you? What did you learn?

Phronesis is a Greek word for a kind of practical intelligence that is based on values and involves careful deliberation, reflection, and the exercise of judgment. It embodies Dewey's concept of "social intelligence," the idea that solutions to common problems rest in rational inquiry carried out by free persons committed to shared understandings. In educational practice, teachers often engage in *collaborative* inquiry into problems and solutions. One of the qualities of a democratic frame of mind is a commitment to shared decision-making, and to processes of consultation, discussion, negotiation, and the democratic sharing of power.

Many people are involved in helping children grow and learn. A topic as important to our survival as climate change necessarily involves practitioners, parents, and community members working together to create holistic learning environments capable of offering children the knowledge they need to live peacefully and productively on an earth that will sustain their lives. Only with such an expanded sense of *practical and ethical wisdom* will it be possible to nurture the development of democratic character in our students, and the corresponding abilities to co-create a world that is just, sustainable, and livable. Consider the following questions:

- Recall a time, such as a curriculum development project, when you worked with a group of people to make important decisions about what and how children should learn. What did you learn about collaborative process work?

- Have you ever been involved in a political action project? What did you learn about the processes of negotiation, deliberation, debate, and compromise?
- How would you be inclusive of parents and community members as you decide how to more effectively teach about climate change?

Praxis, in the ancient Greek, referred to the activity of free people, and in education has come to be known as the intersection of reflection and action, more specifically as critical reflection and action directed towards social structures to be transformed. With critical inquiry, teachers cultivate their awareness of social, economic, and political inequities. Teaching for democratic living requires careful consideration of the overt and covert power relations between people. When critical inquiry is integrated into teachers' reflective practices, it is often called *praxis*. *Praxis* reminds us that we cannot take the "objectives conditions" of a situation at face value, but must begin to dig into the root causes of any perceived problem. What are the underlying economic, political, and social factors that have brought about unjust conditions?

When one digs deep enough into the issues facing communities and their battles against powerful multi-national corporations who seek to "frack" in their backyard or remove the top of their local mountain, one comes to understand the corrupt state of our national politics – which is, according to Klein, "as fossilized as the fuel at the center of these battles" (2014, p. 361). The collusion of big money and big politics is endemic, and this suggests the need to educate our youth on the real workings of democracy. If we are to truly address the environmental crisis, teachers must understand the power dynamics of our economic system, including the inherent tension between sustainability and capitalism, and determine how to educate young people about this in a developmentally appropriate way. Some critical questions might include:

- Can you recall when you first learned about the inequities in our economic system? What were your feelings about this? How have they changed over time?
- Do you think it is within the "power of the people" to combat the policies that serve the interests of immense corporate wealth? What gives you hope?
- Is it possible to educate young people to be critical thinkers without fostering cynicism? What is important to keep in mind?

Polis, the root of all words related to "political," literally means "city" in ancient Greek, but can also mean citi/zenship, and the efforts of citizens to develop "just" forms of association. It signifies the relationship between ethics and politics, and foregrounds questions about what it means to lead a good life and become a good citizen. In a complex, pluralist democracy, competing interests must be weighed against each other. However, citizens who lack the skills to examine their own values and beliefs will be predisposed to making habitual, dogmatic decisions rather than rational, compassionate ones. Teachers need to become skilled facilitators of ethical conversations, with the intention of helping to develop in our students the disposition to weigh the competing claims and ethical considerations in our current situation.

The struggle for climate justice is a complicated grass roots struggle. From indigenous communities protesting the destruction of their native lands, to Appalachian communities raising their voices against the despoilment of hundreds of their mountaintops, to the cries of Pacific Islanders who are suffering the loss of fresh water and land from rising tides, the battle is an epic one between people and their communities and the immense power of not only the fossil fuel corporations, but an entire economic system that holds us all in the thrall of a consumerist ideology. Increasingly, citizens worldwide are demanding greater control over decisions that directly impact the quality of their lives (see Tokar, 2010). The struggle raises important ethical questions that citizens need to discuss and take action on: Should wealthy nations, who have for the past 200 years of industrialization released enormous amounts of carbon into the atmosphere, take greater financial responsibility for cleaning up the mess than developing countries? What are the responsibilities of the rich towards the poor? What about consumption? Do we, as individuals, have a social responsibility to reduce consumption? These questions – about resource use, social inequality, our relationships with other species, environmental justice, and our obligations to future generations – are appropriate questions for young people that can be part of the curriculum in developmentally appropriate ways. We cannot simply provide our own answers to these questions, if we are educators committed to open inquiry. But we can teach young children HOW to engage with ethical questions in ways that will help them grow to be politically engaged citizens. What questions do you have about the politics of climate change to add to this list of discussion prompts?

- What about the idea of "teacher neutrality" – how do you navigate the tension between the impulse to "tell" and the competing impulse to allow for students to "construct" their own knowledge?
- Can we even afford the luxury of teacher neutrality in a time of crisis? If not, how can teachers stand by their values with integrity, respect for others, and an open-minded search for truth?

I have saved *Techne* for last, because in many ways it is the most familiar of our inquiry modes. It could be considered the mirror image of *theoria*. No armchair visions here, but feet-on-the-ground activity, practical activity in and by which we carry out our craft, be it teaching, or pottery, or auto mechanics. As a form of thinking, *techne* identifies problems to be solved, hypothesizes solutions, makes plans based on these hypotheses, implements solutions, and reflects upon the outcome – a classic action-research model. In considering a curriculum for climate change, one must cultivate superb craftsmanship, considering the essential questions, the scientific content, the developmental readiness of students, activities that will engage young people, and imaginative ways to foster expressive outcomes that demonstrate deep learning. Teaching is, at its heart, a skilled craft, refined and revised by the master teacher over many years of trial and error. In and of itself, *techne* could reflect technical, mechanistic activity, but combined with the other inquiry modes, it can demonstrate the mark of a truly wise teacher.

- As you think about designing a curriculum for climate change, what are the essential questions you might frame it around?
- What kinds of activities do you think are developmentally appropriate for the students you teach?
- What "end products" would demonstrate that your students are understanding the multi-faceted problem of climate change?

Final Reflection

As should now be clear, these inquiry modes are distinct, yet overlapping in the kinds of questions they pose. Each mode fosters particular habits of mind, all of which are essential to the cultivation of the democratic spirit. *Theoria* fosters visionary thinking, the capacity to imagine a better world. *Techne* demands that theoretical ideas be put into practice, not merely conceptualized, and subjected to testing in the real world. *Praxis* fosters critique, the ability to pinpoint injustices in the world. *Dialogos* helps us understand these injustices from many perspectives, and to sharpen and refine our own perspectives. *Phronesis* requires deliberation and collaboration in solving problems, knowing that the wisdom of the group enhances and extends the wisdom of the individual. *Polis* reminds us that every situation in life has an ethical dimension, and that the highest calling of a citizen in a society is to think and act ethically, so that the entire society may benefit. *Poesis* sings to us that there is more to life than rational thought and action – that we must engage with the tacit, emotional, creative side of things to bring our world into balance.

In combination, these modes of inquiry offer a high synergy, both epistemologically and socially. *Theoria* alone is an ivory tower activity; without *techne*, good ideas remain ossified in an abstract, idealized world, not enacted in the embodied, experiential world. *Praxis* alone can foster dogma and ideological purity; however, along with *dialogos* and *phronesis* critique is refined, revised, and made more inclusive of many points of view. *Poesis*, with its attention to the emotional and the creative dimensions, counterbalances the strict rationality of *polis* and its precise ethical debates. Such integrated, multi-layered habits of mind and approaches to problem solving are essential for life in a postmodern, complex democracy and especially for meeting the challenges of educating the next generation for active citizenship around issues of climate change.

Now that I have laid out a multi-faceted model for cultivating curriculum wisdom, I would like to push our thinking even deeper. Ancient Greek philosophy was an anthropocentric system of thought, anthropocentrism being the idea that humans (*ánthrōpos*, meaning "human being") are of central (*kéntron*, meaning "center") importance. The most relevant ideas derived from anthropocentrism for this discussion are (1) that we are masters of nature, and (2) that nature exists to serve our needs. Deep ecology, an eco-philosophical perspective that values the inherent worth of all species aside from their usefulness to "mankind," presents us with a strong conceptual alternative to anthropocentrism. What if we were to adopt an "eco-centric" perspective, one which acknowledges the inherent worth of all of nature and its systems? How might this alter and extend our conception of what it means to be wise? What, for example, if we understood *dialogos* as not limited to humans, and we practiced apprehending the world from the perspectives of the non-human species with whom we share the planet? Can we learn to think like a tree? What if we extended our ethical commitments (*polis*) to all of life, and entertained the competing interests of plant and animal species alongside our own? What if we used our voices to speak for other species in our curriculum deliberations (*phronesis*)? What if our analysis of capitalism (*praxis*) extended not just to the exploitation of humans but to the devastation and extinctions that the unlimited growth model has brought to all species? Can we learn to listen to the songs of nature, appreciate the *poesis* in a blade of grass? What if, when we contemplate a better world (*theoria*), we consider what would make it better for all species? And finally, what if every curriculum judgment and instructional decision we made (*techne*) was informed by this multi-layered thought process? How would your classroom and your school look and feel different than it does now?

The idea that all species as well as ecosystems have moral relevance and status is a controversial position, and the philosophical arguments around this topic are much more substantive than this chapter has the scope to address. I want to argue, however, that we can no longer avoid a close examination of our conscious and unconscious beliefs and patterns of thinking, and that we need to align these with the urgent need to help children come to terms with what climate change might mean for their lives, and to foster the dispositions and the agency that will help them be more a part of the solution than a part of the problem.

When teachers work as democratic, eco-centric educators concerned with the big picture, they are committing themselves to the practice of *curriculum wisdom*, a capacity that is similarly concerned with both the practical affairs of daily life (teaching young people to read and write) and with ethical questions (teaching young people values such as respect for all species, social and ecological justice, and right living). Such a practice, though characterized by action, is deeply *philosophical*, from the Greek word meaning *love of wisdom*. To love wisdom is not the same as assuming that one is wise. In fact, it is its humble opposite. To love wisdom is to practice an open-hearted and open-minded life of inquiry. Teaching about climate change calls on us all to develop our best professional selves, to draw out our own deepest values and most compelling visions for the world, and to engage courageously with those who would deny the problem and silence our attempts to speak truth to power.

References

De Vos, J. M., Joppa, L. N., Gittleman, J. L., Stephens, P. R., & Pimm, S. L. (August 2014). Estimating the normal background rate of species extinction. *Conservation Biology*. Retrieved February 23, 2015, from http://onlinelibrary.wiley.com/doi/10.1111/cobi.12380/full.

Dewey, J. (1902) *The child and the curriculum*. Chicago, Illinois: The University of Chicago Press.

Dewey, J. (1934). *Art as experience*. New York: Perigee.

Greene, M. (2004). Learning to come alive. In C. Glickman (Ed.), *Letters to the next president: What we can do about the real crisis in public education* (pp. 223–227). New York, Teachers College Press.

Henderson, J., & Kesson, K. (2004). *Curriculum wisdom: Educational decisions in democratic societies*. Upper Saddle River, New Jersey: Merrill Prentice-Hall.

Jardine, D. W. (1997). To dwell with a boundless heart: On the integrated curriculum and the recovery of the earth. In D. J. Flinders & S. J. Thornton (Eds.), *The curriculum studies reader* (pp. 213–223). New York: Routledge. (Original work published 1990)

Kellert, S. R., & Wilson, E. O. (1993). *The biophilia hypothesis*. Washington, D.C: Island Press.

Klein, N. (2014). *This changes everything: Capitalism vs. the climate*. New York: Simon & Schuster.

Taubman, P.M. (2009). *Teaching by numbers: Deconstructing the discourse of standards and accountability in education*. New York: Routledge.

Tokar, B. (2010). *Toward climate justice: Perspectives on the climate crisis and social change*. Norway: New Compass Press.

23

A RURAL GIRL'S GLOBAL VIEW ON THE ENVIRONMENTAL CHALLENGE

Advice for Elementary Teachers

Amy Krol

Born and raised in rural Eastern Oregon, I am a small town girl who's gone international. I graduated from the University of Oregon, majoring in International Studies and Romance Languages, and I have traveled from Asia to Africa. After graduation, I worked as the outreach, social media, and internship coordinator at the Gabon-Oregon Research Center on Environment and Development at the University of Oregon. The Center facilitates collaborative research between scientific experts and professionals from Gabon and Oregon on common sustainability challenges. It's work that allows me to support people, at both a local and international level, to address climate change.

While my job keeps me in Oregon, I have continued to find ways to both travel and be an activist. I walked door-to-door across Oregon cities to gather support for labeling genetically modified organisms and fight for the right to know what is in our food. I took the People's Climate Train across the country, arriving in New York, dawning a dress of over 150 solidarity ribbons for the People's Climate March in September 2014. Through my role as one of 4,500 facilitators for the Awakening the Dreamer Symposium, I am connected to people all over the world. Though I have developed a deep care for the planet through my travel experience, my values for the environment are rooted in my childhood.

Growing up, nature was very accessible to me. My family lived in a gully with a few neighbors surrounded by hills and creeks. My friends and I were free to adventure outside, which consisted of playing at our tree fort, walking down the creek, or hiking Eagle Caves. While I grew up with 4H kids and summer rodeos, the extent of my agricultural skills was taste-testing my mother's homegrown raspberries. Wild and domestic animals were always around with a cougar or fox occasionally showing itself on the hill. I am grateful that my parents *planted* us where they did because we had a lot of fun growing up in that gully. My mom and dad were the opposite of fearful parents who didn't allow their kids to get dirty or roam. We got our fair share of bumps and bruises but also crossed beaver dams and chased water skippers.

School reinforced these outdoor adventures but was limited by school budgets. There was a program in elementary school where we took field trips across the Columbia River and learned about landscape, ecology, and ecosystems. The school had a gardening program, and we were responsible for taking care of our own plants. However, the school lost program funding and, with it, the plants.

When I started high school, I knew about climate change, although it was not an alarming topic in the community. What did catch my curiosity was study abroad. So I spent my junior year in Ecuador as an exchange student, which exposed me to poverty at a level I found hard to comprehend. At the same time, I attended an elite school with friends of wealthy families who lived so easily next to a poverty that was so normalized. When I left the school, I had many questions about economics, equity, and resource distribution. I asked questions about my own country and how it became so powerful whereas others hadn't.

I came back to the US and joined an environmental club during my first year of college. I came to understand how politics around energy drove the destruction of the environment and those politics were sustained by the profitability of certain political and economic agendas. I learned this through our club activities, not class. We protested local liquefied natural gas pipelines, worked to shut down the Boardman (Oregon) coal plant, installed free compact fluorescent light bulbs, and enforced water conservation in the school cafeteria. These club experiences were exponentially more educational than my classes because I was living what I was learning in regards to environmental issues.

After engaging in these political actions to protect the environment, I began to search for deeper understandings as to why we are in this state of environmental crisis in the first place. I found some answers from the Awakening the Dreamer Symposium, a transformational educational workshop created by the Pachamama Alliance. In the mid-1990s, US environmental activists visited the Achuar people who lived in the Amazon between Peru and Ecuador. The Achuar and the visitors from the Global North formed an alliance in response to the threat of the oil industry to the Amazon.

> The Achuar shared with this group the urgent threat to their lands and culture, their vision for self-determination, and a request for allies from the North who would "change the dream of the modern world"—shifting our culture of overconsumption to one that honors and sustains life.
>
> This group committed to a partnership with the Achuar, and, upon their return to the United States, Bill Twist and Lynne Twist co-founded the Pachamama Alliance to carry out their commitment. (Pachamama Alliance, 2015)

The Alliance has since created the Symposium to educate people of the modern world about values we have, like consumption and individualism, and their impact on ourselves, the rest of the world, and especially the human spirit. Groups like the Pachamama Alliance remind us that the world as it is...was once imagined; therefore, another world is possible. Students need both the space to imagine this world and the encouragement to fight for it!

Teachers are vital in the nurturing of environmental stewardship of children. Unlike my childhood, many kids now grow up in urban areas never seeing vegetables grow from the ground. I believe when children develop a relationship with nature, they will be more compelled to care for it for the rest of their lives. Environmental stewardship starts there. The other key part of an education for this century is the notion that our actions locally have an impact globally. It's important for children to understand their connectedness to people beyond their community. Finally, I think teachers should reflect on their own values and behaviors in the context of Western culture. Non-Western cultures tend to understand humans' relationship to nature and each other differently than we do in the West. We can learn much from non-Western cultures about alternatives to our individualistic and isolating ways of life. I encourage teachers and children to study other cultures that live in more harmonious relationships with nature. By changing our relationship with nature and each other, we can be better advocates for the environment and the human family that it holds.

Reference

Pachamama Alliance (2015). Origin story. Retrieved August 31, 2015, from www.pachamama.org/about/origin.

24

THERE'S NO TIME TO WASTE

Teachers, Act with Courage and Conviction!

Ken Winograd

I believe that the purpose of education is to teach young people to be caring, participatory, and resilient citizens in both local and global community. *Caring* citizens bring an empathy to the suffering of others, including non-human life. *Participatory* citizens are engaged in community, working collaboratively to engage in problems of common interest and then the resolution of these problems, thus improving the quality of life for everyone and everything. And *resilient* citizens have the intra-personal fortitude and sense of connection to persist and endure in tough times. In a future of environmental crises, I would argue that any other educational goals pale in comparison. Certainly, teachers will have subgoals for their students as it relates to learning how to read, write, calculate, and under-stand core concepts of nature, science, civics, and history. But more paramount is a school experience that teaches collaboration and love instead of competition and hierarchy, the sanctity of the web of life instead of disconnected disciplines, and *social* action instead of apathy and isolation. The immediate challenge for elementary teachers is to enhance children's resilience, and the underlying fabric of resilience is children's deepening sense of connection and obligations to all life.

The crux of environmental crises is humans' existential *disconnection*, from each other, from non-human life, from the web of everything. The heart of the educa-tional response to disconnection, therefore, is the enactment of curriculum that seeks *reconnection*, leading children to experience a connection and responsibility to others, and an interdependence with all life. The types of actions described in the chapters aims to teach children this interconnection: by spending more time in nature, reflecting on humans' relationship with nature through talk, art, and play; joining with others to address social and ecological problems in local communities, showing care for all life through these actions; facilitating children's initiatives to engage in projects of a more global nature; and supporting children's

emotions in times of climate stress. Each class, school, and community will con-
ceptualize curricular activity a bit differently, depending on local conditions and
local culture, but in the end it comes down to this roadmap for teacher and children in these early years of the Anthropocene:

- Spending time in nature
- Engaging in civic actions
- Enacting peaceful relations with all life

A popular heuristic for teaching sustainability in US elementary schools is the
three Rs: recycle, reuse, and reduce. Recycling is certainly better than not recycling,
but it has limitations since in no way does it challenge the dominant paradigm
of growth and consumption. In fact, recycling may inadvertently lull people into
a complacency that this action alone is an adequate response to the challenge of
sustainability. The other two Rs, reusing and reducing, as responses to the environmental challenge, are not taken seriously in most public schools. Reusing does
hold much potential in terms of our transition to a sustainable world. A shift
to a barter system, for example, in which people share their tools and objects
of life, and also an ethic of buying 'used,' certainly can help put a *chink* in the
consumption edifice.

Reducing represents the real challenge to the dominant consumer–industrial
complex since serious reduction of consumption is blasphemy for a system that
requires growth in order to survive and thrive. Teachers, if they wholeheartedly
infused concepts and practices of 'no growth' and living simply, would be engaging in truly revolutionary pedagogy. In addition, it is not enough for education to
advocate simply for no growth *for all* given the schism between the rich and poor
nations of the world; perhaps it is the rich who should give up and sacrifice so the
masses of humanity that live on several dollars a day have greater opportunities
for decent living conditions.

The heart of the problems facing human life on the planet is cultural, which
means that these problems require a change in how humans relate to the natural
world and each other; a world that more fairly shares its wealth and resources; and
a change in how we think about 'the good life.' David Selby worries that

> ...even as a discreet subject in the curriculum, climate change is
> relegated to a environmental problem that has technical fixes. There is
> a tendency throughout the present genre of climate change educational
> materials to characterize the global heating crisis...as a CO2 problem
> curable within largely present terms of reference, rather than a problem
> arising out of the crisis of the human condition, a crisis arising from a
> disconnect from the web of life, especially among privileged populations
> and, hence, a crisis of exploitation and violence coupled with denial.
> (Selby, 2010, p. 38)

This broader response to the environmental crisis means a radical rethinking of the dominant myths that have served to organize human civilization for the last several hundred years: progress, growth, and nature-as-resource (Kingsnorth, 2014). Meaningful care for the planet means that we humans turn away from economic growth as *the* core organizing framework for our consumer–industrial complex. The counter-myths and narratives reflected in the book provide a decent point of departure for elementary teachers ready to be in the educational vanguard, teaching children to bring a more critical and caring frame of reference for how to live in the world: with a deep respect and even reverence for all of nature; a participatory democratic worldview that is committed to social equity and equality; and a conception of the good life characterized by modesty, frugality, and love for all life (Elgin, 1981).

So there is much for elementary teachers to think about and act on as it relates to our changing world. I conclude with some final ideas.

1. Our work to teach children to become participatory and caring citizens (as well as our own activism) should begin with small actions, in collaboration with others, ideally reflecting local issues and problems. Teachers should take care not to ask young children to 'save the world' (Sobel, 1998), but, instead, be aware of modest problems or issues in the local environment that might be of interest to children as topics for social action projects. It is also important to remind ourselves, as adults, we ourselves should not become overwrought or paralyzed by the totality of environmental crises. Instead of doing nothing when faced with overwhelming problems outside out of our immediate control, we are more effective as 'defenders of the planet' when participating in smaller projects, like helping raise the minimum wage in our community, supporting some local food initiative, or by testifying to the city council about a proposed development through a wooded area.

2. The quintessential problem underlying environmental crises is humans' disconnection from each other, nature, and the web of life. The emphasis of curriculum that seeks to heal this breach is holistic: transdisciplinary units of study, multicultural studies, nature experiences and nature study, and justice units that raise students' understanding of the 'other,' including non-human life. Certainly, an important learning outcome is that students more wholeheartedly *identify* with others, so 'othering' morphs into deeper forms of relations, like what Buber refers to as 'I-Thou' (fully in relation) instead of 'I-It' (other as an object, a means to an end) (Internet Encyclopedia). The first challenge is to help children begin to understand our collective and personal disconnection, from each other and the web of life. And then, as teachers, we *pull out the stops* and do everything imaginable to help our children reconnect and be in relationship with all life.

3. Teachers who have no therapeutic training can play an important role in supporting children's recovery from the trauma and anticipated trauma stemming from environmental crises. According to Betsy Grove (2002), "The first

and most important principle of helping children is that we must recognize the power of a nurturing, respectful, and caring relationship with an adult to help a child recover from adversity" (Grove, 2002, p. 101). More important than any specific therapeutic strategy is the teachers' willingness to listen and believe in the child's ability to recover and succeed. A second principle in helping stressed children, according to Grove (and Ojala and Brown, this volume), is providing them with opportunities to share stories of what they have experienced. Even when they have not yet experienced the full effects of climate disruption, the *anticipated anxiety* of disruption also warrants teachers' caring response to children as they give voice to their concerns and stories. Especially as civil and natural instability increase in frequency and severity, it is problematic and risky when teachers are silent about the dangers outside the schoolhouse walls. Molly Brown (this volume) reminds us that children *do* pay attention to information about environmental crises in the media, in conversation with peers, and overheard conversations (and anxiety) of parents and adult caregivers. According to Brown, adult silence conveys fatalism and indifference, represses emotions, and unwittingly results in greater confusion and anxiety. The first key element in addressing children's fear of climate change is teachers recognizing and honoring their own emotions and then inviting children to share their own.

4. We live in an economic system that is characterized by violence and domination: e.g., more powerful people using violence against the less powerful; people doing violence to animals and the natural world; men doing violence to women. Violence is structural and institutional, like industries destroying the natural world in order to access timber and minerals, and governments sponsoring wars and terrorism on weaker countries. We cannot have peace and justice in our relations with the natural world without similarly peaceful and just relations in our social world...and visa versa. Therefore, we argue that children must learn peaceful relations, in ways that integrate social and eco-justice. It is crucial that peace be an organizing theme in the elementary curriculum, particularly with a perspective that explicitly examines the relationship between and among peace, violence, and power inequalities.

5. Throughout the book, authors have asserted that teachers have a moral responsibility to address climate change with their students. I agree. Children are required by law to attend public school and be taught by well-intentioned adults. Children are somewhat defenseless, by nature and by law, in relation to the decisions and judgments of teachers who are acting on behalf of the state. Therefore, Soder (1990) argues, "Those responsible for the physical and mental health of children in schools have a *moral obligation to ensure that children are kept from harm*" (p. 73). Children (especially poor children and the elderly) are most at risk of catastrophic climate change. Not doing everything in our power to prepare them for this new world represents a dereliction of our moral responsibility as teachers.

It is a cliché among environmental activists that 'taking action is the best antidote to despair.' The research reviewed in the Chapter 1 about the link between children and youth activism and self-efficacy is compelling. Hilary Whitehead (this volume) reminds us that we need to put aside our traditional ideas about withholding politically sensitive topics from children, calling this 'the New Realism.' Whitehead describes the children of Vanuatu, intimately aware of the existential threat to their island from rising seawaters, as directly involved in the response to this challenge. Children's author and filmmaker Lynne Cherry (this volume) has long observed that action/solution-oriented curriculum helps build self-efficacy and resilience in our youth.

There is no shortage of social and ecological problems, and it is crucial that teachers plan units of study that involve children *in community* doing some form of social action. Certainly, the challenge for elementary teachers is to figure out those topics and forms of engagement that will make sense to their students and families. Teachers have a golden opportunity to help children learn to help each other, to help protect Mother Earth, to act with integrity and care, and be connected in and by love with all life. Children engaged collaboratively as 'agents of change' develop a resilience to proactively tough it out in 'times of environmental crises.' Derrick Jensen (2013) argues that people who actively resist oppressive life conditions are more able to survive. A good example of this is Aliza Vitis-Shomron who as a teenage resistance fighter escaped from the Warsaw Ghetto and then survived the Bergen-Belsen concentration camp (Heller, 2013). "I never saw myself as a victim. I was on the active side, the resisting side," she said. "It helped me cope." As it relates to children, being on *the resisting side* can and should mean their engagement with authentic community problems, including action that promotes justice where, before, there had been injustice. So children can thrive and grow strong in the challenging times ahead, let us engage them in nature, ethical conversations, and the building of caring and peaceful communities, in their schools and beyond.

Environmental activist Bill McKibben (2015) reminds us, "Very few people on Earth get to say, 'I am doing, right now, the most important thing I could possibly be doing.'" Teachers, I would argue that helping children prepare for our changing world, as agents of change, is the most important thing you could possibly be doing.

References

Elgin, D. (1981). *Voluntary simplicity: Toward a life that is outwardly simple, inwardly rich.* New York: William Morrow.

Grove, B. M. (2002). *Children who see too much.* Boston: Beacon Press.

Heller, A. (2013). Warsaw Ghetto uprising remembered by holocaust survivor Aliza Mendel. *Huffington Post.* Retrieved October 19, 2015, from www.huffingtonpost.com/2013/04/06/aliza-mendel-warsaw-ghetto-uprising_n_3029680.html.

Internet Encyclopedia of Philosophy. *Martin Buber.* Retrieved July 23, 2015, from www. iep.utm.edu/buber/#SH2b.

Jensen, D. (2013). Q & A with Arundhati Roy and Derrick Jensen. In D. Jensen & L. Keith (Eds.), *Earth at risk: Building a resistance movement to save the planet* (pp. 237–248). Oakland, CA: PM Press.

Kingsnorth, P. (2014). *Forty days.* Retrieved October 10, 2014, from www .globalonenessproject.org/library/articles/forty-days.

McKibben, B. (2015). *Do the math* (video). Retrieved January 23, 2015, from http:// act.350.org/signup/math-movie/.

Selby, D. (2010). 'Go, go, go, said the bird': Sustainability-related education in interesting times. In D. Selby & F. Kagawa (Eds.), *Education and climate change: Living and learning in interesting times* (pp. 35–56). New York: Routledge.

Sobel, D. (1998). Beyond ecophobia. Retrieved August 23, 2014, from www.yesmagazine .org/issues/education-for-life/803.

Soder, R. (1990). The rhetoric of teacher professionalism. In J. Goodlad, R. Soder & K. Sirotnik (Eds.), *The moral dimensions of teaching* (pp. 35–86). San Francisco: Jossey-Bass, Inc., Publishers.

SUPPLEMENTAL TEXTS AND RESOURCES

Curricular and Teaching Ideas

Bigelow, B., & Swinehart, T. (2014). *A people's curriculum for the earth: Teaching about the environmental crisis*. Milwaukee, WI: Rethinking Schools.

Cowhey, M. (2006). *Black ants and Buddhists: Thinking critically and teaching differently in the primary grades*. Portland, MI: Stenhouse Publishers.

Pelo, A., & Davidson, F. (2000). *That's not fair: A teacher's guide to activism with young children*. St. Paul, MN: Redleaf Press.

Sobel, D. (2004). *Place-based education: Connecting classrooms and communities*. Barrington, MA: Orion Society.

Sobel, D. (2008). *Childhood and nature: Design principles for educators*. Portland, MI: Stenhouse.

Texts for Teachers' Own Learning

Earth Charter. www.earthcharterinaction.org/content/pages/What-is-the-Earth-Charter%3F.html.

Elgin, D. (1981). *Voluntary simplicity: Toward a way of life that is outwardly simple, inwardly rich*. New York: William Morrow.

Louv, R. (2008). *Last child in the woods: Saving our children from nature – deficit disorder*. Chapel Hill, NC: Algonquin Books.

Macy, J. Work that reconnects network. Retrieved October 1, 2015, from http://workthatreconnects.org/.

Macy, J., & Brown, M. (2014). *Coming back to life*. Gabriola Island, British Columbia: New Society Publishers.

Orr, D. (2004). *Earth in mind*. Washington, DC: Island Press.

Assorted Relevant Children's Literature

Beckwith, K. (2005). *Playing war*. Gardiner, ME: Tilbury House Publishers.

Brinkloe, J. (1986). *Fireflies*. New York: Aladdin Books/Simon & Schuster.

Brown, P. (2009). *The curious garden*. New York: LiEle, Brown Books for Young Readers.

Cherry, L. (2000). *The great kapok tree*. New York: HMH Books for Young Readers.

Cherry, L. (2002). *A river ran wild*. New York: HMH Books for Young Readers.

Franklin, K., & McGirr, N. (1995). *Writings and photographs by children from Guatamala: Out of the dump*. New York: Lothrop, Lee & Shepard Books.

Hoose, P. (2001). *We were there, too! Young people in US History*. New York: Melanie Kroupa Books.

Lyons, D. (2002). *The tree*. Vancouver, WA: Illumination Arts Publishing Co.

National Geographic (2009). *Every human has rights: A photographic declaration for kids*. Washington, DC: National Geographic.

Winter, J. (2008). *Wangari's trees of peace: A true story from Africa*. Orlando, FL: Harcourt Books.

Winter, J. (2009). *Peaceful heroes*. New York: Arthur Levine Books.

Woodson, J. (2012). *Each kindness*. New York: Nancy Paulsen Books.

ABOUT THE AUTHORS

Julie Andrzejewski is Professor Emeritus of Human Relations and Multicultural Education at St. Cloud State University in Minnesota, USA, where she co-founded the Social Responsibility Masters Program. Her recent publications include *Social Justice, Peace, and Environmental Education* (Routledge, 2009); and book chapters "War: Animals in the Aftermath" in *Animals and War: Confronting the Military Animal Industrial Complex* (Arissa, 2013), and *The Sixth Mass Extinction*, co-authored with John Alessio in Censored 2014 (Seven Stories Press). Involved with many activist projects over the years, Julie received the 2013 Michael Harrington Award for Scholar-Activism and is a National Judge with Project Censored.

Simon Boxley leads the undergraduate programme in Education Studies at the University of Winchester, UK. He was a teacher in UK state primary schools for 11 years and became an advisory 'advanced skills teacher.' He worked in initial teacher education before becoming part of the Education Studies Team, where his teaching specialties have included 'race,' environment, and recent education policy. His research and publications to date include journal articles and book chapters on critical teacher education, environmental education, the politics of education, and political philosophy. He is also an active campaigner on a range of educational issues and is a trade union officer.

Michael Brody is a member of the faculty of education at Montana State University. He teaches science and environmental education, curriculum development, and educational research. His recent environmental activities include co-editing the *International Handbook of Research on Environmental Education* (Routledge, 2014) and co-authoring The Habitable Planet: Professional Development Guide (www.learner.org/courses/envsci/) and the Flathead Watershed Educators' Guide (www.flatheadwatershed.org/).

Molly Young Brown brings decades of experience in psychosynthesis and *The Work That Reconnects* to her work. She teaches online courses, offers transpersonal coaching by phone, gives workshops internationally, and writes books and essays. Her publications include *Coming Back to Life: The Updated Guide to the Work That Reconnects* (with Joanna Macy); *Growing Whole: Self-realization for the Great Turning, Held in Love: Life Stories To Inspire Us Through Times of Change* (co-edited with Carolyn Treadway); and *Lighting a Candle: Collected Reflections on a Spiritual Life*. More information at *MollyYoungBrown.com* and *PsychosynthesisPress.com*.

Geraldine Burke is an artist, researcher, and teacher-educator at Monash University in Melbourne and Singapore. She lectures on studio and creative/art education. She has an enduring interest in the way local knowledge/s and immersive a/r/t (art, research, and teaching) can be developed for use by schools and community groups to build creative experiences that connect people to place/s and each other. Her own graduate work in Art and Design was awarded through exhibition/exegesis and explored the impact that nature and digital technologies have on image and process. Her recent PhD dissertation was presented through photo-book/exegesis and explored immersive art pedagogy.

Lynne Cherry, author/illustrator of 30 award-winning children's books (*The Great Kapok Tree, A River Ran Wild*), is producer/director of the *Young Voices for the Planet* films championing youth solutions to the climate crisis. Used by National Geographic, PBS, National Wildlife Federation, and the UN Foundation, these films inspire youth to take action (see Lynne's *NY Times* guest blog: http://dotearth.blogs.nytimes.com/2012/05/24/on-the-allure-of-ostriches-and-new-paths-in-climate-communication/?_r=0). Lynne received her BA from Tyler School of Art and her MA in history from Yale University, and has completed residencies at Princeton, Cornell, and the Smithsonian Museum. Her chapter for *Written in Water* was published by National Geographic Books. See YoungVoicesonClimateChange.com.

Helen Clarke is a Senior Lecturer at the University of Winchester, UK, where she teaches on undergraduate and postgraduate Initial Teacher Education programmes. She has particular expertise in learning and teaching science in the early years and primary phases. Committed to celebrating the energy and enthusiasm that children, students, and teachers bring to their learning, she has researched children's early exploration and enquiry, sustainability, environmental education, and teacher development, both in the UK and overseas. She is currently working with a colleague on the notion of 'nature-naivety' as a means to conceptualise relationships with the natural world. Email: Helen.Clarke@winchester.ac.uk.

Carie Green teaches place-based education, child development, and social science research in the graduate programs in the School of Education at the University of Alaska Fairbanks. Her research centers around engaging young children as active researchers on the human dimensions of environmental education research and place identity. She is currently engaged in a forest research project with three- to seven-year-olds in which children use GoPros and other innovative methods (role-playing, modeling, art, and video analysis) to explore their experiences of X marks the spot, sticks, bugs, rosebushes, forts, castles, and houses in the forest.

Ingrid Hakala is an educational anthropologist serving as a program officer of Global Grounds at the University of Virginia, USA. Her dissertation research focused upon contested notions of multilingualism, ethnic identity, and the nation as they intersected with elementary schooling in the context of post-conflict Nepal. In her current professional work, she is interested in developing opportunities for critical examination of the ethics and values underlying models and practices of education for global-mindedness.

Sahtiya Hammell has over a decade of experience in the education sector as a K–12 educator, university instructor, and director of out-of-school time programs. A doctoral candidate in education at the University of Virginia, her undergraduate degree in English from Princeton focused on issues of normativity and post-colonialism in literary curricula in the US and New Zealand. Sahtiya's current research builds upon her earlier work to examine the construction of national identity in textbooks and includes interests in citizenship education and social justice pedagogies. Sahtiya is Co-Chair for the Comparative and International Education Society's New Scholars Committee.

Rhys Kelly is a lecturer in the Department of Peace Studies, University of Bradford, UK. He has taught in the field of conflict resolution for over 12 years and has strong interests in pedagogy and practice relating to peace/alternative education. Rhys' current research focuses on understanding connections between environmental issues and prospects for peace and conflict, with particular interests in grassroots movements seeking responses to climate change and related issues (e.g., Transition Towns, New Economy). Rhys also trained as a forest school leader and is a keen woodworker, food grower, and musician.

Kathleen Kesson is Professor of Teaching and Learning in the School of Education at LIU-Brooklyn, where she teaches graduate courses in the foundations of education and teacher research. She is co-author of *Curriculum Wisdom: Educational Decisions in Democratic Societies* and *Understanding Democratic Curriculum Leadership* and co-editor of *Defending Public Schools: Teaching for a Democratic Society.* She has authored numerous book chapters, book reviews, and academic articles in prominent education journals. Currently, she is researching the personalized learning movement in Vermont public schools and working on a book entitled *The Personalized Learning Revolution: Voices from the Field*.

Gopal Krishnamurthy actively explores J. Krishnamurti's educational philosophy, teacher education, anti-method pedagogies, and reclaiming the wildness in learning. Gopal holds a PhD in Education, masters degrees in Education & Philosophy and a BA (Hons) in Physics. Teaching for over 20 years in school and university contexts, he enjoys a teaching repertoire that includes physics, mathematics, philosophy, Indian music, drama, and education. He is also currently the (curriculum) principal at Brockwood Park School, an international school in the UK. He conducts seminars, conferences, and interactive talks on education in India, Thailand, Azerbaijan, France, the UK, and the USA. Email: gopal.learning@gmail.com. Talk: www.youtube.com/watch?v=hKjwPgrbJl8.

Amy Krol graduated cum laude in 2014 from the University of Oregon with a Bachelor of Arts in International Studies and Romances Languages. She currently works as the outreach coordinator at the Gabon-Oregon Transnational Research Center on Environment and Development. She spends her summers at one of her hometown cherry orchards working the harvest in human resources and management. In the fall of 2014, she knocked on over 2,000 doors for Oregon's Measure 92, a state referendum that requires that families have the right to know what's in their food. She is an activist and artist, and is passionately curious about the world.

Karen Malone is Professor of Sustainability for the Centre for Educational Research at the University of Western Sydney. She is an international researcher and educator on children's environments, child–animal relations, child-friendly and sustainable cities, participatory research with children, learning outside of the classroom, sustainability, and environmental education. Karen has attracted over two million dollars in research grants, awards, and consultancies and has published 5 books, 23 book chapters, and over 47 refereed publications. She has worked for UNESCO international projects supporting the Decade for ESD and researched UNICEF Child Friendly Cities programs in a number of countries around the globe.

Jolie Mayer-Smith is Professor Emerita of Science Education, University of British Columbia, Vancouver, BC. In 2002, she co-founded the Intergenerational Landed Learning on the Farm Project, which she directed until retirement in July 2014. Jolie completed her BSc and MSc in Biology at Stanford University and PhD in Botany at the University of British Columbia. Deep concern for the earth has underpinned her work as biologist, schoolteacher, science teacher educator, environmental educator, and researcher. Jolie lives in Vancouver, where she helps with Landed Learning programs, writes about environmental education, and follows her passions for learning and experience in nature.

Bill McKibben is a founder of the grassroots climate campaign *350.org* and the Schumann Distinguished Professor in Residence at Middlebury College in Vermont. He is a 2014 recipient of the Right Livelihood Prize, sometimes called the 'alternative Nobel.' He has written a dozen books about the environment, including his first, *The End of Nature*, published 25 years ago, and his most recent, *Oil and Honey*.

Nel Noddings is Lee Jacks Professor of Education Emerita, Stanford University. She is a past president of the National Academy of Education, Philosophy of Education Society, and John Dewey Society. In addition to 20 books, she is the author of about 300 articles and chapters on various topics ranging from the ethics of care to mathematical problem solving. Her latest book (2015) is *A Richer, Brighter Vision for American High Schools.*

Maria Ojala has a PhD in psychology and holds a position as research associate/assistant professor, financed by the Swedish research council Formas, at the Department of Education, Uppsala University, Sweden (2011-2016). Maria also works as a senior lecturer at the Department of Psychology at Örebro University, Sweden. Her main research interests lie in the intersection between environmental psychology and education for sustainable development with a focus on emotions and coping. Email: maria.ojala@oru.se; maria.ojala@edu.uu.se.

Ben Paxton is a philosopher and ethicist of education. His academic and professional work has emphasized the centrality of ethics, justice, democracy, and environmental stewardship in education and public schooling. His recent research focuses on the ethics of teaching, school administration, education reform, and policy. He has a BA in philosophy from Middlebury College, masters degrees in ethics from Yale University, and a PhD in education foundations and policy from the University of Virginia. He currently teaches courses in ethics, education, and policy at Virginia Commonwealth University. He lives with his wife in Charlottesville, VA.

Linda Peterat is Professor Emerita of Curriculum Studies, University of British Columbia, Vancouver. She is co-founder of the Intergenerational Landed Learning program. She currently resides in Vernon, BC and maintains research interests in food history, women's history, environmental education, and ecosystem restoration. Email: peterat@mail.ubc.ca.

Christy Radbourne has been an administrator and elementary teacher with the Lakehead District School Board for 15 years and is currently a principal. She holds a BBA from Georgia State University, Atlanta, Georgia, USA, as well as a BEd and M.Ed. from Lakehead University, Thunder Bay, Ontario, Canada. She is enrolled in the Joint PhD program at Lakehead University, Brock University, and the University of Windsor. Christy has presented on Ecological and Aboriginal Education at multiple conferences including the 2013 American Educational Research Association (AERA) and has previously published papers on Aboriginal education, environmental education, and literacy.

Mayeda Rashid is a PhD Candidate at the School of Human Health and Social Sciences, CQUniversity, Melbourne. She completed a masters degree in Disaster Management at the Institute of Disaster Management and Vulnerability Studies, University of Dhaka, in 2013 and has worked in the NGO sector on numerous community-based disaster management projects in her home country, Bangladesh. Her PhD research, which is supported by the Bushfire and Natural Hazards Cooperative Research Centre, involves a cross-cultural analysis of child-centred disaster risk reduction in Australia and Bangladesh. She has been awarded the Australian Postgraduate Award for her current dissertation research.

Mary-Ann Ridgway has been involved in the creation and development of Inwoods Small School, a small alternative rural educational project affiliated with Brockwood Park School in Hampshire, England. She has been heading it since 2004, in particular ensuring that everybody working together sustains a deep and shared sense of responsibility for the place and each individual child. Over the years, she has observed children's incredible capacity to learn when there is freedom from comparison and judgement, and how compassion and sensitivity can be nurtured when there is daily contact with nature and less intellectual striving.

Kevin R. Ronan is Professorial Research Fellow in Clinical Psychology at CQUniversity, Australia. He specializes in hazards and disasters, problems of youth and families, schizophrenia, and program outcome evaluation. He is senior author of a book called *Promoting Community Resilience to Disasters: The Role for Schools, Youth, and Families* (2005, Springer, New York) and coordinating lead author of a Background Paper, commissioned by the United Nations (UNESCO and UNICEF), as part of the 2015 Global Assessment Review on Disaster Risk Reduction. Over two decades, he has authored many publications focused on child-centred disaster risk reduction (CC-DRR). He is the current project leader of a three-year study in CC-DRR funded by Australia's Bushfire and Natural Hazards Cooperative Research Centre.

Candice Satchwell is a lecturer in education at the University of Central Lancashire in the UK, where she is the Course Leader for the masters and doctorate programs in education. She has conducted research with children and students in a variety of educational settings and has a particular interest in literacy practices. Her research in environmental education has examined the perspectives of children on learning about climate change. Her most recent research is a 30-month AHRC-funded project: *Stories to Connect with: Disadvantaged Children Creating 'Phygital' Community Artefacts to Share Their Life-Narratives of Resilience and Transformation (2015–2017)*.

Allen Thompson is an Associate Professor of Ethics and Environmental Philosophy at Oregon State University in Corvallis, OR. His research concerns broadening our conception of environmental virtue and moral responsibility as a part of understanding human excellence in adapting to the Anthropocene. He is the lead editor of *Ethical Adaptation to Climate Change: Human Virtues of the Future* (MIT, 2012) and co-editor of *The Oxford Handbook of Environmental Ethics* (forthcoming from Oxford University Press).

Briony Towers is a Post-Doctoral Research Fellow in Child-Centred Disaster Risk Reduction at RMIT University, Melbourne. Her research is focused on children's knowledge of hazards disasters and child participation in disaster risk reduction and climate change adaptation. She has conducted research with children in Australian, Indonesia, and the Philippines, and her current research on disaster resilience education is being conducted in collaboration with the Bushfire and Natural Hazards Cooperative Research Centre.

Linda Wason-Ellam is a senior professor at the University of Saskatchewan, Canada where she teaches and researches in the area of the multimodal literacies, children's literature, cross-curriculum learning, dynamic assessment, and qualitative research. She uses an ethnographic frame to observe how children of diversity are learning in classrooms in Canada, New Zealand, Finland, the United States, England, and in Indigenous schools. She has authored articles, book chapters, and books that highlight varying pathways to assure that all children have access to success.

Ted Watt is a naturalist/educator and has worked at the Hitchcock Center for the Environment in Amherst, Massachusetts for over 20 years. The areas of natural history where he has the deepest background are birds and plants of northeastern North America. Ted is intrigued by natural systems and enjoys exploring the intricacies and complexities of the natural world. He works with students, teachers, and the public and supports teachers to develop standards-based curriculum in the natural sciences. He has a bachelor's degree in biology from Earlham College. He has worked at four other environmental centers in Massachusetts, New York, and Michigan.

Hilary Whitehouse is a researcher with the Centre for Research and Innovation in Sustainability Education (cRISE) and an educator with the College of Arts, Society and Education at James Cook University in Cairns, Queensland, Australia. She teaches in the Master of Education (Sustainability) Program as well as in early years science education and in postgraduate research education. Hilary is a life member of the Australian Association for Environmental Education and serves as an executive editor of the *Journal of Environmental Education*. In the summer, she raises frogs endemic to the Australian Wet Tropics.

Ken Winograd is an associate professor in the College of Education, Oregon State University, USA. Prior to this book, Ken authored *Good Day, Bad Day: Teaching as a High Wire Act*, a study of his sabbatical year back in the classroom as an elementary teacher (Rowan Littlefield) as well as *Critical Literacies and Young Learners: Connecting Practice to the Common Core* (Routledge). His interests include writing family histories, watching movies, biking, and walking in the woods.

Sharon Witt is a Senior Lecturer in Education at the University of Winchester, UK, where she teaches primary geography on undergraduate and postgraduate ITE programmes. She is currently undertaking doctoral studies at the University of Exeter. Her research includes fieldwork and exploring children's personal geographies through scrapbooking and den building. She is currently working as a member of the Geography Expert Advisory Group to provide guidance on the implementation of the 2014 National Curriculum in England. Sharon is a Primary Geography Champion, a member of the Early Years and Primary Phase committee for the Geographical Association, and on the national moderating team for the Primary Geography Quality Mark. She is currently working with a colleague on the notion of 'nature-naivety' as a means to conceptualise relationships with the natural world. Email: Sharon.Witt@winchester.ac.uk.

INDEX

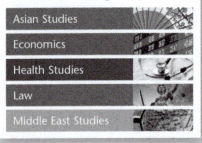
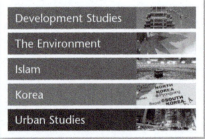